Ruskin's Faithful Stewards:
Henry and Emily Swan

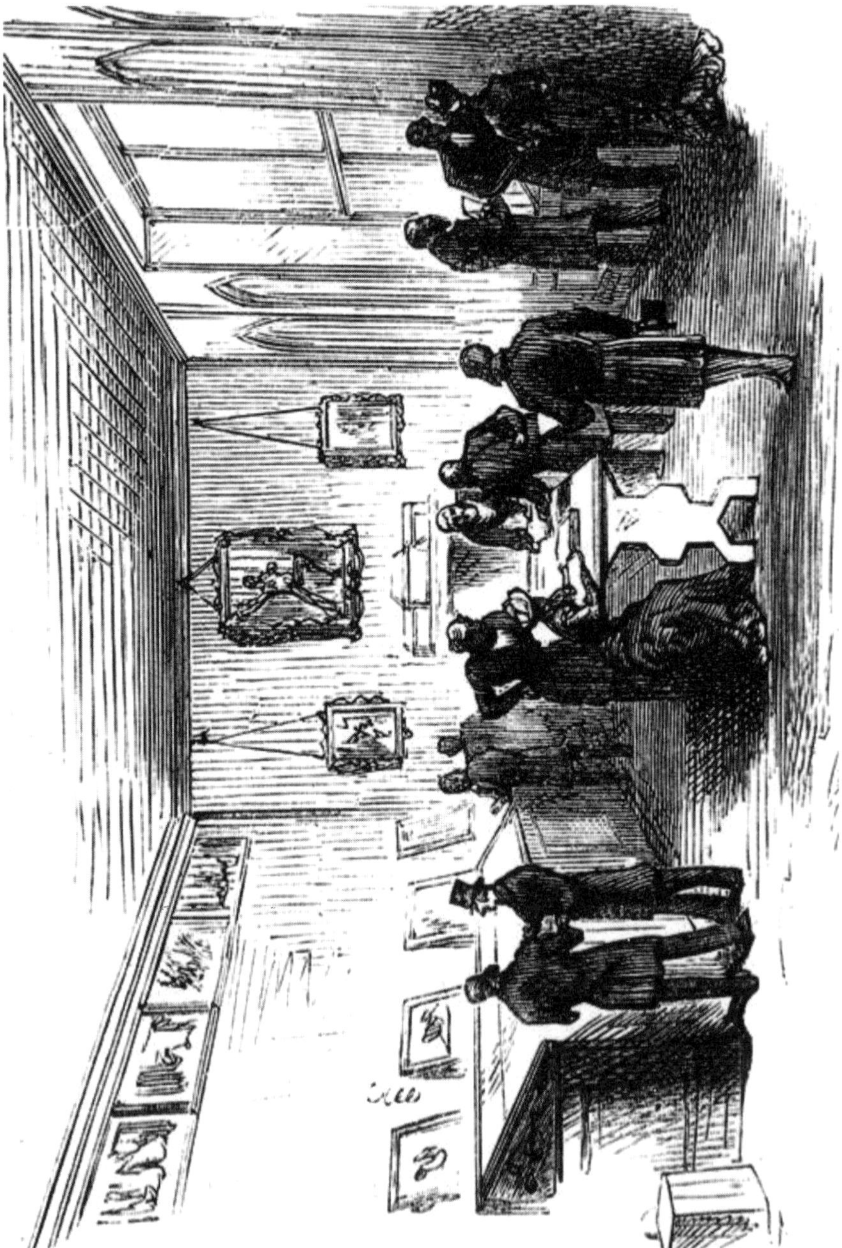

Ruskin's Faithful Stewards: Henry and Emily Swan

Stuart Eagles

2024

Published by
Ruskin Research Blog
2024

www.stuarteagles.co.uk/blog

ISBN 978-1-3999-9049-3

© Stuart Eagles, 2024
The author has asserted his moral rights in accordance with the Copyright, Designs and Patents Act 1988 to be identified as the author of this work.
    All rights reserved. No part of this publication may be reproduced, stored in a retrieval system, or transmitted in any form or by any means, electronic, mechanical, photocopying, recording or otherwise, without the prior consent in writing of the publishers.

Typeset in Garamond
Printed and bound by Short Run Press Limited, Exeter.

*To Ruth Nutter,
Louise Pullen and
Annie Creswick Dawson*

Contents

Foreword	viii
Acknowledgements	xii
List of Illustrations	xiv
A Preliminary Note: On Ruskin's Politics	1
Introduction: 'Practical Power and Faith'	4
One: Remembrance	10
Two: The Boy Hero	14
Three: A New Life in London	19
Four: Vegetarianism & Radicalism	27
Five: The Working Men's College	33
Six: Quakerism	40
Seven: Emily Elizabeth Connell & Married Life	46
Eight: Advancing Photography	50
Nine: Jersey Boys	60
Ten: Ruskin's Museum at Walkley	71
Eleven: Beyond the Museum	84
Twelve: Quaker Networks	93
Thirteen: Life & Death in Sheffield	98
Fourteen: Emily's Retreat	105
Swansong: The Cultivation of Souls	111
Abbreviations	116
Notes	117
Index	135

Foreword

Henry Swan's name will forever be linked to John Ruskin, the Guild of St George, and the Guild's museum, based in Walkley, Sheffield, and justly so. But until Mark Frost's excellent revisionary history of the Guild, *The Lost Companions…*, appeared in 2014, almost everything we knew about Swan came from three obituaries, two published in the *Pall Mall Gazette*, and one in the Sheffield newspapers (and widely syndicated). Some additional information had emerged from other previously unpublished sources, but such material was scarce and widely scattered. Among the few sustained enquiries into Swan's life and work concerned his contribution to photography, but there was little else.

Frost's rediscovery of more than 200 letters from Ruskin to Henry Swan and his wife Emily, written between 1855 and 1887, and preserved at the Rosenbach Museum and Library in Philadelphia, has transformed our understanding. The letters have provided insights into both Henry and Emily's personality and talents. They have shone light on the nature of Ruskin's relationship with his museum curators. They contain numerous fascinating details about the museum and its origins, collection and development, revealing how exhibits were presented to visitors and how the number of art-treasures quickly outgrew the space given to them. Beyond the museum, they uncovered details of Ruskin's agricultural experiments, particularly the project at Totley, just outside Sheffield in the Derbyshire countryside. Our knowledge and understanding has been greatly enhanced, and we will ever remain in Frost's debt.

Yet, as we shall see, and as Frost has himself modestly acknowledged, there has remained much to learn. His hope that his work would whet the appetites of other enquiring scholars fell on fertile ground. I, for one, was intrigued, and set out on a quest for answers.

I was also inspired and provoked by the published suggestions of other modern scholars. For example, it was said that Henry Swan might have been involved in the Political Reform League and, separately, that he joined forces with Rossetti, Morris, Burne-Jones *et al* to help decorate the Oxford Union Society, and even the Oxford Museum of Natural History. Such appealing possibilities were begging to be investigated. And — spoiler alert — even though it turns out that Swan was not involved in any of these campaigns, the process of eliminating him from such enquiries proved interesting in itself.

For much of the 2010s I worked as the Secretary of the Guild of St George. The capital 'S' is justified, I would argue, by the variety and volume of work the role demanded. As well as serving the organisation as company secretary, with all the legal, financial and administrative requirements of such a position, I was the first point-of-contact for director-trustees, members (called Companions), partner groups, public, and media. I edited and designed the Guild's annual magazine, *The Companion*, its website and e-newsletters, and I initiated and maintained its social media feeds on Facebook, Twitter (X), and Instagram. I also gave editorial assistance to Peter Miller in the production of a wide range of Guild publications which explored aspects of the organisation's values, history, and associations.

Under the energetic and imaginative mastership of Clive Wilmer, the Guild embarked on a series of initiatives to — as he put it — 'dig deeper' into its assets. The hope was to engage the public in an exploration of the Guild's heritage which would yield a fuller shared appreciation of Ruskin's ideals and interests. This would help root the Guild more firmly in the communities in which it enjoyed a presence but wished more directly to serve. In the process, the relationship between the Guild, its assets (chief among them, its membership), and local communities would be revivified with mutually beneficial effects. It was an exercise in what I called Applied Ruskin, reaffirming Ruskin's enduring relevance by looking at our world today through his eyes.

The plan was executed with conspicuous success in the Ruskin-in-Sheffield project, which focused on finding new ways to experience the Ruskin Collection of art-treasures originally placed by Ruskin in the care of Henry and Emily Swan at Walkley. A particularly fruitful partnership developed between the project's exemplary creative producer, Ruth Nutter; the deeply knowledgeable and dedicated curator of the Ruskin Collection, Louise Pullen; and a large and enthuseiastic band of volunteers in and around Sheffield, many of whom subsequently became Guild Companions. The Ruskin Collection, now housed at Sheffield Museums Trust's Millennium Gallery, had moved, after the Swans' time, to Meersbrook Hall. Among the numerous programmes the Ruskin-in-Sheffield project initiated in Walkley, Meersbrook, and elsewhere, was one that explored the less well-known history of the Ruskin Museum when Ruskin was incapacitated and in the years following his death. In addition to serving the project's steering committee and attending events, I contributed to the Meersbrook programme by looking into the history of the Ruskin Museum's development, an enquiry which I found both engaging and rewarding. But I kept returning to the Swans and the Walkley years, with Frost's words echoing in my mind's ear. There was so much we still did not know about this apparently well-researched aspect of Ruskin's legacy, Sheffield's cultural history, and the contribution made by the Swans.

I found myself wondering who Henry's obituarists were and whether we could rely on what they had told us about him. More to the point, what hadn't they told us? What was Swan's childhood like in Devizes, for example, and what more could we learn about his family? When did he move to London and in what circumstances? Who taught him how to engrave and what sort of work did he do? Did he really assist Isaac Pitman? If so, in what capacity, and how did the collaboration come about? How did he meet Emily, and what was her background? What were the circumstances that led them to Quakerism? What more might be said of their vegetarianism? What evidence was there of his reputed enthusiasm for bicycles and boomerang-throwing? Did he really invent a system of musical notation and teach it — and, if he did, what was his 'method', when did he devise it, and where did he teach it? Precisely what was this apparently obscure form of photography he experimented with and why was it important?

I wanted to know where he lived and worked, and how it came about that he moved to Sheffield? Was there more to be discovered about his time as a student at the London Working Men's College and the connection he made there with Ruskin? How did Swan come to be appointed curator of Ruskin's museum about 20 years after that initial meeting, and what happened in the years when there was a substantial gap in the otherwise abundant correspondence Frost had rediscovered at the Rosenbach? What was life in Walkley like for the Swan family? What more might be said of their children? Who were the family's friends? What visitors were received at the museum? What more could we learn about the Swans' work at the museum, and their involvement in the Guild and its other projects?

The following pages answer these questions. They also raise some others, and unexpectedly uncover unlooked-for but important new information. I have mined the rich seams of unpublished material in archives, libraries and record offices. I have traced personal, family and business histories, read hundreds of letters, poured over minute and visitor books, searched through nonconformist and parish registers, census returns, civil registration records and calendars of wills. I have scrutinised membership lists and balance-sheets. I have shaken out little gems of information by sifting through school registers, apprenticeship indentures, patent applications, medical records and even criminal proceedings. I have scoured a wide range of contemporary newspapers, journals, and books.

After studying all this material, and much else besides, I decided to start a Ruskin Research Blog <www.stuarteagles.co.uk/blog>. My decision was driven, in part, by the necessarily isolating impact of the coronavirus pandemic. I have published dozens of short articles exploring aspects of Ruskin's writings and legacy, many of them relating to the Guild, and not a few to Sheffield. The current work also draws on research towards two other forthcoming books. The first, *John Ruskin's Sheffield*, will tell the full story of St George's Museum in Walkley and set it in its broader cultural and historical context. The second, *Ruskin and the Communists*, will explore the Totley experiment. Both build on the work of Janet Barnes, Catherine Morley, Robert Hewison, Louise Pullen, Marcus Waithe, Sally Goldsmith and others, most notably Mark Frost. I add previously unpublished, unexplored and unfamiliar material to expand our knowledge and deepen our appreciation of Ruskin, the Guild, and its projects.

I was privileged to share some of my research findings at the Ruskin Society Birthday Lecture in February 2023. An enthusiastic audience gathered at the Art Workers' Guild in Bloomsbury, relieved to be meeting in person, rather than on Zoom, and gratefully mask-free. I express gratitude to Marcus Waithe and Harry Daniels for giving me that encouraging and stimulating opportunity, and for their generosity in jointly awarding my Ruskin mentor and friend, Robert Hewison, and myself, with Lifetime Membership of the society, of which I was formerly the secretary.

I am hopeful that more material will yet be found, and I have no doubt that scholars far more gifted than me will spot connections I have missed and share insights that would never have occurred to me. But here, for the first time in the nearly 200 years since Henry Swan was born, and approaching 150 years since Ruskin founded his Guild museum and set it in Walkley, it is now possible to present a comprehensive and fully referenced biography of Henry and Emily Swan, Ruskin's faithful stewards.

NB. This book is not about the contents of the Ruskin Collection itself. Readers are advised to visit the collection at Sheffield's Millennium Gallery. Janet Barnes's *Ruskin in Sheffield* (Sheffield: Guild of St George, 2011), revised by Louise Pullen, is a well-illustrated guide. Selections of the collection's treasures can be explored online in calendars arranged and edited by me, from material prepared by Louise Pullen: see:
<www.guildofstgeorge.org.uk/ruskin-collection/about-the-ruskin-collection>.

Acknowledgements

This publication draws heavily on documents preserved in archives on both sides of the Atlantic. I express my gratitude and indebtedness to all of them, with particular thanks to the many members of staff who have rendered assistance and guidance. I would especially like to thank Stephen Wildman, Rebecca Patterson, Diane Tyler, the late Jenn Shepherd, and Louise Pullen. Full source information on documents consulted is given in the list of abbreviations (p. 116) and notes (pp. 117-134). I have sought to establish the copyright for all unpublished manuscript material, including that of John Ruskin and Henry and Emily Swan, but have been unable to do so on the basis of all the information known to me. I would therefore welcome contact from any person or persons who can show they hold this copyright.

Special thanks are owing to those archives which have given permission to quote from previously unpublished material: the Rosenbach Museum and Library, Philadelphia; the Borthwick Institute for Archives, University of York; Inspire Nottinghamshire Archives; the John Rylands Research Institute and Library, University of Manchester; the Morgan Library & Museum, New York; and the Ruskin Library, University of Lancaster (the Ruskin Foundation).

Research in many more archives has yielded details which have added to the rich tapestry I have tried to weave in this book. Repositories consulted include The National Archives, the British Library (including the Newspaper Library), the Old Bailey (Central Criminal Court), the General Register Office, Wiltshire and Swindon Archives, the London Metropolitan Archives, the Library of the Society of Friends, Jersey Archive, Sheffield City Archives and Local Studies Library, and Sheffield Museums Trust/the Guild of St George (with special thanks to Louise Pullen).

In some instances, a private archive have been consulted on my behalf by an official. This was the case with John Wilson at the Royal Humane Society, and Celia Wolfe at Ackworth School. Both were unfailingly helpful, courteous, and generous in sharing their knowledge.

For his inspiration, scholarly generosity and friendship, I express unending gratitude to Mark Frost. For helping me to access specific sources of information, I would like to thank the late James Dearden, the late Andrew Russell, Paul Dawson, Matthew Winterbottom, Andrew Melling, and Pavel Chepyzhov.

For reading earlier drafts of parts of this book, and for providing encouragement and feedback, both of which were greatly appreciated,

I would like to thank Annie Creswick Dawson, Sara Atwood, and Mark Frost; and for responding to some of this material, as presented to the Ruskin Society at the Art Worker's Guild in 2023, I'd like to thank my audience at the Ruskin Society Birthday Lecture. For expressing an interest in particular aspects of my work and engaging in useful conversation or correspondence, I give thanks to James Gregory, Philip Stevens, Richard Hoare, and Roy Starkey.

For their Ruskinian friendship and encouragement, I'd like to renew my thanks to Mark Frost, Stephen Wildman, Louise Pullen, Paul Dawson, Annie Creswick Dawson, Sara Atwood, the late James Dearden, the late Andrew Russell, and add Robert Hewison, Lawrence Goldman, Clive Wilmer, Ruth Nutter, Sally Goldsmith, Suzie Doncaster, Bill Bevan, Carrie Leyland, Howard Hull, the late Francis O'Gorman, Dinah Birch, Kay Walter, Jim Spates, Marcus Waithe, Rachel Dickinson, Cynthia Gamble, David Barrie, David Ingram, Jeffrey Richards, Alan Davis, Ray Haslam, Emma Sdegno, Carmen Casaliggi, Janet Barnes, Peter Miller, Jacqueline Yallop, Martin Green, Simon Seligman, Arjun Jain, Michael Wheeler, Robert Whelan and many others too numerous to name.

Without the distraction of family and friends outside the Ruskin world this book would have been completed far sooner, but with infinitely less joy. Without their patience, support, and encouragement, it would never have been written at all. They have inspired me and driven my sense of purpose. My biggest debt will forever be to my parents. I'm enormously grateful, too, to Warren, Wendy, and Val. I'd particularly like to renew my thanks to Pavel Chepyzhov and Andrew Melling, and I add James, Clair, Harrison and Jude Buckley, Will Fradley, Stu Heslegrave, Jo Harris, Ian Mullen, James Corbett, John Beasley, Rob Wilson, Ionnis Dragoumis, Evgeny Korchagin, Quentin Broughall, Paul and Sophie Williams, Oliver Lanning, Sam and Dave Carey, Craig Collins, Matt Tillotson, Matt Roper, Ben Doak, Frazer and Angela Thwaite, Paul Fargher, Scott Doidge, Chris Ballinger, and others too numerous to name. There is no wealth but Life. In my life I've loved them all.

List of Illustrations

Cover image. 'Ruskin's Museum, Walkley — Exterior' (the earliest known image and drawing of St George's Museum), part of a six-image cycle, *HRH Prince Leopold's Visit to Sheffield*, by an unknown artist, reproduced from *The Pictorial World* (1 November 1879), p. 140. Border art by Henry Swan, extracted from Isaac Pitman's *Phonographic Examiner* (1 December 1855), engraved on stone by Henry Swan and printed by F. & H. Swan, Kingsland Green.

Frontispiece. 'Ruskin's Museum, Walkley — Interior' (the earliest known image, and only drawing, of the original upstairs room at St George's Museum), part of a six-image cycle, *HRH Prince Leopold's Visit to Sheffield*, by an unknown artist, reproduced from *The Pictorial World* (1 November 1879), p. 140.

1. John Ruskin photographed by Frederick Hollyer, 1894, reproduced from *The Works of John Ruskin*, eds. E. T. Cook and Alexander Wedderburn (39 vols) (1903-1912), vol. 35, *frontispiece*.

page 2

2. St George's Museum, Walkley, photographed c. 1885 from Bell Hagg Road, photographer unknown. The 1882-83 extension is visible to the left, and the Lyceum Gallery (opened in May 1885) to the right and rear. Sheffield Museums Trust/Guild of St George (Ruskin Collection).

page 4

3. The grave of Hemry & Leonard Swan at Walkley Cemetery, with the new plaque carved by Richard Watts. Alongside stands Annie Creswick Dawson, artist, Companion of the Guild of St George, and a great-granddaughter of Benjamin Creswick, a celebrated student at the museum and a disciple of Ruskin. Photo: Stuart Eagles, 2016.

page 11

4. An example of the bronze medal issued to Henry Swan by the Royal Humane Society, courtesy of the Royal Humane Society (with thanks).

page 14

5. Little Brittox, Devizes, as it looked in 2019. Henry and his siblings grew up here in the 1820s and '30s in the family toyshop. Photo: Stuart Eagles.

page 16

6. An advertisement for Ives & Swan in the *Archaeological Journal*, vol. 3, no. 12 (December 1846), unpaginated.

page 21

7. Isaac Pitman's *Phonographic Examiner*, engraved on stone by Henry Swan and printed by the Swan brothers (author's collection).

page 25

8. George Dornbusch, a leading vegetarian known to the Swan brothers. From Charles W. Forward, *Fifty Years of Food Reform: A History of the Vegetarian Movement in England* (London: The Ideal Publishing Union Ltd, 1898), p. 32.

page 29

9. William Ward, a friend of Swan's and a fellow pupil of Ruskin's at the Working Men's College. From *John Ruskin's Letters to William Ward, with a short biography of William Ward by William C. Ward* (Boston, MA: Marshall Jones Co., 1922), facing p. 18.

page 35

10. J. W. Graham, Quaker and Ruskinian, from *John Bull* (17 September 1927).

page 41

11. Alfred William Bennett, photographed by Maul & Fox, c. 1900, originally published with Bennett's obituary in the *Journal of the Royal Microscopical Society* (1902), Linnean Society, inv. no. PP/B/21.

Page 44

12. An early C20th advertisement for Connell's of Cheapside (author's collection).

page 47

13. An advertisement for Swan's Patent Clairvoyant, from *Bookseller*, no. 17 (25 May 1859), p. 955.

page 50

14. Swan's technical drawing illustrating the 'crystal cube' in his successful British patent application, no. 3249 (4 December 1862).

page 53

15. The reverse of a typical *carte de visite* from Swan's Casket Portrait Co. Ltd (author's collection).

page 56

16. Howard Swan, *A Preliminary Catalogue of St George's Museum, Walkley, Sheffield* (Sheffield: W. D. Spalding & Co., 1888), title-page.

page 76

17. Inside the Lyceum Gallery of St George's Museum, dominated by J. W. Bunney's painting of St Mark's, Venice, photographer unknown, c. 1885, Sheffield Museums Trust/Guild of St George (Ruskin Collection).

page 80

18. Crest of the Ruskin Society of Sheffield (author's collection).

page 91

19. Howard Swan, pictured in W. T. Stead, 'How To Learn a Language in Six Months', in *The Review of Reviews: An International Magazine*, vol. 5, no. 30 (July 1892), pp. 701-708, specifically p. 701.

page 106

A PRELIMINARY NOTE
ON RUSKIN'S POLITICS

THERE IS NO WEALTH BUT LIFE. Life, including all its powers of love, of joy, and of admiration. That country is the richest which nourishes the greatest number of noble and happy human beings; that man is richest who, having perfected the functions of his own life to the utmost, has also the widest helpful influence, both personal, and by means of his possessions, over the lives of others.
—John Ruskin, *Unto this Last* (1860, 1862).[1]

John Ruskin's politics were complex. They developed over time. Yet some fundamentals might be clearly and usefully stated.

Ruskin believed in hierarchy, not equality; order and discipline, not anarchy and rebellion; co-operation rather than competition; the individual and community rather than the nation-state. He advocated strong but wise and beneficent leadership. He required obedience, not of the ruled to the ruler, but of both to Christian tenets of faith, truth, and justice. He opposed democracy, parliamentary party politics and referendums. He drew his authority and inspiration from the Bible, Greek philosophy (particularly Plato and Xenophon), medieval architecture and craftsmanship, pre-Renaissance art, Turner, the Romanticism of Scott, Wordsworth and Byron, the social and political thought of Thomas Carlyle, and above all, the fragile beauty of the natural world, which he believed had been created by God, and given into humanity's care, in a sacred and vital bond of trust.

Ruskin was deeply conservative, even reactionary, yet also profoundly radical, and he was more radical as he aged. He deplored liberalism, despised republicanism, and dismissed socialism. He was, in fact, an Ultra Tory who believed that it was the Christian duty of the rich to care for the poor and disadvantaged. He was out of sympathy with the nineteenth century. He held that industrial capitalism and the utilitarian political economy that underpinned it had, by their demand for mass production and their unbreakable love-affair with steam-powered engines, reduced work to soulless, mechanical drudgery. He found answers to contemporary problems in the wisdom of the past, and sought to weave the fabric of a better tomorrow. He was not a Utopian in the sense of striving for the impossible, but someone who, despite periods of crippling doubt, believed in fundamental but deliverable reform that would, at some point in the future, foster spiritual renewal that would be of mutual benefit to humanity, society and what we now call the environment.

Among his personal influences, apt to inspire love, frustration, and heartache, but also creative energy yet constraint, were his parents (his father's mercantile career and cultural passions, his mother's evangelical Protestant faith) and the young woman to whom he proposed marriage, Rose La Touche. Among the forces that shaped his philosophy were his Scottish heritage, the landscapes of Europe, the social and religious structure of the Middle Ages, and medieval working practices, exemplified in his notion of the nature of Gothic.

1. John Ruskin photographed by Frederick Hollyer, 1894.

He devoted himself to the teaching of what he considered to be timeless truths. He encouraged accurate observation, penetrating perception, perseverance, and the co-ordination of eye, hand, head and heart. By means of education, and as a fundamental matter of justice, he explored and explained the value of beauty in nature and art. His motivating purpose was to engender individual self-fulfilment by releasing the student's best creative potential. This would lead to a truly wealthy society of happy and healthy workers and thinkers, the thinkers sharing in the work, and the workers sharing in the thinking. His mission was nothing short of the cultivation of the soul.

Unpacking all of this would fill a substantial volume. It must suffice here to return only briefly to this summary in order to illuminate aspects of Ruskin's political philosophy relevant to his relationship with Henry and Emily Swan. The reader's attention is directed in particular to discussions in the introduction, in chapters five, nine, and eleven, and in the concluding 'Swansong'.

Ruskin warned that *'no true* disciple of mine will ever be a "Ruskinian"! — he will follow, not me, but the instincts of his own soul, and the guidance of its Creator'.[2] Many of the people who felt most inspired by Ruskin — those charmed by the power of his prose, his personal example, his ideas and values — were of a different political stamp to himself, the subjects of this biography included. Ruskin's disciples were generally not 'Ruskinians' in the sense he described, but if most believed in God, it was not necessarily Ruskin's God. Ruskin was prepared to collaborate with others, regardless of their political and religious views, and social backgrounds, always provided that he believed them to be honest and trusted in the sincerity of their intentions.

Ruskin's legacies are multiple, and he often did not approve of the direction in which his disciples adapted his vision. Most of them, by contrast to Ruskin himself, were politically progressive and believed in popular democracy, such as the founding members of the Labour Party, like Keir Hardie, and the pioneers of the welfare state, including William Beveridge and Clement Attlee. They were joined by a diverse range of famous figures from around the globe who unambiguously acknowledged their debt to Ruskin — William Morris, Leo Tolstoy, Marcel Proust, and Mahatma Gandhi among them.

Above all, Ruskin's gospel taught that we have inherited the earth and that we must be careful to preserve Life upon it, with all its powers of love, joy and admiration. Our most sacred duty as human beings is to be model custodians and exemplary stewards who bequeath to future generations something even greater than we inherited. Ruskin's disciples, in all their diversity, and in their different ways, sought to make the world a better place in which to live. How far they succeeded is a matter of opinion, but the fact that they tried is indisputable.

Few of Ruskin's disciples understood him better than Henry and Emily Swan, fewer still could lay greater claim to his wider helpful influence. As the faithful stewards of his exemplary collection of art, they executed their duties to the fullest extent of their considerable abilities. Together, Ruskin and the Swans bequeathed a priceless educational legacy from which we will continue to benefit for generations to come.

INTRODUCTION
'PRACTICAL POWER AND FAITH'

[T]he right function of every museum, to simple persons, is the manifestation to them of what is lovely in the life of Nature, and heroic in the life of Men.
—John Ruskin, *On the Old Road* (1885)[3]

2. St George's Museum, Walkley, in the late 1880s. The 1882-83 extension is visible to the left, and the Lyceum Gallery (opened in May 1885) to the right and rear.

If we must necessarily resist the temptation to describe the museum work of Henry Swan (1825-1889) as 'heroic', we should, nonetheless, be in no doubt that he and his family were responsible for making a practical success of an educational experiment. It was no mean feat. The Swans were tasked with bringing into being a museum that would realise the vision of its founder, John Ruskin (1819-1900), the famous critic of art and society who was also their friend. Henry Swan's role as curator would demand courage, require personal sacrifice, and necessitate constant perseverance, not only from him, but from his wife and children, too.

Called St George's Museum, it was established towards the end of 1875. It was situated in Walkley, formerly a village, but by then a young and burgeoning suburb on the north-west edge of Sheffield, in the south of Yorkshire. It occupied a liminal space, connecting town and countryside. As such, it formed a symbolic gateway between a rural past and an urban future, yet purposefully rooted in the present. The museum's exemplary collection preserved timeless treasures. A significant proportion crucially demonstrated the joyful achievements of medieval artists and craftsmen whose skill and inspiration Ruskin hoped modern workers would fruitfully, perhaps even transformatively, rediscover and recuperate.

The collection was housed in a modest detached stone cottage on Bell Hagg Road which doubled as the Swans' family home. A notice on the garden gate boldly declared Ruskin's notion of the true function of a museum.

> A museum is, be it first observed, primarily, not at all a place of entertainment, but a place of Education. And a museum is, be it secondly observed, not a place for elementary education, but for that of already far-advanced scholars. And it is by no means the same thing as a parish school, or a Sunday school, or a day school, or even — the Brighton Aquarium.[4]

These words, provocatively humorous but absolutely sincere, also appeared on the reverse of the green student tickets, freely obtained, but required to guarantee admittance. Ruskin intended his museum principally to benefit the artisan metalworkers of Sheffield, an increasing number of whom lived in Walkley itself.

No visitor could reasonably have been in any doubt about the serious educational purpose of this repository for Ruskin's rich collection of watercolour drawings, etchings and engravings recording Europe's fine art, great buildings and outstanding natural scenery; of plaster-casts of Gothic sculpture; of rare books of literature, history and natural science; of illuminated manuscripts, minerals and coins. For those workers willing and able to invest the time and effort to look and learn, their eyes and minds would be opened to the noble moral lessons of creative reverence to be derived from an appreciation of beauty in nature that was reflected in the finest works of art and craftsmanship. Ruskin, who at the time of the museum's inauguration was working as the first Slade Professor of Fine Art at his *alma mater*, the University of Oxford, hoped his museum would be Sheffield's 'working man's Bodleian'.[5]

The collection was moved from Walkley to Meersbrook in 1890, and has since been rehoused several times. It now has its own permanent display-space in Sheffield's Millennium Gallery, where it is cared for by Sheffield Museums Trust. The Walkley cottage has undergone significant alteration. Divided into self-contained apartments, it now fronts Bole Hill Road. The original museum can still be explored virtually, courtesy of an online reconstruction created by scholar Marcus Waithe.[6]

The treasures the Swans curated at Walkley were collected as a vital part of what became the Guild of St George, the association founded by Ruskin in 1871, and still active as a charity today.[7] Ruskin's plans for the Guild and its museum were worked out in *Fors Clavigera*, 96 'letters to the workmen and labourers of Great Britain', which he wrote between 1871 and 1884. *Fors* is complex, allusive, and multi-faceted. It represents Ruskin's fiercest attack on global injustice, self-righteous malpractice, rampant corruption, and the squandering of resources by the unsympathetic, unintelligent and insatiable demands of industry. War in Europe between France and Prussia, and the damage done to the Louvre in May 1871, convinced him that civilization was crumbling. He believed that in the modern world social bonds had been shattered and humanity robbed of honour. 'For my own part,' he had declared, 'I will put up with this state of things, passively, not an hour longer.'[8]

By means of the Guild, Ruskin sought to fight, if not to slay, the dragon of modern capitalism. The factories had swallowed workers' souls by turning them into unthinking, unimaginative machines;, segmented, fragmented — no longer whole. Chimneys furiously belched acrid smoke into the streets of the cities, befouled the rivers, and disfigured the landscape. Lives were blighted and community relationships were undermined. The massive coal-fuelled factories of Steelopolis stood as ugly monuments to degradation. Guild members — called Companions — were enjoined to practice traditional methods of craftsmanship and land management in an effort to promote the honest work of the hands and counter the disruptive and often destructive deployment of steam-powered machinery which churned out unvarying, useless, mass-produced junk.

Henry Swan was acutely conscious that the purpose of Ruskin's Guild, and the Guild's connection with the Walkley museum, was not obvious to local people. He addressed the matter in a letter to Sheffielders published in the local press.

> [... A]s there are many of your readers who will be entirely unacquainted with the relation which the Museum holds to the St George's Guild, the following extracts from the registered memorandum of association of the guild will not be without interest for them:—
>
> Object 3. 'The acquisition by gift, purchase, or otherwise, and the erection of schools, museums, and other educational establishments, in different parts of Great Britain and Ireland';

Object 4. 'The acquisition by gift, purchase, or otherwise, of such pictures, sculptures, books, and objects of art and natural history, as may be properly adapted for the cultivation of taste and intelligence among rural labourers and among craftsmen.'[9]

Moreover, in a letter written to one of the Guild's earliest Companions, Ruskin epitomised his belief that 'to divide pretty things fairly is the first duty of justice — and to me whether things are *truly* pretty or not, the finest power of truth'.[10]

There were many reasons why the northern manufacturing town of Sheffield was specially chosen as the location for the museum. Ruskin explained that England generally, and Sheffield in particular, had mastered the 'always necessary and useful' art of ironwork in 'sword, tool, [and] ploughshare'.[11] He judged that Sheffield's ironworkers were uniquely suited to benefit from the ennobling influence of a cultural granary that would serve as a 'national store' in sharp contrast to the Government's debilitating 'national debt', and would stand for the true wealth of Life, which had nothing whatever to do with money.[12] Yorkshire, moreover, was 'old English' — 'capable therefore yet of the ideas of Honesty and Piety by which old England lived'.[13] Sheffield was 'within easy reach of beautiful natural scenery' and of the great man-made monuments to Faith at 'Lincoln, York, Durham, Selby, Fountains, Bolton, and Furness'.[14]

The unique and ever-growing collection at Walkley was assembled solely by Ruskin himself, and was an expression of his personality, interests, and concerns. It was vital that its curators knew and understood Ruskin if they were to communicate the significance of the objects in their care, and explain their interconnections. Henry Swan and his family were uniquely placed to serve Ruskin, the Guild, and the museum to the fullest extent. Swan was a former pupil of Ruskin's at the London Working Men's College. Ruskin had recognised his eye for colour and skill in copying illuminated manuscripts. Henry had entered the college as an accomplished artisan who had engraved on stone some of Isaac Pitman's periodicals in shorthand. Already a Quaker and a vegetarian, Swan would go on to invent equipment and pioneer processes in the development of stereoscopy — a form of three-dimensional photography. The fact that the Swans were living in Walkley at precisely the moment Ruskin's mind turned to the founding of a museum was the deciding factor in settling its location. Swan's work at the museum was the crowning success of a life of energy and experimentation. He was ably and enthusiastically assisted in the work by his wife, Emily (1835-1909). The eldest of the couple's children, Howard (1860-1919), even compiled a creditable museum catalogue.

The cottage in Upper Walkley was never big enough to serve satisfactorily as both family home and public art gallery. Furthermore, its location, a couple of miles from the centre of Sheffield and perched high on a steep hill, was widely decried as too remote, especially for many of the hard-working and time-poor artisans based in the town centre and especially those living in a suburb of the town other than Walkley. Public transport links and local roads, though they improved during the 14-year life of the museum, were poor. But the museum's beautiful setting had much to commend it, as Howard Swan recollected in reminiscences published on the death of Ruskin in 1900.

> Out beyond lay the hills — Bolehills — where stone was quarried and the men played knurr and spell, a kind of golf and trap and ball game peculiar to the North. Further, the woods and the rocky escapements of Elliott's Retreat, the Elliott of Corn Law rhyme fame, show dusky green in the distance.[15] Down below the valley of Rivelin, gleaming with reservoirs of water for grindstones, and across more hills over to Bradfield, where the great dam burst in the Sheffield flood, and below the murky cloud of Sheffield itself, the climb was steep.[16] 'It was symbolic', Ruskin said; 'the climb to knowledge and truth is ever steep, and the gems found at the top small — but precious and beautiful.'[17]

The cottage was described in 1879 by the journalist Edward Bradbury (1853-1905) as 'square, grey; bleak, ugly, English, and,' he added in modest consolation, 'comfortable'.[18] For half its existence, the museum was squeezed into a single upstairs room — 'a mere bandbox of a place; a cupboard of curiosities', Bradbury called it.[19] Yet, he went on, 'everything in the room bears an obvious impress of earnest art. There is nothing sham or showy; all is honest, thorough-going, and valuable.'[20] Swan was not misty-eyed about the situation, as he demonstrated in a private letter to the artist, John Wharlton Bunney (1828-1882), whom Ruskin employed as a copyist for the collection. The context was that Queen Victoria's youngest son, Prince Leopold, who had been Ruskin's pupil at Oxford and had become a personal friend, had recently visited the museum. It was an occasion which had generated a great deal of publicity and — according to Swan's good-humoured testimony — not a little attendant exasperation, too.

> The whole space we have at command for displaying either to royal princes or to nascent genius, is — one room, 13 ft. square [...] I dare say thou hast seen the report in the 'Times' that tells folk that the museum consists of a small mansion situated in its own grounds. Well that's reporter's English for a five-roomed cottage lying in a freehold land allotment.[21]

Lack of space at the museum would be a constant source of frustration, even irritation, and it came to dominate discussion and appraisal of the place.

The Swans' living quarters were extended in 1882-83 and in September '83, 'a corner of the museum grounds' was 'roofed over in a sufficiently substantial manner', Henry Swan explained in a letter to the local press, to provide 'a small temporary gallery'.[22] No image or drawing of the structure appears to have survived. In May 1885, it was superseded by a more solid ground-floor conservatory-like extension to the main cottage, called the Lyceum Gallery, which did something, but still not enough, to alleviate the cramped conditions. Notwithstanding, Swan was excited to tell the public, through the letters-pages of the local newspapers, that J. W. Bunney's large painting of the western façade of St Mark's, Venice (1877-82), would soon be on display there.[23] It remains central to the collection today. As to what Swan called the 'allotment', visitors to Walkley found that the wicket gave access to 'a garden-plot of about an acre in extent, with a miniature apple-orchard, and bushes of evergreens and old-fashioned flowers' and strawberry beds,[24] cared for by Emily Swan and a gardener whose enthusiasm was such that he joined the local Ruskin Society.[25]

Several dozen people a week found their way to Ruskin's domestic shrine to art. Some were local labourers and craftsmen; others were art students and young teachers. Many made pilgrimages from across Britain and the globe. Leading figures in Victorian cultural life, royalty included, elected to make the journey up the hill, though they did so in varying degrees of comfort.

In 1886 Ruskin told the Huddersfield woollen manufacturer and Guild Companion, George Thomson (1842-1921), that, 'without your practical power and faith — nothing could have been yet done' of St George's work.[26] If that was true of the man who became the Guild's junior then senior trustee, and one of Ruskin's successors as Master, it was even more emphatically true of his curators, Henry and Emily Swan. In planting the museum in the community, and entrusting it to the Swans' nurturing care, Ruskin gave his experimental ideal every chance to take root and flourish. The Swans' vital importance to the success of Ruskin's project has never been in doubt, yet no substantial biography has hitherto been published. Now that nearly 150 years has passed since the founding of Ruskin's museum in Sheffield, and we prepare to nark the bicentenary of Henry Swan's birth, it is time to make amends.

ONE
REMEMBRANCE

Tuesday, 2 April 1889 was a typical spring day in south Yorkshire. Short, sunny intervals were interrupted by squally showers, and there was a cold edge to the north-westerly wind. A group of mourners huddled on the edge of the steeply sloping grounds of Walkley Cemetery on the outskirts of Sheffield. They were there to pay their respects to a remarkable local resident, Henry Swan.

For the previous 13-and-a-half years Swan had served as the curator of one of the most eclectic provincial art collections in England. It had been initiated and assembled by the nation's leading art critic, John Ruskin — a generous philanthropist, celebrated teacher and controversial social commentator. A large crowd watched as Swan's body completed the quarter-mile journey from his home and workplace, St George's Museum, at 75 Bell Hagg Road. The coffin was carried by the Swan family's neighbor and friend, Frank Shelley, and other members of the Shelley family. Following behind were Swan's grieving widow, Emily, the couple's eldest son, Howard, and their only daughter, Mabel.[27] Another son, Godfrey, politically the most radical of the Swans' offspring, was abroad, working on an orange farm in Florida, having emigrated to America in 1887.[28] Henry was to be interred with the youngest of the Swan brood, Leonard, who had been buried three Christmases earlier.

At three in the afternoon a 'simple but impressive' Quaker service was presided over by the lay minister, James Henry Barber (1820-1902), a Quaker Elder, a banker, a hugely respected figure in the local community, and a close friend of Henry's. Following the interment, Barber offered 'a few words of consolation to the family'.[29] Emily spoke for a few moments at the graveside, but her words of tribute to her husband were not recorded. Likewise, those of the congregationalist, Rev. Thomas William Holmes (1836-1915) who, supported by the presence of his daughter, also delivered a short address. A close friend of the Swans', Holmes was an admirer of Ruskin, and — like Barber — an advocate of improved educational provision in Sheffield. Holmes had met Ruskin at the Walkley museum of which he was a keen supporter, and he had signed the visitor books there no fewer than 15 times, including on the day Swan died.[30]

The eulogies were heard by the 'large number of persons' who had assembled 'to pay a last mark of respect to the deceased gentleman, who was very much liked in the neighbourhood'.[31] Among them were

Elijah Howarth (1853-1938) (the curator of the Weston Park Museum), and Joseph Gamble (1824-1905) (a cutlery manufacturer, councillor, and — six months later — a founding member of the Ruskin Museum Committee). Two students of the museum whose talents Swan had recognised and helped to nurture were also there to pay their respects: the sculptor Benjamin Creswick (1853-1946) and the artist Frank Saltfleet (1860-1937).[32] Wreaths and crosses from those who had been unable to travel to the funeral brightened the scene. 'Mrs Severn, on behalf of Mr Ruskin' — she was Ruskin's cousin and carer — had written 'sympathising with the family on the great loss they had sustained'.[33]

> In the assessment of the *Sheffield Independent* Swan had forwarded, by explanation and all means in his power, the social and art teaching of Mr Ruskin; carried out as far as possible the arrangement and exhibition of Mr Ruskin's art treasures; and, in connection with Mrs Swan and the whole of his family, strove to bring home to Sheffield and the world in general the teachings of helpfulness, and beauty, and joy in life, which are the great principles in Mr Ruskin's life and writings.[34]

The paper made an important point in emphasising that Swan was very much a family man who was assisted in his work by his wife and children. The reporter added that Swan's 'passing from this life, even at his fairly advanced age' — he was 64 — would 'come as a shock to his many friends in Sheffield and elsewhere'.

3. The grave of Henry & Leonard Swan at Walkley Cemetery, with the new plaque. Alongside stands Annie Creswick Dawson, artist, Companion of the Guild of St George, and a great-granddaughter of Benjamin Creswick.

On 27 June 2015, a warm and sunny day, Companions (that is to say, members) of Ruskin's Guild of St George, the organisation founded by Ruskin in which custody of the art-collection was vested, gathered in Walkley to remember Swan's achievements. It was part of the five-year Guild project, Ruskin-in-Sheffield, which sought to reaffirm the connections between the collection and the community in the twenty-first century. It was piloted with flair by Ruth Nutter, ably assisted by curator, Louise Pullen, and a broad range of volunteers, many of whom subsequently became Guild Companions. Swan's simple gravestone, weather-worn and neglected in the 125+ years that had passed since its erection, had been repaired by the Guild that spring, and a new plaque of Lakeland slate installed, inscribed by local carver, Richard Watts. At the head of the inscription are the words 'A Faithful Steward', a phrase taken from an obituary of Swan published in the *Pall Mall Gazette* and adapted for the title of the present volume.

A second plaque, also carved by Watts and made of Lakeland slate to reflect the life Ruskin led by Coniston Water, marks the site of the museum, which today is a greatly expanded and altered building comprising private apartments, and entered from Bole Hill Road at what was originally the rear of the property. In an address delivered near the graveside, the Master of the Guild, the poet, critic and Cambridge academic Clive Wilmer, described Swan as 'warm, humorous, loyal, original and careless of the opinions of others' and bade the gathering, of which I was myself a part as the Guild's secretary, to remember both Henry and his wife, Emily, with 'honour and gratitude'.[35]

Scholar and Companion Mark Frost had delivered the Guild's annual Ruskin Lecture two years earlier in 2013, and I was privileged to introduce him. Frost shared the fruits of his extensive research into Ruskin's correspondence with the Swans, which he had recently rediscovered in America, and he argued that Henry Swan deserved to be taken altogether more seriously than he had been in the studies published hitherto, and that Emily Swan should be seen as an equal partner in the museum work, having also provided Ruskin with crucial emotional support. He ended his lecture, entitled 'Curator and Curatress', a formula taken from the Ruskin-Swan correspondence, by expressing the hope that he had left the audience with 'an inclination to get to know [the Swans] a little better'.[36]

For me, at least, a seed had been sown. Theirs is a remarkable story, and such was the character and extent of their combined contribution that an understanding of St George's Museum is incomplete without an appreciation of who they were — of where they came from and what they became. This is the personal story of the family that laid the foundations on which a Ruskinian heritage has been developed in Sheffield over the course of nearly 150 years.

TWO
THE BOY HERO

The aptly named Winter Randell, a lively lad who had recently turned 12, was out ice-skating. He was having fun on a bitterly cold day in the middle of January. Returning home along the towpath, he stumbled, slipped and fell, plunging deep into the partially frozen waters of the canal. A few yards away, at the wharf, a man stood motionless, muttering to himself that the boy was done for. A young friend of Randell's who had witnessed the accident and may have been his companion that day, hurriedly threw himself to the ground in an effort to help him. Winter's friend reached out and grabbed his hand, the only part of the boy that could be seen above the cracked ice. And, with a heave, the rescuer pulled Winter to safety.

The year was 1838, and the location was the charming Wiltshire market town of Devizes. The scene of the rescue was within sight of the now-forgotten Drewe's Wharf on the Kennet and Avon Canal, probably close to where a theatre and canal museum stand today. Completed in 1810, the 87-mile-long waterway helped Devizes to thrive commercially, connecting it to the Bristol docks to the west and the River Thames at Reading to the east. Thanks to what a local newspaper called the 'praiseworthy actions' and 'the presence of mind and courage' of the skater's friend, a tragedy had been averted.[37] The young hero was Henry Swan, less than a week away from his 13th birthday,

It was suggested in the press that Henry had previously saved one of his brothers from drowning, though no details of this incident were given. Apart from having the satisfaction of saving a life, perhaps for a second time, the brave boy did not go unrewarded. Nine months after the dramatic episode occurred, Henry was presented with a handsome bronze medal for his intrepidity by the Royal Humane Society, a charitable organisation set up by two London doctors in 1774 to promote efforts to save people in danger of drowning.[38] The successful appeal to the Society had been advanced by the Whig MP for Devizes, Capt. James Whitley Deans Dundas (1785-1862), a Royal Navy Officer who had served in the Napoleonic Wars, and later became a knighted Admiral. His letter of support

4. *An example of the bronze medal issued to Henry Swan by the Royal Humane Society.*

was addressed to Admiral Sir Edward Codrington (1770-1851), also of the Royal Navy, a veteran of the Battle of Trafalgar and the MP for Devonport.[39]

In Henry Swan's case it may truly be said that the boy was father to the man. This youthful act of selflessness anticipated the final period of his life which was dedicated to the stewardship of Ruskin's museum at Walkley, and spent in devoted service of Ruskin's ideals, shepherding the workmen and labourers of Great Britain as they studied the collection. We will probably never know whether Swan ever told anyone about this heroic episode in his boyhood. There is no evidence that he told Ruskin about it, none of his obituarists mention it, and it has evaded researchers until now.

Before proceeding to an account of Swan's background and upbringing, it is worth noting that his friend, Winter Randell, went on to study medicine at the University of London. He graduated as a medallist with honours in chemistry in 1845. But such are the vicissitudes of fate that he died late the following year, aged only 20.[40] By contrast, Winter's elder brother, James Saunders Randell (1813-1903), whose stone-quarrying business, Randell and Saunders, which was based in Corsham, was eventually later incorporated into the Bath Stone Firms Ltd, died just a week before his 90th birthday. He remained an active company director until his death. Coincidentally, he lived for over a decade in Portland Place, Reading, in premises until recently part of the University of Reading's London Road campus (St David's Hall), where the Ruskin Collection, first in Henry Swan's care at Walkley, was stored between the 1960s and 1980s. It was also but a short distance from where Ruskin's friend, assistant and biographer W. G. Collingwood (1854-1932) resided when he served as the first Professor of Fine Art at University College, Reading.

Swan and the Randell brothers were born into nonconformist families, and they were all baptised at St Mary's Independent Chapel on Northgate Street, Devizes. Their respective fathers were tradesmen and presumably knew each other. Winter and James's father, James Randell (c.1786-1842), was a prominent local citizen, a coal merchant, brick-and-tile maker and tallow chandler (candlemaker) with premises on Market Street. A councillor, he was 'greatly respected for [his] integrity and public spirit'.[41]

Henry's father, John Swan (1790-1871) owned a toyshop in Little Brittox, a narrow alleyway lined with shops leading from the corner of Market Place to the top of the High Street in the commercial centre of Devizes. It was here, among brightly coloured and curious contrivances of all kinds, that young Henry and his siblings spent a cheerful and playful childhood. The children were not short of stimulation, and it seems reasonable to speculate that this upbringing helped inspire Henry's prodigious capacity for invention and his love of new things in later life. John Swan and his wife Elizabeth had seven children in total: Elizabeth, Ann, Francis Benet, Henry, Emma, John, and Fanny. Henry, born on 20 February 1825 (and baptised 31 July), was therefore the couple's middle (fourth) child. Two of his siblings died as children: Ann, in 1822, aged 17 months, and Emma, in 1827, aged 20 months; Elizabeth and John both lived into adulthood but died at the ages of 19 and 20 respectively. Fanny remained single into her forties, when she married a mariner, Samuel Leaman. Francis Benet Swan — known as Frank — was closest to Henry in age and spirit and plays a more substantial role than the others in the story that follows.

5. Little Brittox, Devizes, as it looks today. Henry and his siblings grew up here in the 1820s and '30s in the family toyshop.

The toyshop was certainly in the family's hands by the late 1820s, and probably shortly after Henry's christening in July 1825, the last time that John was described as a (commercial) clerk. Thereafter, he was referred to in parish registers as a (commercial) traveller. He was specifically acknowledged as a toy dealer in *J. Pigot's Commercial Directory* for 1830. In late October 1837, less than three months before Henry's heroic rescue of young Winter Randell, John Swan tried to sell the business, placing an advertisement in the local newspapers.

> To be DISPOSED OF,
> A FANCY and TOY BUSINESS, in decidedly the first situation in the Town of DEVIZES. It has been conducted upwards of 14 years by the present Proprietor, and is capable of much improvement. Is now parted with on account of his leaving the Town.
> Apply (post paid) to Mr SWAN, Little Brittox, Devizes. — N.B. *Terms Moderate*.[42]

Evidently unsuccessful in selling the business to begin with, further advertisements were placed in March and May 1838, in which John Swan made it clear that he wished to let the 'house, shop and premises' as a whole.[43]

The Swans may well have known Dr Robert Herbert Brabant (1781-1866), a physician, and his wife, Elizabeth née Hughes (1785-1864), a native of the town. The Brabants, who lived at Sandcliff, an elegant eighteenth-century townhouse two doors down from the chapel where the Swans and Randells regularly worshipped, would play host in 1843 to a young Mary Ann Evans (George Eliot), a friend of their daughter's, Elizabeth Rebecca (Rufa) Brabant (1810-1898). Evans was one of Rufa's bridesmaids at her wedding to the Christian apologist Charles Christian Hennell (1809-1856) in November 1843. Eliot's balanced but positive view of Ruskin was expressed memorably in her review of the third volume of *Modern Painters* (1856) — the book, coincidentally, which contained Henry Swan's first published engraving for Ruskin. She wrote:

> The truth of infinite value that he teaches is *realism* — the doctrine that all truth and beauty are to be attained by a humble and faithful study of nature, and not by substituting vague forms, bred by imagination on the mists of feeling, in place of definite, substantial reality. The thorough acceptance of this doctrine would remould our life; and he who teaches its application to any one department of human activity with such power as Mr Ruskin's, is a prophet for his generation.[44]

It has been asserted that Brabant was one of the models for the character of Edward Casaubon in *Middlemarch* (1871-72), that most important of English novels.[45] It is a book, as Victoria Mills has noted, that portrays the visits paid by Dorothea Brooke to the historic sites, museums and galleries of Rome as significant steps towards her creative liberation.[46] The parallel with the museum at Walkley is self-evident. It proved its power to inspire in real life and was helped inestimably to do so by its curators, Henry and Emily Swan.

Henry's mother, Elizabeth Swan (1789-1882), was also a religious dissenter baptised at St Mary's Independent Chapel. Her parents,

Joseph and Eliza Baster, ran the town's sack office, an important post in a semi-agricultural town with a significant corn market.[47] John Swan, likewise christened at St Mary's, was the son and grandson of nonconformists in Devizes. His father and grandfather, both named William Swan, and his uncle, John Swan, worked as ironmongers, and his great grandfather, another William Swan, was a whitesmith and sometime blacksmith, all trades Henry would come to know well in Sheffield. One of these William Swans, probably John's grandfather, also registered his home in the New Port area of Devizes as a nonconformist independent meeting house in 1773.[48]

In Henry Swan's boyhood and background, then, were sown the seeds of his selflessness, inventiveness and religious nonconformism, three of the defining characteristics of his fascinating life.

THREE
A New Life in London

The Swans had moved from Devizes to London by July 1838 and settled in the Kingsland area of Shoreditch (modern-day Dalston).[49] Initially, they lived at 79 Pleasant Place, off Kingsland Road, now demolished. On 27 July, soon after the family arrived, Henry's sister, Elizabeth, then aged 19 and nine months, sadly died of consumption at her parents' home. Present was a family friend from Devizes, Margaret Eden, who registered the death.[50] It must have been a terrible loss for the family, and a shockingly unwelcome and foreboding way to start their new life more than a hundred miles east of their old home in Wiltshire.

Henry's brother, Frank, quickly found work as a shop assistant for a neighbour, George Hinde Smith, a young draper. On 19 September 1840, the area proved to be anything but pleasant. Frank noticed that 19 yards (15 shillings'-worth) of flannel, which had been tied by string just outside the shop door, was missing. He later told a jury at the Old Bailey:

> I looked out, and saw the prisoner with something under his arm, covered with his great coat — I ran up — three or four persons ran, and when I got up, the flannel was on the ground, and the prisoner running away — the flannel was taken to my master's, and it was his property — it was dropped about fifty yards from the shop — I did not see him drop it.[51]

Under cross-examination, Frank added, 'I had never seen the prisoner before — he was about thirty yards from me — he had his back towards me — he said it was not him'.

A passing warehouseman, John Togue, was in no doubt that the accused man was the thief, however. He saw the robbery at close quarters and witnessed the man in the dock drop the roll of flannel. Another witness, William Neal, had run after the accused, caught him after a chase over a distance of 30 yards, and escorted him to the shop where he was handed to a policeman named William Hodge. The defendant, Thomas Crump, a 20-year-old labourer, was pronounced guilty as charged and sentenced to transportation for seven years.

This incident, together with Elizabeth's death, can scarcely have failed to underline to the Swan family that, for all the promise and opportunity London offered, life there was more hazardous than in Devizes. Whether the experience of this robbery put paid to Frank's job as a draper's assistant is not clear, but by 1841 he was working as an engraver's apprentice, articled to John Wilson at 325, The Strand, Frank's home and place of work for the next few years[52] Wilson's father, William, had been a printer, and it is clear that Frank became a specialist in lithography. By 1851, Wilson had moved on to become a hatter.

In common with his brother Frank, Henry Swan was apprenticed to the printing trade. Generally described by scholars as a copper-plate engraver,[53] Henry was indeed apprenticed as a writing engraver, articled from 2 April 1839 for a consideration of £63.[54] His master was William Richard Royle (1811-1886), of 56 High Holborn. By the mid-1840s Royle's business premises had moved along to no. 251. Royle grew up at his father's fancy-stationer's business and paper manufactory on Pall Mall and later on King Street, Holborn. He was apprenticed to Henry Dixon Smith, originally a haberdasher, of Rolls Buildings, Fetter Lane. According to his great grandson, Royle quickly 'gained a reputation as the finest lettering engraver in the country'.[55] He set up in business in 1833, and his printing firm (W. R. Royle, and from 1865, W. R. Royle & Son) survived into the twenty-first century.

Following tradition, Royle was made a Freeman of the City of London on becoming a liveryman at the age of 28 in 1838, and the following year Swan appears to have become his first apprentice. Royle is described as walking to work each morning 'in top hat and frock coat, changing into working clothes before getting down to the bench', and his apprentice's appearance, if less resplendent, was probably not much different.[56] As a writing engraver working mainly with copper, perhaps also with steel, Swan would have toiled to fulfil the company's orders for visiting or calling cards, share certificates, headed notepaper, invoices, receipts and so on.

In the early 1840s the Swan family moved the short distance from Pleasant Place to 44 Mayfield Road, Dalston. Henry's father, John Swan, who had continued to work as a commercial traveller, set up a theological bookselling partnership with Samuel Ives. Their company, Ives and Swan, was based at 14 Paternoster Row, in premises previously occupied by Benjamin Wertheim (c.1795-1856), also a specialist in theological books — and a printer and publisher, as well as a bookseller. This was a prestigious business address in the heart of London's publishing world around St Paul's Cathedral. Swan and Ives placed advertisements in a range of national, cultural, and religious journals, and in the newspapers of the university cities of Oxford and Cambridge, 'most respectfully invit[ing] the attention of Clergymen and Gentlemen preparing for Holy Orders' to view 'their extensive collection of Books in BRITISH and FOREIGN THEOLOGY, a Catalogue of which, containing nearly 5,000 articles, may be had on application to the publishers': 'Ives and Swan give the utmost value for Libraries or small parcels of Theological Books', they boasted in 1842.[57]

IVES AND SWAN,
Theological Booksellers, No. 14, Paternoster Row.

IVES & SWAN have constantly on Sale a large Collection of Theological and other Works in excellent condition, and marked at low prices, from which a liberal Discount is allowed. Catalogues of which will be regularly forwarded to Clergymen and Gentlemen favouring the Publishers with their address.
Orders for Old and New Books executed with immediate and careful attention.

---

6. *An advertisement for Ives & Swan in the* Archaeological Journal *in 1846.*

A few years later, they trumpeted 'a large Collection of Theological and other Works, in excellent condition, marked at low prices, from which a liberal discount is allowed'.[58] Whether the enterprise proved unsuccessful, or conversely so successful that in a short time John Swan could afford to retire, or whether other and unknown factors may have been at play, is not clear, but it is evident that the partnership was dissolved on 12 August 1848.[59] The business was perhaps pushed over the edge by its publication of a monthly journal, the *Gospel Banner and Biblical Treasury*, edited by W. J. Dawson, which they had taken on in February that year.[60] Ives retained the premises at Paternoster Row and continued to run the business alone. On 12 April 1851, however, the stock of books was sold by literature auctioneers, Puttock and Simpson, but records of its value and all other particulars do not appear to have survived.[61]

Decades later, in May 1882, St George's Museum at Walkley was visited by Robert Bagster (1847-1924), of 15 Paternoster Row, next door to where Ives & Swan had been based.[62] The bookseller, publisher and printer, Samuel Bagster & Son, had been based there since 1816. The firm had been founded by Robert's grandfather, Samuel Bagster the Elder (1772-1851), most famous for Bagster's polyglot Bible. Whether the Swans and Bagsters always kept in touch, or this visit to the Walkley museum was merely a happy if improbable coincidence, we cannot know, but Henry Swan would surely have remembered the family and the business.

Henry's younger brother, John Swan Jnr, died at the age of 20 on 17 July 1849. Tragically, he had succumbed to typhus fever, which developed into phthisis, a fatal disease of the lungs.[63] Notoriously, there was a cholera epidemic raging at the time and contagious diseases were threateningly commonplace in the metropolis. John was still living at the family home in Dalston. His father, in attendance at his death, reported his son's passing to the authorities on 19 July. Young John had been working as a pianoforte maker, a fact which reveals a musical interest in the family that Henry would later develop in an interesting and innovative way. According to one of Henry's obituarists, he was

> the inventor of a system of musical notation, which he taught for many years, being a staff notation of the movable doh. That is to say, a tonic sol-fa system, but with notes as easily or more easily recognisable as those of the tonic sol-fa system [… and he was] also a great student of musical instruments, especially early forms. [...][64]

There are several things to unpack here. First, it implies that Swan was possessed of a thirst and a skill for communicating knowledge, and that he had an interest, even a passion, for history and heritage as well as music. Moreover, Swan had a flair for distinguishing the fundamental elements of an issue and combining them in the simplest and most accessible of ways. Such preferences and accomplishments would be characteristic of his approach in the multifarious endeavours of a lifetime.

To be more precise about Swan's musical inventiveness, it is evident that by October 1855 Henry had developed 'the Regent Method of teaching singing at sight', and advertised his teaching services in *The Musical Times*.[65]

> A class designed especially for those engaged in tuition, or for pupils who already have some knowledge of Music, is in course of formation by the inventor of this method of training the voice and ear in singing from the notation in ordinary use. [...]
>
> For the practice of interval, for *solfeggio*, with the 'moveable Do' [*sic*], for the employment of the flats and sharps in transposition, or change of key, and for the study of modulation, composition, and harmony, the Regent Method affords facilities hitherto unknown, and is applicable either to classes or private teaching, placing within the reach of the youngest scholar points of study and practice till now confined to the advanced student.[66]

Swan charged 10s. 6d. for a course of no fewer than 12 lectures. Free tickets for the first lecture, together with other particulars, were obtainable on receipt of a 'stamped, directed envelope'. How many people signed up, and how successful it was judged to be, remains obscure. If Swan persisted with this for years, as his obituarists claimed, then his services appear to have been promoted by word-of-mouth.

Shortly after John Swan Jnr's death, the family moved the short distance to 6 Shrubland Grove.[67] By 1851, they had moved a mile north to 6 Kingsland Green, Dalston, where they remained for the next 14 or 15 years, Frank and Henry re-joining their parents' household when their apprenticeships were successfully completed.

In the latter half of the 1840s, Frank and Henry Swan set up business together in an engraving, lithography and printing partnership, F. & H. Swan. From 1847 to late 1849 they were based at 1 Rolls Buildings, Fetter Lane, a location with which, as noted, Henry's master, Royle, had been associated during his own apprenticeship, perhaps suggesting a helping hand from that quarter.[68] By October 1849, the brothers had relocated to 13 Liverpool Street, and an advertisement appeared in the Quaker journal, *The British Friend*, in May headed

ENGRAVING, PRINTING AND
LITHOGRAPHING OFFICE.
13, LIVERPOOL STREET, BISHOPSGATE, LONDON

and continuing:

F. and H. SWAN respectfully inform their friends, that they have removed their business to the above address, where they hope to execute all orders entrusted to their care to the satisfaction of their employers.

It will be the endeavour of F. and H. S., in all the branches of their trade, to ensure work of the best description for the prices charged, the moderation of which may be seen on reference to the following List [...].[69]

Said list is instructive, both for indicating the type of work they undertook, and the prices charged for it. A thousand plain cards would cost between 14s. and 20s.; a thousand enamel cards, 22s. 6d. to 35s.; a thousand invoices, in octavo, 9s. to 20s., and the same in quarto, 14s. to 24s.; a thousand note-circulars, in octavo, 20s. to 30s.; a thousand letters, in quarto, 27s. to 40s.; and the same as a single sheet, 29s. 6d. to 32s. 6d. Henry's side of the business promised 'Copper and Steel-plate Engraving. Maps, Plans, &c. at equally moderate prices. Brass and Zinc-plates, Seals, Spoons, &c., Engraved.' By August 1850, the pair addressed their advertisements both to the trade and to private customers, with 'checks', and 'glazed' address cards promising 'great beauty of texture, and purity of colour', added to the range.[70] The variety of media with which Swan had learned to work by the age of 25 was impressive.

In 1851, having presumably established their reputation more firmly, the partnership could declare simply: 'F. and H. SWAN thank their Friends for Favours hitherto received, and trust, by their care and attention, to continue to give satisfaction. Patterns and Estimates forwarded free of expense.'[71] They remained at Liverpool Street until at least 1853, when it appears the firm relocated to the brothers' residential address at Kingsland Green where they still lived with their parents. The company was in business until at least the end of 1855.[72]

Swan's obituary in the *Sheffield Independent* stated that, 'He was for some time an assistant of Isaac Pitman, the inventor of phonography, and engraved many of his plates'.[73] (Sir) Isaac Pitman (1813-1897) was, like the Swans, born in Wiltshire — Trowbridge, about 18 miles from Devizes. It is also worth noting another commonality with the Swans to which we shall return, namely the fact that from 1837 Pitman was a vegetarian, and later served as vice-president of the Vegetarian Society; also in common with the Swans, he abstained from alcohol and tobacco. Politically Pitman was a Liberal who in the course of his lifetime supported the extension of the franchise, Irish Home Rule, and the peace movement, and he was a member of the Anti-Corn Law League, and was opposed to vivisection and compulsory vaccination. Pitman was a committed Pestalozzian teacher. He rejected Methodism to become a dedicated disciple of Swedenborg. He promoted his own method of spelling reform; but he will always be remembered as the man who devised what became the most popular method of shorthand: he tirelessly promoted both.

Frank and Henry Swan were listed as members of Pitman's Phonographic Corresponding Society from 1847.[74] This places the brothers in the vanguard of students to benefit from Pitman's pioneering distance-learning programme. Postcards written in shorthand were sent to students who returned them translated for assessment, thus providing mutual feedback intended to encourage continuous improvement. Frank and Henry were also members of the Phonetic Society, founded in 1843. To call Henry Swan Pitman's 'assistant' is possibly misleading. Indeed, given that Pitman was living, teaching and publishing in Bath, it is unlikely that they often met, if they ever did so at all. The Swans evidently proved themselves to be exemplary students, though, and were among the few people entrusted to engrave and print lithographically some of Pitman's shorthand publications.

Henry engraved 'on stone' the third volume of *The Phonographic Examiner (and Aspirants' Journal)* (1855), and Frank printed it, facts declared on the title-page of each issue.[75] Volume I of the same journal, which began publication in February 1853, was printed by F. & H. Swan, too. The Swan brothers also printed the new series of Pitman's *Phonographic Magazine* from their Liverpool Street office between May 1852 and April 1853, as well as some numbers of *The Phonographic Star* in 1853. The *Star*, which began publication in 1844, was originally published by the Quaker Charles Gilpin, perhaps suggestive of a later connection, as we shall see. In the same year the Swans printed *The Book of Common Prayer* lithographed in phonography by Pitman's friend, ally and eventual biographer, Thomas Allen Reed.[76] Like most of the

Pitman periodicals, this book was published by Isaac's youngest brother, Frederick Pitman (1828-1886), at 20 Paternoster Row, again connecting the brothers back to their father's bookselling business. In common with his siblings Isaac, Benn and Henry, Frederick Pitman was a vegetarian; he published the Vegetarian Society's journal, *The Dietetic Reformer and Vegetarian Messenger*.

According to Wilfrid Hargrave — a journalist on the *Pall Mall Gazette* since 1888, a friend of Edward Carpenter's and Swan's, and one of Swan's obituarists[77] — when Swan was in Sheffield he preferred and adopted the shorthand system devised in 1877 by the physicist, Joseph Everett (1831-1904), the professor of natural philosophy at Queen's College, Belfast.[78] Swan shared with Everett a love of the bicycle: Everett invented a spring hub attachment for the spokes of bicycle-wheels that made the contraptions less uncomfortable to ride. Extant notes in the archive of the Ruskin Collection, including a list of workers involved in the farming experiment at Totley which Ruskin facilitated, proves that Swan continued to use Pitman's shorthand, or at least his version of it, into the mid-1870s when he was the curator of St George's Museum.

7. *Isaac Pitman's* Phonographic Examiner, *engraved on stone by Henry Swan and printed by the Swan brothers.*

Swan's obituarists make the further claim that

[h]e had also perfected a system of writing English words phonetically, as they are pronounced, while practically not altering in appearance to the ordinary reader, by the systematised use of Tudor or Early English letters and signs, which he proposed to utilise in teaching children to read.[79]

Owing to a want of evidence, it is not possible to assess whether this is accurate, let alone to expand on it. However, as both Frank and Henry were certainly involved in Pitman's own phonetic spelling-reform efforts, it must be regarded as plausible. In August 1853, for example, Henry Swan's name appeared in the *Phonetic Journal* (written using reformed, simplified spelling). He was one of the gentlemen prepared to consider a case of potential copyright infringement of

Pitman's phonography, and in 1859 Frank joined the London Committee of the Phonetic Institute Building Fund.[80]

Life in London had nurtured an enthusiasm and talent for learning and teaching, engraving and printing, shorthand and spelling reform, and even musical innovation. It would also introduce the brothers to new ways of living and learning, as we shall see in the following chapters which focus in turn on their adoption of vegetarianism, their attendance of drawing classes at the Working Men's College from which their friendship with Ruskin developed, their embrace of the Quaker faith, and their experiments in photography.

FOUR
VEGETARIANISM & RADICALISM

Rev. Thomas Hancock (1833-1903) related a revealing anecdote in the obituary he wrote of his friend, Henry Swan. Before looking at it, it is instructive to consider Hancock himself. Like the Swan brothers, who were between eight and 10 years older than him, he lived with his parents when he first got to know Frank and Henry in the 1850s. The Hancock home, at 48 Milner Square, Islington, was just a mile-and-a-half west of the Swans' residence. Thomas was the son of Charles Hancock (1800-1877), a mould maker turned gutta-percha manufacturer. In common with the Swans Hancock attended classes at the Working Men's College. He later worked with the Christian Socialist, Canon Henry Carey Shuttleworth (1850-1900). Hancock was a prominent member of the Guild of St Matthew and was a frequent contributor to the *Church Reformer*, published by his friend, Rev. Stewart Headlam (1847-1924), himself an admirer of Ruskin. The Christian Socialist campaigner, the Hon. Rev. James Adderley (1861-1942) reckoned Hancock 'one of [the] greatest prophets' of the church, adding parenthetically '(whom the Anglican authorities left unrequited all his days)'.[81] Hancock did most of his work as an Anglican clergyman in Harrow.[82]

As for Hancock's revealing anecdote about Henry Swan, he recalled a scene from the early 1850s:

> I remember calling one day upon Henry Swan in his bachelor days, when he lived in an old house in Kingsland-green. 'Thomas', said he, 'I am curing a cold'. He was sitting in a very small room, before a very great fire, with a blanket around him, and the largest can of cold water at his side. He said, 'When I have emptied the can['] — which would have been a task for a bullock — 'my cold will be gone'.[83]

Hancock does not say if Swan was proved right. Swan's attitude to his health, however, is evidence of his preference for an alternative, unorthodox lifestyle which is symptomatic of the perceived eccentricity that was one of the hallmarks of his extraordinary life.

Correspondence between Ruskin and the Swans shows that from April to July 1879, and at various points later in the year, Swan suffered prolonged bouts of ill-health, the nature of which remains obscure. Ruskin told Henry's wife Emily in September that he was 'glad that Henry thinks of trying water-cure' but added that 'as long as he is resolved to do only so much as he likes of what doctors order

— I have no hope of his restoration to useful health'.[84] If Ruskin was relaxed about an element of quackery, or at any rate, alternative approaches to medical care, he did not tolerate Swan's evident suspicion of medical professionals which was one of the defining characteristics of nineteenth-century radicalism, expressive of a sceptical view of authority. Swan insisted that he knew his illness to have a 'definite cause', though what that was is not disclosed.

Ruskin persistently blamed Henry's ill-health on his diet: 'I imagine that Henry's illness', he told Emily in April that year, 'is the result of prolonged mismanagement of himself in diet — and that he needs stimulus steadily given, in small quantities but for a long time to come'.[85] Ruskin meant Swan's vegetarianism. The stimulant he proposed was meat, as we shall see later.

Swan's obituarists wrote that at the time of his death he had been 'a vegetarian for the last 40 years'.[86] More specifically, and by contrast to Ruskin's assertion, as '[a]n ardent vegetarian since 1850, [Swan] attributed much of his "wiriness" to that ascetic regimen'.[87] As previously hinted, Frank and Henry may have been attracted to vegetarianism by Isaac Pitman's example. What is certain is that the brothers visited the Vegetarian Cottage in Malvern Road, Dalston, not half-a-mile east of their family home. They were both named as doing so in September 1853 in the diary of the wealthy French socialist and radical reformer, Pierre Baume (1797-1875), whom the leading figures in the vegetarian movement were keen to recruit to their cause around this time. Baume established an 'experimental garden' in Pentonville, and was also associated with Manchester where he promoted alcohol-free public houses, and with the Isle of Man where he lived the last part of his life and left a charitable bequest in the form of a generous educational fund.[88] As Baume's example suggests, vegetarianism was often bound up with radical politics as well as alternative ideas of personal health and wellbeing.

Henry was not, however, the 'Mr Swan' referred to in biographies of the radical politician Charles Bradlaugh as having represented the Political Reform League with Passmore Edwards (himself a vegetarian) in November 1858: contemporary newspapers reveal that *that* Swan was the League's secretary, William T. Swan (no relation).[89]

The Vegetarian Cottage visited by the Swan brothers was the home of George Dornbusch (1819-1873), an Austrian émigré who settled in London in the mid-1840s. A successful corn dealer, viewed with suspicion by Richard Cobden, he quickly became secretary of the London Vegetarian Association and hosted meetings at his home.[90] Resisting calls to introduce subscriptions and admission charges, he was instrumental in promoting vegetarianism to precisely that class of thrifty, self-improving artisan workers, interested in progressive social and political ideas, to which Henry and Frank Swan belonged.[91]

Dornbusch embraced a raft of causes which, partly in consequence of his advocacy, became associated more generally with vegetarianism as a movement, and it is striking to note the affinity of allegiances between Dornbusch and Henry Swan in particular. Dornbusch abstained from tea, coffee and tobacco as well as alcohol. He also keenly supported the peace movement, and this was characteristic of vegetarians from non-conformist backgrounds.[92] As a Quaker Swan certainly embraced the cause of peace, and we know that Swan was a teetotaller later in life, when he was married, because Ruskin wrote unsympathetically about it to Emily Swan in 1879:

8. George Dornbusch, a leading vegetarian.

> **You** are both of you very good — but considerable geese — in nothing more than in attempting to defend teetotalism to *me*, after what I have written of it. — It humiliates me to find all my St G[eorge's Guild] people more or less idiotic — here's Creswick been and tumbled himself off the rocks at the back of his house[93] — and hurt his stomach — I never saw such a parcel of babies as you all are.[94]

Ruskin's father had been a sherry merchant, and his freedom to study and draw and write was largely derived from the fortune his father amassed as a result. It was with the money his father made in trading alcohol that Ruskin funded the bulk of his philanthropic undertakings.

Swan also shared with Dornbusch a belief in spiritualism — though apparently Swan 'never sought unduly to put forward his opinions on the subject'.[95] Ruskin was certainly aware of this aspect of Swan's beliefs and was sympathetic to it. In November 1876, Ruskin told Henry, 'I hope Emily and you had spiritual accounts of me, when I can't give any of myself.'[96] Ruskin became keenly interested in spiritualism as he tried to come to terms with the untimely death in 1875 of his love-interest, Rose La Touche. Together with many eminent Victorians, Ruskin joined the Society for Psychical Research founded in 1882. He took the subject seriously. In 1879 he responded earnestly to Swan's contemporary at the Working Men's College, William Ward (1829-1908), who had evidently told him that his daughter (Helen) had experienced 'a vision of her brother' in which he had repeated certain verses, and Ruskin keenly asked what they meant and requested other particulars, if it would not pain her too greatly to give them:

> All evidence of this kind has hitherto failed for want of distinctness; — can you find from her the accurate time — manner of appearing and vanishing — dress — (this very important[)] — expression and gesture — and if the form was light-surrounded by darkness — or naturally dark, surrounded by light?[97]

More broadly, there is no direct evidence that Swan joined with those radicals who opposed the Anti-Contagious Diseases Act and agitated against compulsory vaccination, campaigns with which Dornbusch and others were associated. But he probably supported some of Dornbusch's other causes, such as the Sunday League promoting rational recreation on Sundays for the particular benefit of workers (for whom Sunday was typically their only day off), support of female suffrage (*i.e.* votes for women), and opposition to capital punishment and vivisection.

One might also see an unsuccessful scheme of Dornbusch's to establish a fruit-growing colony in 1858 as sowing the seed of an idea that took Ruskinian form in the 1870s in Totley, Derbyshire, to which Swan's contribution was pivotal, as we shall see.[98] Sheffield, with its tradition of radical politics, educational openness and opportunity, and religious nonconformism, was particularly receptive to community experiments. An early expression of this was a new kind of workhouse set up by Sheffield Town Council on a 45-acre site at Hollow Meadows where paupers were permitted to farm the surrounding land, an initiative of the Owenite socialist, Isaac Ironside (1808-1870), a Chartist, freethinker, trade unionist, and vegetarian. Edward Carpenter (1844-1929) would provide a rallying point for socialists on his small farm at nearby Millthorpe from the early 1880s. And a group of six young workers formed what the historian James Gregory has called 'a Kropotkinite tomato-growing colony in Norton' in the late 1880s: its founders were hailed by the *Vegetarian* magazine as pioneers of a true socialism, though not unusually, and as with Hollow Meadows, the utopia proved to be short-lived.[99]

Ruskin notoriously teased Emily Swan in the postscript to a letter written during one of Henry's minor illnesses: 'Tell Henry I should be glad to hear that he had eaten a mutton chop'.[100] Ruskin was not, however, entirely unsympathetic to vegetarianism. In Letter 90 of *Fors Clavigera* (May 1883), he published a missive from Helen Nisbet, née Currie (1850-1901), the wife of the artist, art critic and poet (James)

Hume Nisbet (1849-1923), both from Stirling in Scotland. Ruskin judged her argument 'the shortest and sensiblest I ever got yet on the vegetarian side'.[101] She described herself in her note to Ruskin as a 'mother of four vegetarian children' (she does not name them, but they were Margaret, Catherine, Iverlyn and Andrew — a daughter Noel would follow later).

Mrs Nisbet recommended the vegetarian diet to promote 'good rest at nights' and 'robust healthy children who are never fevered with fatty soups'.[102] The beneficial appeal of vegetarianism was also one of 'economy' (cost), and 'health, comfort, and cleanliness'.[103] The regimen she described was remarkably bland and austere, porridge providing the principal source of sustenance in her household, with an orange often serving as a main meal. Nevertheless, she argued compellingly that the time and money saved by adopting a vegetarian lifestyle left space to pursue more important interests and could make the crucial difference in saving the poor from starvation or destitution. She implicitly characterised deprivation as synonymous with vice, however, revealing an unattractively judgmental, even snobbish side to her character, apt to undermine the effectiveness of her otherwise evidently well-intentioned intervention.

The *Dietetic Reformer and Vegetarian Messenger* took a keen interest in this publicity for their cause. In the same month as the correspondence appeared in *Fors* (May 1883), the journal publicised Hume Nisbet's latest exhibition at his own studio on South Castle Street, Edinburgh. The notice included the words of a letter Nisbet had received from Ruskin, who was described as 'a very high authority' on art, in which he had told Nisbet

You have a real faculty for colour and sensibility to beauty, and you may be entirely independent of any help or applause. I have great hope that your gift for colour will make you an extremely popular, prosperous, and, in a true sense, excellent artist.[104]

Ruskin's letter concluded by giving Nisbet permission to use the testimonial any way he liked. The fact that Ruskin was well-disposed to Hume's work as an artist may help to explain why he was sympathetic to Helen Nisbet's advocacy of vegetarianism. 'To the surprise of all, and to our great delight,' the journal reported in July, 'Mr Ruskin has at length given attention to the subject of Vegetarian diet'.[105] Faithfully reproducing what Ruskin wrote in *Fors* — but not Mrs Nisbet's letter, which had appeared in their journal the previous August — they included the whole of Ruskin's concluding paragraph, complete with its gently mocking reference (once more) to a mutton chop.

I am in correspondence with the authoress of this letter, and will give the results arrived at in next *Fors*, only saying now that

Walter Scott, Burns, and Carlyle, are among the immortals, on her side, with a few other wise men, such as Orpheus, St Benedict, and St Bernard; and that, although under the no less wise guidance of the living Æsculapius, Sir William Gull (himself dependent much for diet on Abigail's gift to David, a bunch of raisins), I was cured of my last dangerous illness with medicine of mutton-chop, and oysters; it is conceivable that these drugs were in reality homeopathic, and hairs of the dog that bit me. I am content to-day to close the evidence for the vegetarians with Orpheus' Hymn to the Earth.[106]

Unlike Ruskin, the journal's editors did not reproduce the testimony from the 26th of the Orphic Hymns. As Cook and Wedderburn note, the 'results arrived at' by Ruskin's correspondence with Mrs Nisbet never appeared, nor was the matter pursued by the *Dietetic Reformer*.

FIVE
THE WORKING MEN'S COLLEGE, LONDON

Henry and his brother Frank attended lessons at the London Working Men's College (WMC) at 31 Red Lion Square. They were among the group of 176 students who enrolled in its first term of operation which began on 23 October 1854.[107] It was here that they quickly came under Ruskin's direct influence as students in his drawing class. Frederick Denison Maurice (1805-1872), the Unitarian turned Anglican theologian, author and Christian Socialist who founded the London WMC, wrote in 1855 that 'Mr Ruskin has procured for our Drawing class a reputation that has been reflected on the whole society, of which it forms a most important part'.[108] The Swans attended Maurice's lectures, and according to one report they were temporarily attracted to Anglicanism by his example.[109]

Maurice put his finger on the central power of Ruskin's teaching several years before their professional collaboration, when he wrote to Archdeacon Julius Hare on 13 September 1851:

> We have been reading Ruskin's chapters on clouds and water, trying a little to verify his observations. I do not know that we have done that, but at all events he is very instructive and sharpens one's own faculty of seeing, which I find is naturally very dull.[110]

Maurice's son, Frederick, wrote later that, 'To the no small delight of all, Mr Ruskin, on a circular being sent to him, volunteered to join [the WMC] and to take a drawing-class'.[111]

That is not to suggest that Ruskin shared the political outlook of the college's founders any more than he did Swan's. On the contrary, Ruskin remained a committed Ultra Tory. Nevertheless, he did consent to the college's publication of 'The Nature of Gothic', the central chapter of the middle volume of *The Stones of Venice* (1851-1853), which was produced as a standalone pamphlet, priced fourpence but initially given out free, and later sold for sixpence to raise funds. The pamphlet was subtitled 'And Herein of the True Functions of the Workman in Art', wording suggested by the formidable Frederick Furnivall (1825-1910), a friend of Ruskin's and another keen supporter of the college.[112]

This vital recent work of Ruskin's conveyed a message about the value of the artisan and his work, which Ruskin argued had reached its apotheosis in the pre-capitalist world in which masons collaborated creatively and harmoniously to produce the infinitely varied and reverential sculptures carved by hand for the medieval Gothic cathedrals. The modern industrial economy demanded mass production which reduced the workmen to slavish, dull, profane and mechanical conformity. The pamphlet took on the status of something akin to a manifesto for the college. When the same chapter was finely printed and published in 1892 for William Morris's Kelmscott Press in collaboration with George Allen, himself a graduate of the WMC, it was also absorbed into the more radical socialist revival of the late nineteenth century.[113]

Maurice told Ruskin's colleague, Charles Kingsley (1819-1875), on 3 January 1855, that 'Ruskin is doing capitally in the drawing-class at the college'.[114] Ruskin's class became a recruiting-ground for some of the key participants in his projects, notable among them George Allen, who became his publisher, and George Butterworth, John Wharlton Bunney, Arthur Burgess, William Ward and of course Henry Swan himself, all of whom went on to contribute so much to the educational work of Ruskin's Guild of St George through the museum at Sheffield, many of them by their exquisite copies of works of art, memorial studies of architecture and exemplary landscapes. Among other students was Ebenezer Cooke, who succeeded Ruskin as a drawing master at the college.

William Ward, who would excel in copying Turner's watercolours, later recalled that

> [s]ome time in 1854, a friend — Mr Henry Swan, late curator of the Ruskin Museum at Sheffield — called upon me, bringing with him Ruskin's *Seven Lamps of Architecture,* of which he read a few pages. The words came like a revelation and made a deep impression upon me. I longed to know more; and, learning that the author was actually teaching a drawing class at the Working Men's College [...] I as soon as possible enrolled myself as a pupil. I well remember the first evening. [...] entering the classroom, full of the expectation of seeing the man whose words had so charmed me [...]. [115]

A brief summary of Ward's biography will serve to elucidate the character, experiences and opinions of many students at the WMC. He was a linen merchant's clerk in London, and like Swan, was the son of a nonconformist and commercial traveller. Although Ward was from a Wesleyan background, his father, William — who was also inclined to mysticism — converted to Quakerism, and young William Ward was for a short time educated at the Friends' School on Park Lane in Croydon.[116] Previously, Ward had attended the Pestalozzian Alcott House School, in Richmond, named after the American transcendentalist and vegetarian, Amos Bronson Alcott (1799-1888), most celebrated today as the father of the author of *Little Women*. Supporters of the school played a key role in the formation of the Vegetarian Society in London in 1847. Ward and his father were both vegetarians, but later abandoned the practice.[117]

9. William Ward.

Ward's drawings very much impressed Ruskin who employed him as a copyist and supported his artistic development by sending him to study under William Holman Hunt (1827-1910). Ward later acted as an agent distributing photographs for Ruskin. In 1894 he would sell to the Corporation of Sheffield Turner's watercolour of *Sheffield from Derbyshire Lane* (c.1797) for the Ruskin Museum's collection, then at Meersbrook.[118]

Ward's recollections of life at the WMC are valuable in suggesting what the Swan brothers would also have experienced.

> A delightful reminiscence of old times is that of some pleasant rambles a few of us (who could command the leisure) had with Mr Ruskin through Dulwich Wood — now [...] covered with villas. On these occasions we took our sketching materials, and sitting in a favourable spot, perhaps opposite a broken bank partly covered with brambles and topped by a few trees, spoiled a few sheets of paper in trying to make something of it. The result on paper was not worth much; but Mr Ruskin's criticisms, and a few touches on our work, gave us some ideas that were worth a great deal. As a wind-up to these sketching parties we adjourned to the Greyhound to tea and some very interesting talk.[119]

Ruskin lost little time in employing both Swan brothers to copy illuminated manuscripts in the British Museum. Henry excelled at this work. His apprenticeship as a writing engraver must have been a considerable advantage. Henry taught Illumination to Adelaide Anne Proctor (1825-1864), the poet published by Dickens and whose parents were exceptionally well connected in the literary world. She was a student at Queen's College in Harley Street. Ruskin sent Swan to her in December 1855.[120] Around the same time, Ruskin was writing to William Ward about his 'Protestant Convent Plan' to develop a publicly funded mission of art copyists.[121] He also referred to the scheme briefly in a letter to Swan of October 1855 in which it is evident that Ruskin had consulted him on the matter.[122] The editors of the Library Edition of Ruskin's *Works*, Cook and Wedderburn, described the 'mission' as

> a community of art-workers, who were to carry out under modern conditions the labours of a mediæval *scriptorium* — bound together in some sort of brotherhood and engaged in copying illuminated manuscripts and making records of old pictures or buildings.[123]

Although nothing quite like it was ever initiated in practice, Ruskin effectively bankrolled a private version of the same scheme, and eventually formalised it in the institution of the St George's Copying Fund in the 1870s, many of the contributors to which he first got to know at the WMC, and most of the products of which would fill the museum at Walkley run for him by Henry and Emily Swan.

Although Ruskin saw merit in the work that both of the Swan brothers undertook for him, Henry proved to be more talented than Frank. Ruskin praised Henry's 'true eye for colour' in capturing a 'depth and intensity' that he found 'very delightful'.[124] Notwithstanding, in May 1856, Ruskin explained to him that he wanted to engage others in the work, and that there was a limit to the number of people whom he could so employ:

> The person whom I want to try, Miss [Octavia] Hill, will send you her address, which I forget. Please send her the folio book of illumination of different ages and show her the best types in it. I may perhaps be able to find more employment for your brother after August, but am not sure. Even if I did not try Miss Hill, I would not keep *two* workmen at illumination, now I see how little can be done. I do not say this because I think you, or he, would be ungenerous in your feeling about the matter: but that you may be free from any idea of my thinking your brother incapable of good work. It is not so, but I find the production is too slow for me to be set to it, and I want to give the work to women, who cannot do anything else.[125]

Ruskin would later feel compelled to change his mind on this last point, both in respect of women's talent in art, which he came increasingly to admire as he advanced in years, and their wider accomplishments. But the fact that Ruskin's 'brotherhood' was also a 'Protestant Convent' that could accommodate sisters as well as brothers, or in fact sisters in preference to brothers, speaks to his trust in artistic merit above social convention and other considerations.

Ruskin had met Octavia Hill (1838-1912) in November 1853 when she was aged 15. By 1855, she was secretary to the working women's classes of the WMC. If Swan ever did get to know her at all well, he would also doubtless have identified with her involvement in the making of toys for ragged school children, her first contribution towards providing for London's poor. Hill would receive a salary from Ruskin for doing copying work for the best part of a decade, providing her with a modest but steady income that helped empower her to develop the charitable activities for which she is remembered. In Hill, Ruskin had found a pioneer of social work who graduated from managing some properties bought by Ruskin in Marylebone, to overseeing one of the first, and one of the biggest, social housing schemes in England. The connection between Ruskin and Hill, though it later ended in acrimony on his part and bitter disappointment on hers (albeit, a partial reconciliation was later effected), was one of the most important in both their lives.[126] She would go on to co-found the Kyrle Society (with her sister Miranda) and the National Trust which together saved so much of the British countryside from destruction and helped so many of the least advantaged members of society to access beauty.

The fact that Swan was involved in the early days of this Hill-Ruskin relationship is further evidence of his own centrality to Ruskin's life and legacy. Ruskin sufficiently respected Swan's skill as an artist by 1856 to entrust him with the task of engraving plate 9 of the third volume of *Modern Painters* (1856) — an example of missal-painting from 'Botany of the Fourteenth Century'.[127] Moreover, Swan's engagement with the London WMC may in part explain why he went on to move his family to Sheffield in the early 1870s. This is important because it was largely owing to the fact that Swan was living in Walkley that Ruskin chose to place his museum in that suburb and to put Swan in charge of it. The connection between Sheffield and the London WMC also provided Ruskin with a reason to put his museum there.

When Maurice was hoping to set up what became the WMC, he gave a series of six lectures at Willis's Rooms in June and July 1854. In the last of them he explained:

The experiment of a Working College, which some of us wish to make in London, has been made already in Sheffield. The history of that experiment, as I have heard it, is very interesting. The necessity for it in that great manufacturing town was felt by various benevolent persons, as well as by many of the workers themselves. [...] Last autumn so eminent a man as Dr Lyon Playfair [(1818-1898), the scientist who later became a Liberal politician] proclaimed it as one of the greatest movements in modern scientific education. Nearly all the London newspapers, I believe, commented on his words, and noticed the Sheffield institution as a striking phenomenon of this age [...;] above all, the proof which the Sheffield people have given that they care for education, and will have it, and can conduct it, in an orderly, intelligent manner, increasing their numbers and their range of studies, as I hear they do, each year, is a fact to be dwelt upon with serious thankfulness. [...] I am glad that anywhere, in any town of England, manual workers should have shown the spirit which they have in Sheffield.[128]

Maurice was referring to the People's College, set up in Sheffield in 1842 by the independent minister, Robert Bayley. The college particularly attracted artisan workers keen on self-improvement, but it was also open to women. Instruction was given in a broad range of subjects, including art. Classes were taken early in the morning, before the working day began. A letter from the secretary of the college had been read out by Vansittart Neale (1810-1892) at one of the London college promoters' meetings in January 1854. This led to a motion being passed recommending that 'the Committee of Teaching and Publication [should] frame, and so far as they think fit to carry out, a plan for the establishment of a People's College in connection with the Metropolitan Associations'.[129]

It does not seem fanciful to speculate that Sheffield's radically progressive tradition in politics, education and religion — a tradition in which Swan had indirectly shared and benefitted through the London WMC — was one of the attractions that eventually called him north, though his work as an artisan engraver probably provided the more immediate incentive to move there. Nor does it seem improbable that such words of Maurice's, and of Playfair's, might have planted a seed in both Ruskin's mind and Swan's which the vicissitudes of fate — or Fors — would nurture into fruition in the years that followed.

An intriguing connection between Ruskin, Henry Swan and Oxford has been proposed in recent years. Scholars including William Frede- man, Alison Chapman, Joanne Meacock and John Holmes have speculated that Henry Swan was part of the 'jovial campaign' of 1857-58 to decorate the original Debating Hall of the Oxford Union Society.[130] The band of Pre-Raphaelite artists involved, which included William Morris and Edward Burne-Jones, was led by Dante Gabriel Rossetti, who assisted with Ruskin's classes at the WMC. Holmes has further speculated that in 1859 Henry Swan was also responsible for designing a decorative scheme for the area at the Oxford University Museum of Natural History occupied by the entomology collection donated by Frederick William Hope (1797-1862).[131] A museum news release in 2018 announcing the conservation and revitalisation of the British Insect Collection unhesitatingly ascribed the decorative work to Henry Swan.[132]

Contemporary references to 'Mr Swan' did not identify his first name, but a reference by Georgiana Burne-Jones to the Swan involved in decorating the Oxford Union reveals, on investigation, that the Swan in question was a little-remembered Irish artist, Joseph Swan (1831-1902).[133] It is most likely that Joseph Swan also worked on the University Museum, though it is not absolutely certain that the same 'Mr Swan' worked on both the Union and the University Museum. The distinctive Gothic Revival buildings, however, were designed by the Irish architects Deane & Woodward and several artists worked on both, such as Alexander Munro (1825-1871) and John Hungerford Pollen (1820-1902). No contemporary records of these buildings or of Henry Swan hint at a connection between them.

Moreover, Joseph Swan was certainly responsible around the same time for richly decorating a room in Drawda Hall, then part of University College, and now part of Queen's, using Celtic and pre-Raphaelite *motifs* and symbols that have been misidentified as the work of Morris and Burne-Jones.[134] It is implausible to argue that Henry Swan's obituarists and Ruskin scholars alike have overlooked what would otherwise have been a vitally important episode in Henry Swan's life, the story of his association with Ruskin and, by extension, our assessment of the impact of the WMC and Ruskin's broader legacy.[135]

SIX
QUAKERISM

Henry and Emily Swan were Quakers by permission — that is to say, they converted to Quakerism as adults. The *Working Men's College Journal* suggested that Henry and his brother Frank converted first to the Church of England as a result of their studies under Maurice and Ruskin, and later, to Quakerism: "'Henry and his brother Frank,' says a friend, 'were probably almost the only Englishmen who were converts to Quakerism in our time'", by which the friend presumably meant 'our time at the college'.[136] This suggests conversion in the mid-1850s, which is certainly inaccurate.

As we have seen, Frank and Henry Swan advertised their printing services in the Quaker journal, *The British Friend*, in 1849. Moreover, the records of the Society of Friends reveal that Henry first took an interest in Quakerism in 1844 around the time he completed his apprenticeship and returned to his parents in Kingsland Green. It is probable that he attended the increasingly popular Meeting House in Park Street (now Yoakley Road) in Stoke Newington, which had been founded in 1827. Swan gradually came fully to embrace Quakerism. From 1848 he was associated with the Friends' monthly meetings at their leading centre in the City at Devonshire House on Bishopsgate, very near the premises out of which the Swans came to operate their business partnership from 1849.[137] By July 1855 Henry was listed as one of two correspondents in London responsible for reporting to the conference of the Friends' First-Day School Association.[138]

From 1864 Henry and Emily Swan attended the monthly meetings of the Westminster Meeting House, which occupied large, galleried premises in Peter's Court, Hemmings Row, off St Martin's Lane.[139] The site was redeveloped in 1879 as the Duke of York's Theatre. The move from Devonshire House to Westminster was almost certainly a practical one, as a change in Henry's career had taken him west across town from Bishopsgate to Charing Cross, as we shall see. With all the zeal of a convert, Swan addressed people throughout his life using the traditionally preferred Quaker pronouns of 'thee', 'thou' and 'thine' — a practice he continued long after it had become a rather old-fashioned matter of choice for Quakers, directed by personal preference.

It is worth remarking how far removed from their roots in the Devizes toyshop Henry and Frank Swan's wholehearted embrace of Quakerism must surely have taken them. Notwithstanding, Henry Swan later appeared to find little difficulty reconciling Quakerism with playfulness, music, inventiveness, and the demands of running Ruskin's art museum. As *The Working Men's College Journal* commented, '[...] Henry Swan was a Quaker with a difference. He was a devotee of Art, and ended his life some six years ago as Curator of the St George's Museum (Mr Ruskin's) at Sheffield'.[140] On the surface, this observation, pointing out a certain contradiction between Quakerism and the work of an art-museum curator appears valid, but the bridge between them, if one were ever needed, was arguably provided by Ruskin himself.

Thomas Dixon (1831-1880), the Sunderland cork-cutter, inveterate letter-writer, and friend of so many notable figures of his day, told Ruskin, who addressed *Time & Tide* (1867) to him: 'The only religious body that approaches to your ideas of political economy is Quakerism as taught by George Fox.'[141] There is much truth in this assertion, as an important study, *The Harvest of Ruskin*, published in 1920, attests. Its insights into Ruskin and Quakerism are worth considering at some length, because the Swans' religious beliefs played an important part in their dedicated service at Sheffield. Moreover, Ruskin's ideas resolved a potential contradiction in the Swans' lives.

The author of *The Harvest of Ruskin* was John William Graham (1859-1932). Graham was himself a somewhat distinctive Quaker and a devoted Ruskinian. He was a university mathematics lecturer, and served as Principal of Dalton Hall, Manchester, from 1897 to 1924. He was a Companion and later a trustee of Ruskin's Guild of St George, and for several years from the summer of 1910 he sat with the Guild's then Master, George Thomson, on Sheffield's Ruskin Museum Committee, a role for which Thomson nominated him.[142] 'For a man who, in the name and for the sake of spiritual things, fought the good fight of a reformer during two generations', Graham wrote, 'Ruskin was but little brought into personal friendship with members of the Society of Friends.'[143] Two notable exceptions, however, were Henry Swan, and the Birmingham blacking manufacturer and local politician, George Baker (1825-1910), a Companion, trustee and Ruskin's successor as Master of the Guild, and one of its most generous benefactors.[144]

10. J. W. Graham.

Graham's insights are those of an insider — a Quaker with personal knowledge of Ruskin himself. When he, 'as one of a party of Friends, was kindly shown over [Ruskin's home,] Brantwood, by its owner in 1884', he recounted:

the only things [Ruskin] had to say to us about Quakerism in the course of a forty minutes' talk, were a little homily on sectarianism, contrasted with a church of 'God-fearing people', including Catholics and Turks — a little chaff about our failing in the matter of usury to literally obey our Bibles, as he supposed we thought we always tried to do — and an astonishing pronouncement that 'Your early Friends would have carried all before them, if they had not opposed that which is obeyed by the whole of the animal creation — the love of colour.' We must take this as one of the characteristic plunges into emphasis (some well-balanced people would use a stronger term perhaps), which are a cause at once of his strength as a stimulating teacher, and of his insufficiency as an infallible oracle, to be mechanically interpreted.

These three utterances, however, slight as they are, show a misreading of Quakerism. We are, I trust, the least sectional of little sects. The religion of the Light Within is at the basis of all other religions too; it is the absolute religion, religion reduced to its simplest, and it brings us into sympathetic connection with Evangelical, Ritualist, Jew, Mohammedan and 'heathen', so far as these have the Divine Spirit shining through their particular forms of thought and practice. Also, of all people, we are the least prone to unintelligent Biblical literalism, and are quite unlikely to be stumbled by the Mosaic regulations about usury. There is a measure of truth in his third statement about 'colour', if by that he meant, in a comprehensive sense, those recreations which relieve the strain of a severely ruled life. We have become less numerous, I doubt not, through our restrictions (now abandoned) on art, music, 'the theatre and the ball-room'. But there have been compensations to those who have stayed under the discipline.[145]

Despite Ruskin's expressed opinion, Graham nevertheless saw him as the one person in whom Quaker beliefs and concerns harmonised most closely and effectively — unintentional and unrecognised though this harmony was on both sides: Quakerism was 'a coherent system, all [of] whose parts hang together as they all appear together when they rise up in Ruskin'.[146]

This is not the place to attempt a Quaker exegesis of Ruskin's vast and varied *oeuvre*, but it will suffice here to point out some of the Quakers other than Baker and Graham who, devoted to Ruskin, contributed to the Guild's work quite independently of the Swan family: T. E. Harvey, J. E. Southall, William Doubleday, Silvanus Wilkins, A. B. Ramsay, and Sydney and Juliet Morse, for example.

Each deserves ample space, but let us focus alone on the last of those listed, namely Mrs Juliet Morse, née Tylor (1852-1937). She first became acquainted with Ruskin through her father, Alfred Tylor (1824-1884), a Quaker and geologist whom Ruskin respected. In the early 1870s Ruskin entrusted to the Tylor family management of his project to cleanse and beautify the ponds and streams of the Wandle Basin at Carshalton where they lived — specifically an area now known locally as Margaret's Pond but originally named Margaret's Well by Ruskin in memory of his mother.

Ruskin called Juliet 'a rich girl, but a very nice one' when electing her to an education committee of the Guild in order, as Catherine Morley has commented, 'to put middle class Quaker opulence in touch with provincial poverty'.[147] She went on, 'Juliet's preconceived religious ideas got in the way [...]. Attracted by [Ruskin's] radical approach but mystified, like everyone else, by his religious and philosophical views, the Quakers treated him with just enough misgiving to make all the difference.'[148] She added that Juliet 'was a conservative Quaker, choosing to wear Quaker bonnet and mauve or blue flowing Quaker silks all her life' and she points out that such dress was optional after 1859.[149]

Juliet's husband, Sydney Morse (1854-1929), in common with Juliet, was admitted as a Guild Companion by Ruskin himself before 1884. Morley points out that Morse's law partnership, which mainly handled parliamentary business, 'only put his extensive intellect to minimal use for the Guild'.[150] Morse was himself a compelling character, a keen rugby player who won three caps for England. He was an enthusiastic art collector, particularly of Blake, Whistler and the Pre-Raphaelites. It was Juliet Tylor, together with Dora Livesey of Moss Side, Manchester, and Mrs Talbot in Barmouth, Wales, whom Ruskin hoped would take legal possession of the Guild's property in the early days (1876) though Swan apparently suggested alternative arrangements, according to a letter from Ruskin: 'That "Quaker's Dozen plan" is a very pretty one, but more complex than I at present feel to be needful, or care to try. My three will do very well, and the property is to be made over to them without any reserve whatsoever, except only the condition that in the event of the decease of any one of them, their right in the property becomes vested in the surviving two: and in the event of the decease of two, in the surviving one.'[151]

Following the closure of the F. and H. Swan business partnership, Henry moved on to become a bookseller's clerk. At face value, this appears to represent a significant diminution of status, especially given his experience as an engraver which included work for Isaac Pitman,

11. Alfred William Bennett.

and bearing in mind all that he had learned from Ruskin. But the reality was somewhat different. By November 1858 Swan worked for the Quaker publisher and bookseller, Alfred William Bennett (1833-1902), at 5 Bishopsgate Street Without (opposite the Church of St Botolph without Bishopsgate), which Bennett had taken on from William and Frederick G. Cash in December 1857. These premises were near Devonshire House whose Quaker monthly meetings Swan appears to have attended. Bennett was given a Pestalozzian education which equipped him for entry into University College, London. Like his father, the Quaker tea-dealer and botanist William Bennett (1804-1873), Alfred was a vegetarian and championed a variety of progressive causes. One such cause was female education: Alfred's sister, Mary (1835-1928), whose life was dedicated to peace work and child welfare, was the first Quaker woman to go to Bedford College. Alfred and Mary's eldest brother, Edward Trusted Bennett (1831-1908), was one of the last Quakers to be expelled for heresy, and devoted his life to the Society for Psychical Research of which he was the founding secretary.

Swan probably assisted Alfred Bennett in a variety of tasks as a publisher and bookseller, but it was the photographic side of the business in which he was most involved, as we shall see. Bennett sold a wide range of photographs, especially 'stereoscopic goods': 'the largest stock in the world of first-class English Scenery', he boasted.[152] Swan worked for Bennett until at least late 1863. Bennett published no fewer than eight books with photographic illustrations during the five or six years that Swan assisted him. Among them was William Despard Hemphill's *Stereoscopic Illustrations of Clonmel, and the Surrounding Country* (1860) with 80 plates showing the abbeys, castles and scenery of this part of Ireland. S. Thompson's *Waverley Series of Cabinet Photographs* (1862) included 50 plates, and am edition of Sir Walter Scott's *Lady of the Lake* (1863) and *Lady of the Lake Album* (1863) had 14 and 24 plates respectively.

It was as a botanist rather than a publisher that Bennett would be remembered by posterity, however. He came to the attention of Charles Darwin in the early 1870s and went on to earn acclaim for his work on the flora of the Swiss Alps, a major study of which he published in 1897. A sub-editor of the journal, *Nature*, he was later a Fellow of the Royal Microscopical Society, was three times its vice-president, and he also edited its journal. Given Swan's association with Bennett and Ruskin, and the considerable overlap of their interests, it is surprising not to find any evidence of a direct connection between these great men who so influenced Henry Swan.

In 1858 Bennett had taken over the publishing business of the Quaker Liberal and moral reformer, Charles Gilpin (1815-1874). Gilpin, as we have noted, was a publisher of Pitman's *Phonographic Star*, some copies of which the Swan brothers printed. Gilpin and Bennett were both members of the Society for the Abolition of Capital Punishment. Swan may have briefly worked for Gilpin and stayed on to work for Bennett. There was certainly some continuity of business, with Bennett taking on from Gilpin the publication of the weekly Quaker journal, *The Friend*, which he also edited.[153] Gilpin was politically active as a member of the Court of Common Council of the City of London, a connection to which we shall return in the next chapter.

SEVEN
EMILY ELIZABETH CONNELL & MARRIED LIFE

By the conventions of the day, Henry Swan was quite an old bachelor at 34. The woman he married, Emily Elizabeth Connell (1835-1909), was 10 years his junior. Bride and groom lived with their respective parents until their wedding day on Thursday, 2 June 1859. Their homes were a few streets apart in Dalston and Shacklewell. Emily arrived for the wedding at Hackney Register Office from Warwick Lodge, on Amhurst Road. Henry's father and both of Emily's parents were present and signed the register as witnesses.[154] Neither bride nor groom yet knew it, but their union would prove vital in the success of Ruskin's most audacious challenge to Victorian society, the Guild of St George. Together they would successfully pilot one of the most innovative private museum projects of the nineteenth century.

Born in Clerkenwell, Emily was the third child of William Connell (1803-1863) and his wife Mary Hamlin Adams (1808-1888). There is no doubt that Emily's upbringing was significantly more comfortable and cosmopolitan than Henry's. At the time of Emily's baptism at the Church of St Mark's the Evangelist, Myddelton Square, on 11 October 1835, the Connells were living nearby, just off Goswell Road. The family had moved by 1851 to Clay Street (now Forest Road), Walthamstow, the thoroughfare on which was situated William Morris's birthplace, Elm House, and his home from 1848, Water House (now the William Morris Gallery). Of Emily's eight siblings, one did not survive infancy and young adulthood — one tragedy too many, of course, but in sharp contrast to the deaths of four of Henry's young siblings, and a poignant reminder that differences in social status did not merely mean a more or less comfortable lifestyle, but significantly impacted health outcomes, child mortality and life expectancy.

Emily's father, William Connell, was a distinguished citizen of London, described in the local press as the 'well-known and veteran Reformer' and 'the master of the Clerkenwell Watchmakers'.[155] The son of George Connell (c.1778-1815) and his wife Elizabeth Hinds (1778-1856), William was born and brought up in Camberwell. He was apprenticed in 1817. He married Mary at the iconic Anglican Church of St Bride's, Fleet Street (with the spire that reputedly spawned the multi-layered wedding cake). Around the time Emily was born he established a firm of chronometer, clock and watch makers, based initially at 22 Myddelton Street, Clerkenwell, in the centre of London's watch-making district. The company quickly achieved success and in 1845 Connell took on the business of Richard Ganthony, Master of the Clockmakers' Company, and relocated to fashionable Cheapside (no. 83).

As a member of the Worshipful Company of Clockmakers William Connell was granted the Freedom of the City on 7 April 1846. In the same year, Connell's firm was listed as supplying chronometers and watches to the Royal Navy. Connell sent chronometers for display at the Great Exhibition in 1851.[156] The business was continued and developed by Emily's younger brother, William George Connell (1837-1902), and in turn by his son, George Lawrence Connell (1876-1933), and was eventually wound down in the 1930s. In 1917, under George Lawrence Connell's ownership, the business became a public liability company, having expanded to produce fine Arts and Crafts silverware.[157] (Mary) Christine Connell (1865-1938), George Lawrence's sister, was a respected artist, sculptor, silversmith, and art critic; she married the artist John Arthur Mease Lomas (1862-1950).

12. An early C20th advertisement for Connell.

The broad business and philanthropic interests of Emily's father, William, eventually included the Provident Benefit Building Society of London, of which he was a trustee. He was evidently a shrewd tradesman. He managed to foil a pair of swindlers who attempted to defraud him of a gold watch by proffering a forged cheque, an example of deft business practice that earned him the commendation of the Lord Mayor.[158] He was involved in City of London politics from the mid-1850s onwards, serving as Common Councilman for Cheap Ward on the non-party-political Court of Common Council, the principal decision-making body of the City of London. It seems likely that he knew the Quaker Charles Gilpin, a possible mutual contact of Henry's and Emily's, through whom the couple might have met each other.

In 1859, Connell took the Chair of the Coal, Corn and Finance Committee, and in 1862 proposed that his contemporary, the Liberal statesman, and anti-Corn Law campaigner, Richard Cobden (1804-1865), who had established a successful calico printworks in Manchester, should be granted the Freedom of the City of London.[159] Connell was a keen supporter of the Ward Benevolent Fund, the Clockmakers' Pension Society, and a trade-related asylum which he helped to found, serving the last two bodies as a trustee. He also supported Kingsland Ragged School, another possible point of common interest between the Connells and the Swans. Suffering from liver problems that led to paralysis, he was increasingly confined to Warwick Lodge and was unable to conduct business. When he died, he was said to be 'deeply lamented by a very large circle of friends, including his colleagues in the Court of Common Council, who entertained for him the highest respect'.[160] His 'earnestness of manner and strict rectitude of conduct' had 'earned the cardinal esteem' of his peers.[161]

After their wedding, Henry and Emily Swan lived at 12 South Grove East, Mildmay Park, Islington, now renamed Mildmay Grove, and not far from their respective families. It was here that their first child, Howard Swan, was born on 7 March 1860.[162] The family was still living there over a year later when the census was taken on 7 April, which reveals that the Swans were one of three families with rooms at the property — probably occupying one floor of this three-storey townhouse. Another of the residents was the author, John Sutton Dell (1800-1872) and his wife, Fanny, parents of the landscape artist and illustrator, John Henry Dell (1830-1888).

The Swans would live in several houses in the 1860s, moving in order more comfortably to accommodate their growing family, and in line with Henry's increasing income. The couple's second child, Godfrey, was born on 29 January 1862 at their home, 1 Devon Villas, off Buckingham Road, De Beauvoir Town, back near Kingsland.[163] By the time their third and fourth children, Mabel and Leonard, were born respectively on 8 December 1863 and 21 May 1866, the Swans were living at Belgrave Road, Upper Holloway, though originally at no. 6 and later at no. 7.[164]

As we have seen, in the early 1860s Swan worked for Alfred Bennett in Bishopsgate. In 1864 Bennett published *Wharncliffe, Wortley, and the Valley of the Don*, followed in 1865 by his publication of his friend William Howitt's *The Ruined Abbeys of Yorkshire* and Theophilus Smith's *Sheffield and its Neighbourhood*, which contained 16, 16 and six photographic plates respectively. Although Swan had probably left Bennett's employment by the time these books were published, it is possible that he did some of the preparatory work on them. It would be a stretch to argue that these photographic books helped propel Swan northwards to Sheffield in the 1870s, though the possibility that they played their part by affording him a glimpse of the region's attractiveness cannot be discounted.

What is certain is that Swan's work for Bennett provided the context in which he experimented with photography. In the 1850s and '60s, Swan successfully adapted and advanced stereoscopy, a technology which had only been invented in 1838 by the remarkable London-based inventor, Charles Wheatstone (1802-1875). Swan's innovations constitute a significant contribution to Victorian science.

EIGHT
ADVANCING PHOTOGRAPHY

Photography was at the height of fashion in the late 1850s and early 1860s. In the competition to attract customers, inventors flourished and innovations abounded. It was in this frenetic atmosphere that in November 1858 Henry Swan came to patent 'improvements in stereoscopes and stereoscopic pictures'; 'stereoscopes and other optical instruments, stands or supports for stereoscopes'.[165] Stereoscopy made use of lenses to exploit binocular vision and create an illusion of three-dimensionality from flat images. This was typically achieved by looking through a stereoscope which separated two versions of a single image, taken from slightly different angles, with one image channelled to the viewer's left eye, and the other to the right. The buzz of excitement around the technologies associated with this form of virtual reality is not difficult to imagine. The impulse to create a sense of life in the form of animated or dynamic imagery would lead later in the same century to the invention of cinema.

Swan's initial contribution to the marketplace was his 'Registered Clairvoyant Stereoscope'. The name clearly implied something futuristic and out-of-this-world, and perhaps deliberately nodded towards his belief in spiritualism. The contraption was a handheld device described in promotional material as the 'model drawing-room stereoscope', the purchase of which promised 'a merry Christmas' in 1859, and advertisements quoted testimonials from the *Athenaeum*, *Morning Post*, and *Art Journal* which declared it 'elegant in construction and design', compact, easy to use, and convenient.[166] Images on glass, paper or in books could be placed on a stand to which a separate lens panel was attached by rods and partitioned by ribbed glass. Focus was achieved by sliding the lens panel on the rods, pushed through a thumb-sized aperture labelled 'Swan's Patent Clairvoyant'. The equipment came in a lockable, domed case, the more expensive model being made of walnut and lined with rich silk velvet, and compartmentalised for the storage of stereoscopic cards. It was labelled 'The Stereoscopic Treasury'. Some stereoscopes and boxes have survived and occasionally come up for auction today.

13. An advertisement illustration for Swan's Patent Clairvoyant.

Alfred Bennett appears to have been the sole contemporary retailer. A second and third patent for 'stereoscopic pictures and cameras for taking the same', dated 3 September 1859 and 29 February 1860 respectively were, like all of Swan's photographic patents, registered to Swan at Bennett's business premises at 5 Bishopsgate Street Without, but none bore any reference to Bennett himself.[167]

It is instructive that Henry's sister, Fanny, was described as a photographic artist in the census of 1861 — the only time an occupation was ever recorded for her. She was still living at home with her parents and brother, Frank, and neither sibling was yet married. It seems likely that Fanny was working with Henry and Bennett at this time, and she probably continued to provide assistance to her brother as he sought to make more of his inventions.[168] Frank, who ultimately pursued a longer career in photography than Henry, is likely to have come on board at an early stage, too.

Possibly dissatisfied with the modest improvements in the existing, rather clunky stereoscopic equipment which he had achieved hitherto, Swan succeeded in inventing apparatus and devising a process which offered a marketable self-contained stereoscopic portrait (an autostereoscope): he called it a 'casket portrait' or 'crystal cube miniature'. Again, Bennett was initially the sole retailer. The invention was once more patented by Swan. A successful application for an 'improvement in stereoscopic apparatus' was dated 4 December 1862 and sealed 12 May 1863.[169] The caskets or crystal cubes comprised two hand-coloured miniature photographic portraits which were typically placed in a casket or locket and fixed with precisely positioned lenses. This created the illusion of 'a solid bust in an enclosed cube of crystal', according to the *Morning Post*.[170] In a busy marketplace, it nonetheless attracted a great deal of interest. It provided a similar effect to standard stereoscopy, but with the stereoscope built-in to the bespoke portrait itself, and it was small enough, in some instances, to wear about the person or carry in a pocket or handbag. Some examples survive in the collections of the Science Museum and Victoria & Albert Museum in London.[171]

> According to the *London Evening Standard*
> The casket portrait is a still further and more effective development of the photographic process than has yet been discovered — indeed, as far as truly realistic portraiture is desired, this method, which has been discovered by Mr Swan, must meet the requirements of the most exacting in that style of individual representation. In that entirely new and original adaptation of optical illusion to the ordinary portraits taken by the photographer the head and features of the sitter have all the

distinctness and projection of a bust in marble, with the advantage of preserving the natural tints of the countenance in the most life-like manner.[172]

Reading this description, it is not difficult to imagine how Swan was motivated to mix and blend what he knew about stereoscopy, with what he had learned about art and sculpture from reading Ruskin and attending his drawing classes at the WMC, in order to make beneficial advances in photography.

As well as a 'bust' portrait, 'a whole length figure — in fact, a very minute statuette portrait' could be obtained in the form of a locket 'small enough to be worn as an elegant appendage to the watch-chain of either a lady or a gentleman'.[173] An advertisement in the *Morning Post* indicated some of the options available, and the prices charged for them.

> ON VIEW THIS DAY. — The CASKET, or CRYSTAL CUBE MINIATURES and LOCKETS patented for Great Britain, Belgium, and the United States, presenting a solid, life-like Bust in an enclosed cube of crystal, with a degree of beauty and truth wholly unattainable in a flat portrait. Lockets in finest gold of 22 carats the standard for sovereigns four guineas each; jewelled, from five guineas; set with diamonds, ten guineas. Miniatures, in morocco case, from one guinea.[174]

These were luxury, or at least high-end items, incorporating a significant amount of jewellery, and it must surely be a probability that Henry's in-laws, the Connells — experienced clock, watch and chronometer makers of Cheapside, familiar with cases and lockets of all kinds — played a role here. It is probably no coincidence that the commercial aspects of the venture came to public attention within six months of the death of Henry's father-in-law, William Connell, who left a not inconsiderable estate worth £9,000 on 16 March 1863.[175] Nevertheless, the standard '*Cartes de Visite* and *Vignettes*' were also made available on the usual terms.[176] One *carte de visite* which has survived is a portrait of the Quaker poet, Mary Howitt (1799-1888), one of Bennett's friends, and most famous for *The Spider and the Fly* (1829).[177]

In the second half of 1863, Swan seems to have left Bennett's employment. He founded the Casket Portrait Company to serve as the commercial vehicle for his invention. Its premises were at 40 Charing Cross. It is worth pausing to note the address — 'near the Admiralty' as advertisements boasted — not Regent Street as Swan's obituarists claimed. When he registered the birth of his daughter, Mabel, who was born on 8 December, Swan described himself on her birth certificate as a photographer.[178] The photographic business had clearly become a full-time commitment, and Bennett was now a customer rather than an employer. Swan's old vegetarian friend, George Dornbusch, endorsed both company and product.

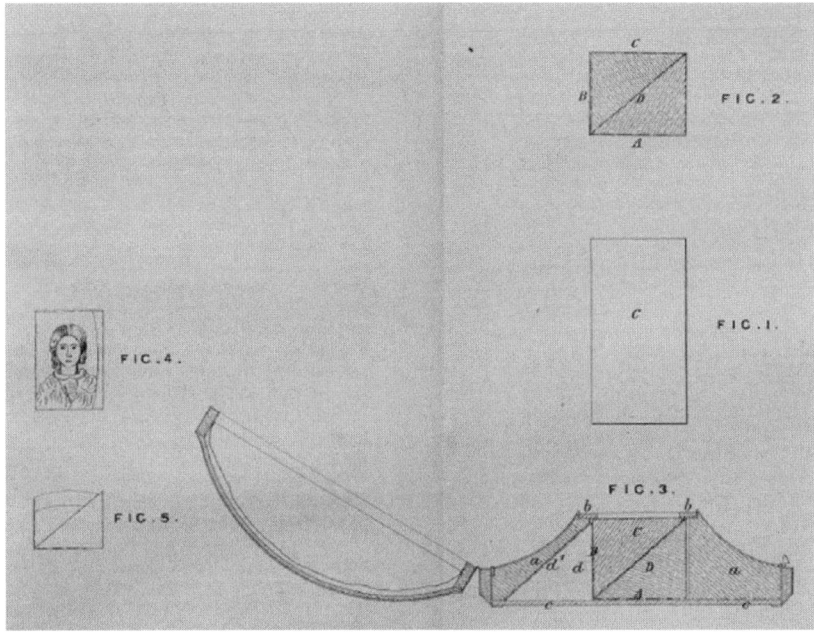

14. Swan's technical drawing illustrating the 'crystal cube' in his successful patent application.

An advertisement in *The Athenaeum* in September 1863 added France to the list of countries in which Swan's patent applied.[179] A favourable column in the *Art Journal* praised the invention, though it noted that the matter of colour had not yet been perfected. Presumably the quality of the coloration depended on the work of individual artists. Notwithstanding, the writer saw a special application for the product.

We can see many uses to which Mr Swan's portraits may be put.
There is a foreign sculptor who executes statues of celebrities from half-a-dozen photographs, back, front, and side views of the subjects. Working from these portraits enlarged would be all but working from the life, and much more suggestive than photographs in the flat.[180]

The public was invited in numerous advertisements to visit Thomas Edward Golding, the secretary of the company, at the business premises in Charing Cross, to view examples of these photographic miniatures and to judge the results for themselves. With more than a hint of hyperbole, the *London Evening Standard* declared that 'likenesses which cannot be successfully rendered on the ordinary flat photograph, are unmistakeable when produced by that method'.[181] It would be revealing to know what Ruskin thought of them. According to William

Harrison Riley, who would eventually manage the Guild's estate at Totley, Ruskin told him in the 1870s, '[...] remember, a photograph gives nearly always the worst of a face; its best insufficiently'.[182]

Swan presented his invention to the 33rd meeting of the British Association for the Advancement of Science, held in Newcastle-upon-Tyne in August and September 1863. His own description is worth quoting at length. We can almost hear his voice as Henry Swan, in his late thirties, held forth, listened to attentively by a learned and distinguished audience.

> By means of this invention is obtained a miniature representation of the human form or bust appearing as a perfectly solid figure, the image being apparently embedded in the thickness of a small, enclosed block of glass or crystal, and with a form and expression far more beautifully defined than is possible in a flat portrait. This is effected by a new application of the principles of binocular vision. A pair of transparent pictures (taken at an angle available for the effect to be produced) are obtained by the ordinary photographic process.[183] To effect the combination of these, the block of glass, or crystal, in the interior of which the solid image is to appear, is composed of two rectangular prisms ground to an angle of about thirty-nine or forty degrees. These are placed together so as to form one solid quadrangular prism, divided lengthwise by a thin film of air. If now we place one picture at the back of this combination, and the other at the side of the prism nearest to the eye, we shall find, on attempting to look through the combination, that the two images are superposed on each other, the union of which form one perfectly solid figure [...] presenting a most extraordinary and even magical effect, as though the real living being had been conjured into the centre of the solid crystal.
>
> The reason of this curious phenomenon is, that all the rays which fall on one side of a line perpendicular to the surface of the prism next the eye suffer total reflection at the oblique inner surface of the prisms, while the rays which fall on the other side are transmitted unaltered through the body of the combination. Thus it is that one of the eyes only perceives the object at the back of the prism, while to the other the picture at the side is alone visible, that apparently being at the back also. It necessarily follows that, if the pictures have been taken in accordance with the principles of binocular vision, the resulting image seen in the interior of the crystal will be quite solid, every detail appearing wrought in perfect relief with the most exquisite delicacy.

To the scientific observer it will be evident that, to produce the effect intended, care must be taken, not only that the picture shall not be misplaced, so as to produce the pseudo-scopic effect, but also that the image which suffers reflection shall be reverted, to compensate for the reversion which takes place when reflection occurs.[184]

Such a description leaves no doubt about the scientific and technical competence on which Swan's invention depended. But Swan was of course also marketing a product, and hyperbolic references to its 'magical effect' — the subject of the photographic portrait conjured in miniature and suspended in a cube — are indispensable elements in the promotional vocabulary of commercial advertising.

Yet Swan was far from alone in exalting the merits of the crystal cube miniature. *The Intellectual Observer* declared in November 1863 that 'Mr Swan's is one of those happy inventions in which art and science join, and his labours will be appreciated to the extent that they are known'.[185] In June 1864, when Golding showed a series of the company's portraits at an exhibition in the library at the Royal College of Physicians, attended by the Prince of Wales, *Saunders's News-Letter* and the *Morning Post*, which described them as 'much admired', hailed 'a new era in photographic portraiture'.[186]

In May 1866 Swan published a pair of articles about his invention in both *The Photographic News* and the *British Journal of Photography*.[187] The precision of his account reveals an acuteness of observation and a clarity of thought that demonstrate a well-developed scientific understanding and artistic sensibility. Moreover, his crystal cube miniature was an imaginative and innovative response to a commercial opportunity, and it was founded on a solid grasp of the scientific principles of optics. Yet there is a childlike playfulness both in the invention itself, and in some of the language he used to describe it, which is apt to recall a childhood spent in a toyshop. As an adult, Swan embraced innovations of many kinds. Among them, as we have seen, were his enthusiasm for phonography and phonetic spelling reform, and the 'Regent Method' of simplified musical notation he devised for teachers and pupils of singing. He clearly enjoyed developing new ways of doing things. Moreover, Swan relished a challenge.

A little more than a year after his product came on to the market, and despite the protection of his intellectual property rights that his patents were meant to afford, imitations were rife. It had become a problem, and he was forced to state in the *Morning Post* and *The Times* that

> SEVERAL Cases having occurred in which persons have been induced to purchase various settings of crystal as being the same

or possessing the same properties as SWAN'S Patent 'CRYSTAL CUBE' MINIATURES and LOCKETS, the public is hereby CAUTIONED that the only London address where these are procurable is the PATENT CASKET PORTRAIT COMPANY, 40, Charing Cross near the Admiralty.

Signed HENRY SWAN Patentee.[188]

Partly as a result of this difficulty, it is likely that Swan focused increasingly on the apparatus and technique by which the portrait was produced, rather than on the physical product itself. In December 1865 he was congratulated for the 'very ingenious and beautiful application' of his 'optical principles', with the 'hair and flesh' of the sitters for the portraits which he exhibited at the Russell Institute on Great Coram Street described as being of the 'proper tint', suggesting that some early difficulties with coloration had been overcome.[189] In September 1867 Swan attended the Paris Universal Exhibition and received 'honourable mention' by the jurors.[190] The *Illustrated London News* reckoned the crystal cube 'a new optical invention for binocular relief in miniature. [...] The object represented has all the relief as if viewed in the ordinary stereoscope'.[191] Less happily, his exhibits arrived too late for the Dublin Exhibition in August 1865 and, as a consequence, could not be seen to advantage.[192]

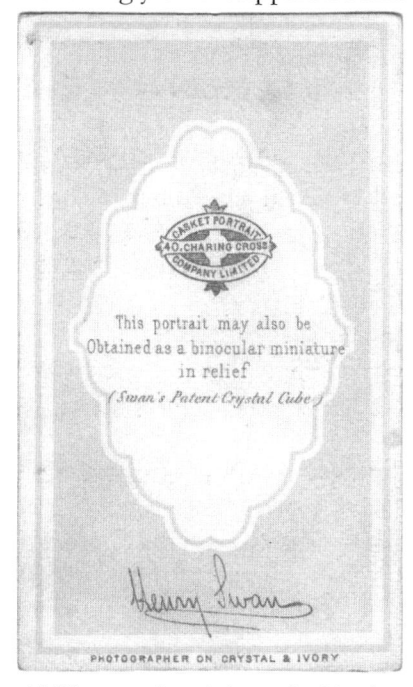

15. The reverse of a typical carte de visite from Swan's Casket Portrait Co. Ltd.

According to the widely syndicated obituaries published of Swan, 'Lord Brougham and Louis Napoleon were among his [photographic] studies'.[193] *The Photographic News* for 20 July 1866 reported that a 'marvellously life-like [portrait] of Lord Brougham' was on display at Swan's business premises in Charing Cross.[194] It had been shown at the exhibition hosted by the Photographic Society of Scotland at Edinburgh in 1864, together with a portrait of Robin Hood from a statue by Susan Durant (1827-1873) who had originally exhibited her sculpture at the Art Treasures Exhibition at Manchester in 1857.[195] A casket portrait of John Bright for the Historic Society of New York was described as 'equally a triumph of resemblance of expression and of binocular reality'.[196] Brougham and Bright were both notably radical politicians who had made great contributions to progressive causes: Brougham to the abolition of slavery, Bright to the abolition of the Corn Laws. Bright was also a Quaker. It is not difficult to appreciate how Swan thus came to photograph these famous men.

The report reproduced from the *Morning Star* concluded that Swan's photographic 'process deserves to be far better known than it is, for though somewhat more expensive than ordinary photography, it is so vastly superior in effect, and so infinitely capable of decorative and monumental use, that its special advantages more than compensate for its trifling excess of cost.' Furthermore, a 'visit to Mr Swan's rooms suffices to suggest the employment of photographic portraiture for drawing-room decoration to an extent and with an effectiveness impossible on any other principle'. Later in the year, the executive committee of the Yorkshire Fine Art and Industrial Exhibition held in York was sufficiently impressed to award Swan a certificate of merit for his 'new instrument for showing photographs in relief'.[197]

The Casket Portrait Company seems to have endured until 1868, and Swan always remained its manager. The *British Journal of Photography Annual* for 1895 noted that, along with all stereoscopic innovations, Swan's had fallen into 'desuetude a score of years ago'.[198] Contrary to the assessment of the *Morning Star*, and the many commendations and accolades the crystal cube received, the fact that its success was limited and short-lived was mainly due to its exclusivity: it was an expensive, high-end product that, in an intensely competitive and fast-moving market, fell foul of cheaper imitations which reduced Swan's market-share and perhaps helped undermine his reputation. There were other factors, too, which will be explored in the next chapter. But a large part of the responsibility for the failure belonged to Swan himself. He was not, at heart, a businessman. In 1866, he gladly shared 'instructions' about his invention for the benefit of 'the amateur or such professional photographers' interested in experimenting with it. Although he hinted at a degree of confidence that his expertise would not be easily matched, experience having taught him the 'considerable amount of judgment and precision' necessary to produce a successful result, there is no evidence that he took account of the potential commercial impact of such a gesture of openness and generosity.[199]

Additional evidence of Swan's approach to commercial competition is to be found in a letter he wrote about photographic printing in 1872. He disparaged both 'high-flown and pretentious advertisement[s]' and 'trumpet-sounding', deplored a lack of honesty in the everyday conduct of business which he implicitly seems to have regarded as inevitable in a specialised market-place motivated by the competitive pursuit of profit, and he expressed scepticism about how effectively 'advantage against rivals' might be afforded by 'the Patent Office'.[200] First and foremost, Swan was an innovator — a 'man of ideas' with the practical nous to make a reality of them.[201] But he was not competitive. There was about him a restlessness of mind and a constant energy that drove him to embrace new challenges. On the flipside, this made it difficult for him to stick at anything for long. At a basic level, he seems to have become dissatisfied with his invention. He wanted to improve it, but he yearned for new opportunities, too. One of the advantages of his constitutional bias was that he was well equipped to deal with disappointments. He had the capacity to roll with the punches and move on.

By the age of 40, Swan had excelled at engraving, phonography (in both of these reaching a standard that satisfied Isaac Pitman), the teaching of singing, drawing (copying illuminated manuscripts sufficiently well to impress Ruskin), bookselling and stereoscopic photography. He moved in radical and alternative circles buzzing with unorthodox ideas. He preferred water-cures and consumed a vegetarian, or in fact a frugivorous and teetotal diet, and he had fully embraced both Quakerism and spiritualism. According to the *Pall Mall Gazette*, he was also, in the course of his life (though precisely when is not clear), 'one of the first to introduce the now familiar bicycle into this country, and at another time made an attempt to popularize the throwing of the boomerang as an athletic exercise'.[202] Both claims seem credible though further evidence has proved elusive. A Bicycle Club was promoted to velocipede enthusiasts in Sheffield by Thomas Ibbotson, of Times' Buildings, Bow Street, as early as May 1869, before Swan arrived in the town and used Times' Buildings himself for his business premises.[203] If Swan was ever successful in riding up the steep gradients of Walkley on the sort of bicycle available in the 1870s and 1880s, with their rudimentary mechanisms, he must have been a formidably fit man for someone over 50.

As for the boomerang-throwing, two possibilities suggest themselves. When the first national cricket team from Australia visited England in 1868 on an overseas tour, the Aboriginal player known as Twopenny made such a sensational hit when batting at Bramall Lane that a record nine runs was scored from one ball (with no overthrows), a feat not quickly forgotten in Sheffield — and neither was the players' display of agility in throwing the boomerang, a sight that wowed crowds throughout the tournament.[204] Whether this influenced Swan, who was yet to move to Sheffield, or if he ever came to be aware of it, is not known. An equally uncertain second possibility is the fact that one of the leading self-styled communists involved with Ruskin's farm at Totley in the late 1870s had spent time living in Australia in the mid-1860s, namely George Shaw, whom we will meet again later. Swan certainly got to know him well, and it is plausible that Shaw brought back a boomerang on his return to Sheffield. In the absence of evidence, we are confined to speculation.

In any case, the sheer number and variety of uncommon pursuits Henry Swan enjoyed not surprisingly gave rise to a view that he was eccentric, even cranky. There is some truth in this, but Swan was a man of character and substance, skilful and intelligent in both art and science, a dreamer adept at practical execution. Any attempt to dismiss him as a Victorian oddball underestimates his seriousness of purpose, level of attainment, and his earnest sense of morality. He showed his mettle aged 12 when he saved his friend from drowning in the canal. Yet there is also, undeniably, a childlike wonder and playfulness about him, qualities that make more sense in light of the discovery that his childhood was spent in and around his father's toyshop in Devizes. Swan's photographic inventiveness combined to laudable effect that playfulness and seriousness with a scientific understanding of optics and an artistic eye for colour and form.

One regrettable observation must yet be made. This family of photographers appears to have left behind it not a single traceable picture of themselves. They seem always to have been behind rather than in front of the lens. Indeed, we do not know what Henry Swan looked like, save for a scarce and brief piece of pen portraiture by his obituarists which alludes vaguely to his physical appearance. Wilfrid Hargrave wrote that

> one saw [Swan] trudging up the steep hills that abound in the neighbourhood [of Walkley], Scotch cap on head, and coat-tails flying, [...] carrying home over his shoulder a sack of potatoes or apples (for there was 'no nonsense' about him, and he was always a very active man)[.][205]

This was, the writer understandably thought, difficult to reconcile with the thought that Swan had once been a fashionable London photographer.[206] Hargrave also remarked that Swan was '[g]entle-voiced, unassuming, and enthusiastic'.[207]

NINE
JERSEY BOYS

The Casket Portrait Company seems to have been deliberately wound down by Swan. He would write in a letter to the *British Journal of Photography* in November 1872 about 'withdrawing [his] invention from public notice'.[208] He hinted that the main reason for the decision was connected with 'some troublesome internal reflections which disturbed pleasurable vision and disgusted the eye', though he wrote in again to insist that 'disgusted' was a printer's misreading for 'disquieted', the word which more accurately described the effect and conveyed his meaning.[209]

According to the census of 2 April 1871, Henry was then employed as an engraver, but whether this was the sort of work in which he had been trained or something different is not clear. He and Emily had moved south from Islington to the Old Town area of Clapham, where they occupied 28, The Pavement, on the eastern boundary of Clapham Common.[210] They were raising a family of four children: Howard (1860-1919),[211] Godfrey (1862-1913), Mabel (1863-*aft* 1912) and Leonard (1866-1886). At the time of the census, the family was assisted by one domestic servant, which was not at all unusual for better-off artisan families.

Only Howard, then aged 11, was not living at home. He was boarding at the College House School at Chase Side, Southgate, founded in 1806, and since at least 1851 'conducted' (as advertisements had it) by Scotsman, Matthew Thomson FGS (1805-1888), and his son, James Rodway Thomson BA (1833-1893), deacon of the local independent chapel with which College House was connected. 'The situation is healthy and pleasant, premises commodious, the diet is of the first quality and unlimited', they boasted, the fee ranging from 25 to 40 guineas, depending on the pupil's age and desired range of studies.[212]

The previous half-decade had brought about significant changes for Henry's siblings, Frank and Fanny, and their parents. In the mid-1860s, all four had moved away from Kingsland to live in the Channel Islands. By 1866 the elderly parents and their middle-aged, unmarried children, who all continued to live together as a family, had settled at 28 David Place, an ample townhouse to the north of the centre of St Helier, in Jersey.[213] This private residence doubled as Frank's business premises, being only a short distance from the Royal Hotel and St Mark's Church in a busy part of town. From 1866 to 1873 Frank advertised as a photographer there. This suggests that he had probably taken an active interest in the Casket Portrait Company earlier in the decade, and it is possible that his (and Fanny's) withdrawal was another contributory factor in the company's failure. In 1867, Frank advertised in the *Jersey Times* his 'new process (hitherto unknown in the Island)', raising the possibility that he introduced the crystal cube miniature to Jersey. Moreover, the building at 28 David Place, had been associated with photography since 1850 when it was the premises of the Portrait Establishment.

John Swan died aged 81 on 28 October 1871 and was buried three days later at St Helier's nonconformist Almorah (or General) Cemetery, on Richmond Road. In 1873/4, Frank moved with the rest of the family to Langley House, a six-bay, two-storey detached villa on Rectory Lane, St Saviour, just north-east of St Helier; and, in 1879, to Undercliff, Old St John's Road, St Helier. By 1881 the family had moved again, this time to Nora(h) House, Les Marais, Grouville, a few miles east of St Saviour. The 1881 census suggests that the family unit remained solid, with Elizabeth, Frank, his sister Fanny, and her husband, English master mariner Samuel Leaman (aged 56) all living together under one roof.

Elizabeth died on 14 May 1882 at the formidable age of 92 years and six months and was buried with her husband in St Helier. At about this time, or shortly afterwards, Frank appears to have retired from business. He remained a convinced vegetarian and had re-subscribed to the national society in 1877.[214] In April 1882, shortly before his mother's death, he advertised in the pages of the *Dietetic Reformer* his willingness to 'accommodate Vegetarian travellers on reasonable terms'.[215] What happened to him thereafter remains a mystery, likewise the fate of his sister and brother-in-law. He may have been the same Frank B. Swan found in US naturalization records who emigrated to America in 1883, and settled in North Dakota by 1886. There is insufficient information to be sure, but it might explain how Henry's son, Godfrey, came to emigrate to America later in the decade — following in his uncle's footsteps. In any case, in continuing the Swan family's association with photography into the early 1880s, Frank carried the connection, which had begun in the 1850s, into a fourth decade.[216]

There is no doubt that Henry visited Jersey to see his family. It is very likely that he attended his parents' funerals. But it is almost certain, too, that he lived there for a while, possibly minded to move there after the death of his father in October 1871. It would have meant that he could be closer to his elderly mother, and he may well have joined Frank's photography business. Henry's letter to the *British Journal of Photography*, quoted in the opening paragraph of this chapter, was dated

9 November 1872, and was sent from Mont à l'Abbé, a district northwest of the centre of St Helier. Henry had been prompted to contact the editors of the *BJP* after another correspondent had asked for information about the 'cube miniature'. Henry pointed out that he had patented the product, and referred the reader to an article in an earlier issue of the journal in which he had fully described it. What he went on to say makes it clear that he continued to experiment with his stereoscopic invention. Having acknowledged the shortcomings of the original crystal cube, he explained that he had since 'devise[d] an arrangement' which remedied them, 'while presenting the same perfect appearance of relief on a larger scale' and, he concluded,

> this new mode of construction possesses peculiarities which point to a much wider range of popular use than was possible for the old form under the most favourable circumstances, and I trust at no very distant date to bring the matter before the photographic public in a more explicit form. [217]

Sadly, it does not appear that this promise was ever fulfilled.

By March 1876 the *BJP* reported that 'so far as we know, there is no one who now produces such portraits, and this is to be regretted'.[218] Yet people were still asking about it in 1893, after Swan's death.[219] It seems unlikely, given the hope Henry expressed in his letter, that he would have used for publication an address other than that of his permanent residence. Moreover, as we shall see, in a letter of April 1873 also addressed from Jersey, in which he scrutinised the island's economy, he refers to 'the landlord of the house I live in'.[220] This is language and content which is emphatically not suggestive of a short visit to see a relative, or make a holiday. This letter, and another not yet mentioned, together supply vitally important evidence which we shall now examine.

The letter sent from Mont à l'Abbé, Jersey and dated 17 April 1873 was quoted anonymously by Ruskin in the pages of *Fors Clavigera*. Ruskin wrote that the letter provided an 'account of the changes produced by recent trade in the country life of the island of Jersey'.[221] He reproduced it in the body of the text of Letter 30 of *Fors* (June 1873) because it was, he declared, 'of the highest value' and 'quite as important as anything I have myself to say'.[222] Before scrutinising the contents of that letter, let us consider what evidence there is, besides Henry's proven stay at Mont à l' Abbé in November 1872 and his family connections with Jersey, to suggest that he was the author of this important letter to Ruskin. This is crucial because no Ruskin scholar, Cook and Wedderburn included, has ever identified the author of the letter before now. Ruskin told his readers that the letter about Jersey had come from 'the correspondent who directed me to Professor Kirk's book'. Unhelpfully, said correspondent was also unnamed in the text, but Ruskin explains that the tip about Kirk was contained in a 'letter of great interest' of late 1872, from which he quoted at length in the 'Notes and Correspondence' section following Letter 29 of *Fors* (May 1873). It emerges that the correspondent was a Quaker and a temperance man.[223] Furthermore, the letter about Jersey was from someone who addressed Ruskin as 'Master' and described himself as an 'essentially [...] frugivorous animal', a clear reference to vegetarianism.[224] It is possible that Ruskin's correspondent was Frank Swan, since he also matches this description, except that there is no evidence that Ruskin and Frank had direct contact after the Working Men's College years, and Frank would have been well advised to use his business and residential address at David Place. Only Henry was provably connected with Mont à l'Abbé.

The two letters quoted by Ruskin, which touch upon matters of social and economic interest, and evidently impressed him greatly, would seem to offer vitally important pieces of the jigsaw puzzle which have hitherto been missing, though hiding in plain sight. They are significant because they show that Swan and Ruskin kept up an important correspondence in the early 1870s. They reveal a great deal about Swan's interests at this time, and how far they coincided with Ruskin's own. And they demonstrate that Swan was a dedicated reader of *Fors*. It is vital to examine the letters and Ruskin's responses to them in detail because they represent a public conversation about the state of the world in which these interlocutors lived. Moreover, they bring into focus how and why Ruskin came to have so much faith in Henry Swan that in 1875 he entrusted him with the task of curating his exemplary educational museum for the benefit of the workmen and labourers of Great Britain, and chose to locate it in the spot where Swan was then living.

Swan's interest in the Rev. Prof. John Kirk's *Social Politics in Great Britain and Ireland* (1870) related to 'the robbing of the poor by the rich, through temptation of drink'.[225] Ruskin had drawn on the book's arguments in Letter 27 of *Fors* (March 1873).[226] Swan took issue with Kirk: 'to my mind the inquiry does not reach deep enough', he wrote, and he asked two questions. First, why should 'the workers have so little control over their appetites in this direction' (*i.e.* the consumption of alcohol); second, why 'those who wish to drain the working men are permitted to govern them': in both cases, he asked what might be the remedy, adding, 'The answers to each question will, I think, be found to be nearly related'.[227] Ruskin responded that workers were hindered by the nature of their work from rational and domestic pleasures, and given that manual work made people thirsty, 'Intoxication is the only

Heaven that, practically, Christian England ever displays for them'.[228] England was not truly Christian at all, in other words, and Ruskin's irony was that of the son of a sherry merchant, albeit that the intoxicant under discussion here was of an altogether different character.

Ruskin proceeded in a characteristic vein, blending Ultra Toryism and radicalism. He criticised working-class politics for seeking equality, disparaged the naivety of its representatives, and denied the merits of popular democracy. Yet such disapproval of the ruled was matched, and in fact surpassed, by his contempt for the rulers — the middle and upper-class politicians whom he denounced as irredeemably corrupt. Ruskin lamented the fact that for 50 years (a duration he does not explain) the workers had been told that 'one man is as good as another', so 'they never think of looking for a good man to govern them' and the only people who volunteered to govern them 'intend to pillage or cheat them' and it was only such people that could

> succeed in doing so, because as long as they trust in their own sagacity, any knave can humbug them to the top of his bent; while no wise man can teach them anything whatever, contrary to their immediate notions.[229]

If Ruskin's anti-democratic, hierarchical, Platonic politics of wise leadership were not clear to readers, including Swan, he pointed them to the 'republican correspondent's observations on election, [discussed] in the next letter' where Ruskin warmed to his theme in response to a letter, quoted anonymously, but in fact from the socialist William Harrison Riley whom we will meet again in chapter eleven.[230] As to the remedy for the problems about which Swan had asked, Ruskin drew on the Bible and his Christian sense of morality to advise only that one's duty was always to remain 'cool and fearless', and to 'do what is instantly serviceable to the people nearest him, and the best he can, silently, for all.'[231]

How far Swan was persuaded by Ruskin's reactionary yet radical analysis is difficult to assess, though the Christian moralism of the (albeit vague) remedy certainly did appeal to him. Ruskin's politics were at odds with those of the radical circles in which Swan had previously mixed. Yet it was not uncommon for Ruskin's disciples to harbour quite different political views to the man whose social and economic insights they nonetheless valued, Riley being another case in point. Given that Swan was on the verge of dedicating the rest of his life to Ruskinian projects associated with the Guild of St George, he presumably felt sufficiently comfortable with Ruskin's point-of-view that he could reconcile it with his own outlook. Swan was keenly attracted by Ruskin's notion of quiet and unobtrusive influence, which held that exemplary personal conduct and neighbourly service would reap benefits for the wider community. This is where Ruskin's Christian moralism substantially overlapped with socialistic ideals, and where differences in motivation, analysis and even intent dissolved into a shared communitarian concern for the commonweal — that is to say, the welfare of all. Ruskin, and many people within a more straightforwardly radical tradition, such as Swan, viewed society as an organism, and identified industrial capitalism and commercial competition as their common enemies — the deadly diseases poisoning the body politic.

'The possibility of a watchful and exacting, yet respected, government within a government,' Swan told Ruskin, 'is well shown by the existence and discipline of the Society of Friends, of which I am a member.'[232] He wondered if the public's opinion of Quakerism, which had been injured by 'narrow views of religious truth', had been more severely harmed by 'their change from an agricultural to a trading people' which had 'sap[ped] the vital strength of their early days'.[233] Ruskin remarked that this 'sentence respecting the corrupting power of trade, as opposed to agriculture, is certainly right, and very notable.'[234]

Swan's letter ended by quoting from an obituary of the Quaker philanthropist and Bristol-based pin manufacturer Robert Charleton (1809-1872). 'In him', the notice claimed,

> the poor and needy, the oppressed, the fallen and friendless, and the lonely sufferer, ever had a tender and faithful friend. When in trade, he was one of the best employers England could boast. He lived for his people, rather than expected them to live for him; and when he did not derive one penny profit from his factory, but rather lost by it, he still kept the business going, for the sake of his workpeople.[235]

Swan clearly regarded such selflessness as admirably noble, but Ruskin, reminded no doubt of his attack in 'The Nature of Gothic' (the text vital to the origins of the WMC) on Adam Smith's advocacy of the division-of-labour in the manufacturing of pins, as advanced in the *Wealth of Nations* (1776), asked whether 'keeping useless work going on, for the sake of the workpeople, be not the wisest thing to do for the sake of *other* people?'[236] Here we have the radical Ruskin that appealed to William Morris and other socialists. Ruskin wished to see a fundamental re-organisation of society that would reject redundant mechanical efficiency in favour of recuperating the useful, creative and soulful work of the medieval artisan, imperfect but reverential, individual but collaborative rather than atomized, and manageable in scale and scope. Keeping people at useless work was destructive for everyone, because it perpetuated a broken system that undermined health, happiness, and social good.

Swan's politics, the nature and extent of his understanding and appreciation of Ruskin's purpose in setting up what became the Guild of St George, and his own obsessions (notably his opposition to the consumption of meat, alcohol and tobacco) emerge most strongly in his long letter about social and economic conditions in Jersey. As such, it merits quotation in full, exactly as it appeared in *Fors*, with Ruskin's emphasis marked by the use of italics. Ruskin's response to it is equally instructive, as we shall see. Swan's focus is on what today we might call a 'cost-of-living' crisis, the distorting impact of modern trade and finance, specifically in the rural economy and, his chief concern, the disproportionately negative effects of both on the lives of the poor, specifically their opportunities for rational recreation.

'The lesson I have gathered here in Jersey as to the practical working of bodies of small landowners,' Swan wrote,

> is that they have three arch-enemies to their life and well-being. First, the covetousness that, for the sake of money-increase, permits and seeks that great cities should drain the island of its life-blood — their best men and their best food or means of food; secondly, love of strong drink and tobacco; *and* thirdly (for these two last are closely connected), want to true recreation.
>
> The island is cut up into small properties or holdings, a very much larger proportion of these being occupied and cultivated by the owners themselves than is the case in England. Consequently, as I think, the poor do not suffer as much as in England. Still the times have altered greatly for the worse within the memory of every middle-aged resident, and the change has been wrought chiefly *by the regular and frequent communication* with London and Paris, but more especially the first, which *in the matter of luxuries of the table, has a maw insatiable*.[237] Thus the Jersey farmer finds that, by devoting his best labour and land to the raising of potatoes sufficiently early to obtain a fancy price for them, very large money-gains are sometimes obtained, — subject also to large risks; for spring frosts on the one hand, and being outstripped by more venturous farmers on the other, are the Jersey farmers' Scylla and Charybdis.
>
> Now for the results. Land, especially that with southern aspect, has increased marvellously in price. Wages have also risen. In many employments nearly doubled. Twenty years ago a carpenter obtained 1s. 8d. per day. Now he gets 3s.; and field labourers' wages have risen nearly as much in proportion. *But* food and lodging have *much more* than doubled. Potatoes for

ordinary consumption are now from 2s. 6d. to 3s. 6d. per cabot (40 lb.); here I put out of court the early potatoes, which bring, to those who are fortunate in the race, three times that price. Fifteen years ago the regular price for the same quantity was from 5d. to 8d. Butter is now 1s. 4d. per lb. Then it was 6d.; and milk of course has altered in the same proportion. *Fruit, which formerly could be had in lavish, nay almost fabulous abundance, is now dearer than in London.* In fact I, who am essentially a frugivorous animal, have found myself unable to indulge in it, and it is only at very rare intervals to be found in any shape at my table. All work harder, and all fare worse; but *the poor especially so.* The well-to-do possess a secret solace denied to them. It is found in the 'share market'. I am told by one employed in a banking-house and 'finance' business here, that it is quite wonderful how fond the Jersey farmers are of Turkish bonds, Grecian and Spanish coupons. Shares in mines seem also to find favour here. My friend in the banking-house tells me that he was once induced to try his fortune in that way. To be cautious, he invested in four different mines. It was perhaps fortunate for him that he never received a penny of his money back from any one of the four.

Another mode by which the earnings of the saving and industrious Jerseyman find their way back to London or Paris is the uncalculated, but not unfrequent, advent of a spendthrift among the heirs of the family. I am told that the landlord of the house I live in is of this stamp, and that two years more of the same rate of expenditure at Paris that he now uses, will bring him to the end of his patrimony.

But what of the stimulants, and the want of recreation? I have coupled these together because I think that drinking is an attempt to find, by a short and easy way, the reward of a true recreation; to supply a coarse goad to the wits, so that there may be forced or fancied increase of play to the imagination, and to experience, with this, an agreeable physical sensation. I think men will usually drink to get the fascinating combination of the two. True recreation is the cure, and this is not adequately supplied here, either in kind or degree, by tea-meetings and the various religious 'services,' which are almost the only social recreations (no irreverence intended by thus classing them) in use among the country folk of Jersey.

But I had better keep to my facts. The deductions I can well leave to my master.

Here is a fact as to the working of the modern finance system here. There is exceedingly little gold coin in the island; in place thereof we use one-pound notes issued by the banks of the island. *The principal bank issuing these, and also possessing by far the largest list of depositors, has just failed. Liabilities, as estimated by the accountants, not less than £332,000; assets calculated by the same authorities not exceeding £34,000.*[238] The whole island is thrown into the same sort of catastrophe as English merchants by the Overend-Gurney failure.[239] Business in the town nearly at a stand-still, and failures of tradesmen taking place one after another, with a large reserve of the same in prospect. But as the country people are as hard at work as ever, and the panic among the islanders has hindered in nowise the shooting of the blades through the earth, and general bursting forth of buds on the trees, I begin to think the island may survive to find some other chasm for their accumulations. Unless indeed the champion slays the dragon first.[240]

Swan's optimistic notion that the banking crisis might result in a beneficial recalibration of Jersey's economy was in vain. He had witnessed a financial crash, the consequences of which were only beginning to show. It was a symptom of a wider problem, and Jersey, and the whole United Kingdom, would experience a prolonged period of economic depression.

In a modest parenthetical flourish at the end of Swan's letter, he responded to what Ruskin had written at the start of Letter 24 of *Fors* (December 1872). Ruskin had declared that he would neither call his readers or anyone else, his 'friends', and would not sign off his letters 'faithfully', because it was not honest to do so, and he then speculated about the origins of his surname.[241] Swan responded with a charming compliment: 'As far as one of the unlearned may have an opinion, I strongly object both to "Rough skin", and "Red skin", as name derivations. There have been useful words derived from two sources, and I shall hold that the Latin prefix to the Saxon *kin* establishes a sort of relationship with St George.'[242] Ruskin, flattered by this 'pretty' philological speculation, insisted that derivation from two languages was untenable. More significantly, he declared that neither Swan 'nor any of my readers, must think of me as setting myself up either for a champion or a leader'. They should read the first issue of *Fors*, he told them, and proceeded to outline what he saw as his true role, acknowledging his limitations, and underlining the two lessons upon which the Guild was founded. Written in reply to Swan, it is a memorable expression of Ruskin's prophetic vision. His readers, he claimed,

> will find [*Fors*] is expressly written to quit myself of public responsibility in pursuing my private work. Its purpose is to state

clearly what must be done by all of us, as we can, in our place; and to fulfil what duty I personally acknowledge to the State; also I have promised, if I live, to show some example of what I know to be necessary, if no more able person will show it first. That is a very different thing from pretending to leadership in a movement which must one day be as wide as the world. Nay, even my marching days may perhaps soon be over, and the best that I can make of myself be a faithful sign-post. But what I am, or what I fail to be, is of no moment to the cause. The two facts which I have to teach, or sign, though alone, as it seems, at present, in the signature, that food can only be got out of the ground, and happiness only out of honesty, are not altogether dependent on any one's championship, for recognition among mankind.[243]

We cannot know if Henry Swan read this as a call to action. Nor whether he perceived the note of warning, particularly about Ruskin's suitability as Master of the Guild, and his capacity to steer the organisation. But in what Ruskin *was* able to do in the years that followed, Swan would be central to the effort.

A letter of Swan's that appeared in the *British Journal of Photography*, written in November 1872 when he lived in Jersey, provides further evidence of the extent to which his political views were in sympathy with Ruskin's.[244] Swan's avid reading of *Fors Clavigera* expressed itself in a Ruskinian attack on commercial competition in the world of printing and publishing in which he justifiably claimed to have had practical experience for more than 20 years. One could not expect a commercial copper- or steel-plate printer to turn away a large order simply because he knew that lithographic transfer 'would serve equally well at half the cost or less'. Rather, he would accept the order and wait till his customer knew better. But if the printing-house could undertake both types of work, the more appropriate form would be offered, depending on whether 'clearness' or 'low price' was the customer's priority. The letter was titled, 'Monopoly through Coalition', and in what it recommended about combining the various branches of photographic printing in a single business — calotype, carbon printing, lithography etc. — Swan sought to promote an honesty of conduct that he believed would obviate the need for wasteful and meaningless advertising.

Swan was arguing a Ruskinian case and did it in language familiar to readers of *Fors*, not that many readers of the photographic journal would probably have recognised it. Swan wrote, for example, of publishers 'flying from one suburb of the metropolis to another to compare testimonials and specimens of most puzzlingly-superlative quality', but his 'time and thought' could yet be saved 'with profit to himself and the public' if only Swan's recommendations were adopted. The amalgamation of existing companies would provide 'a coalition of interests' which 'would be for the good of all concerned' and would optimise the advantage of experience and commonsense, but if such combination proved impossible because of existing vested interests, new businesses should form to offer the full range of services. In this last admission — though it was not Swan's preference — we have a hint that he adopted a generally more flexible and pragmatic approach than Ruskin. He would, for example, subsequently be more sympathetic to the co-operative movement than his master.

This previously unexamined evidence of Swan's views, from his hitherto unknown period of residency in Jersey, provides the best clue yet as to how Ruskin came to place him in such a pivotal role in the Guild of St George. Ruskin wrote to him in July 1875, 'It is very wonderful to me the coming of your letters just at this time. The chief point in my own mind in material of education is the getting a museum, however small, well explained and clearly and easily seen.'[245] This is the germ of an idea that would immerse Henry Swan in the fruitful collaboration with Ruskin that proved to be the crowning glory of his life's work. Sheffield beckoned, and in turn Swan drew Ruskin there, a fact Ruskin acknowledged in 1876 when he wrote of Swan's 'dream that brought me to Sheffield'.[246]

TEN
RUSKIN'S MUSEUM AT WALKLEY

No definite account of why the Swans moved to Sheffield has come to light, but it is likely that the promise of work the town offered an engraver of Henry's skill and experience was part of the attraction. However though nobody yet knew it, the country was entering a period of prolonged economic depression. The family was certainly living in Sheffield by February 1874,[247] but they probably moved there in the summer of 1873. Ruskin wrote on 8 August that he marked the Swans' address, suggesting it had changed since April when he received the letter from Jersey, and he had written in early July that something could wait 'till you are well on your legs', implying recent change.[248]

Swan found work as a silver engraver, and was apparently employed by one of the town's many manufacturers of designed silverware. He may have worked with Ernest Hill (1834-1917), a skilled silver chaser from Nether Edge whom he certainly got to know well. Hill produced fine silverware with ornamented design-work, and patented machinery for engine-turned metal engraving which produced results that were sufficiently impressive to be exhibited internationally. Ruskin referred to a 'pen drawing reduced by mechanical engraving' in a letter to Swan in November 1873.[249] Hill was the branch secretary of the National Education League, campaigned for longer library opening times for the benefit of workers, and was one among the group of working men whom Swan introduced to Ruskin in April 1876.[250]

A response from Ruskin to Swan quoted by Mark Frost implies that Henry was not wholly content with the type and quality of work in which he was engaged: 'don't fret over your work — whatever you think of it. It may be useless and vulgar; but need not be deleterious'.[251] Whether these were originally Swan's adjectives or Ruskin's insensitive selection is unclear. By August 1875 Swan was linked to 33 Times Buildings, on Bow Street (today's West Street), suggesting that he may have set up by then on his own account.[252] This was a commercial address: the architects Hill and Swann (two 'n's and unrelated) were among companies based in the same building.

Ruskin wrote to Henry in May 1875, 'I will really come to Walkley one of these days', indicating that the Swans were by then resident in that north-west district of Sheffield.[253] The 1876 edition of *White's General and Commercial Directory of Sheffield* lists Swan in Bell Hagg Road, Walkley, still working as an engraver.[254] Ruskin's museum was not yet up and running at the time of the directory's compilation. Walkley was a young and growing suburb populated mainly by metalworkers, a large proportion of them artisans of the same stamp as Swan himself. Construction of its parish church of St Mary's had only begun in 1861 and was then enlarged and consecrated in 1869. The museum was set high on the hills leading out of Sheffield into the surrounding countryside, a cultural beacon on the edge of the town.

In a long tribute to Ruskin published on his death, the *Sheffield Independent* told its readers that Swan 'was not long in discovering the class of men by whom he was surrounded, and by whom Walkley is chiefly inhabited' and, believing that Sheffield in general and Walkley in particular would provide the perfect location for the sort of museum Ruskin had long contemplated, Swan had written,

> informing him of the skill, intelligence, and industry of the artisan class with whom he had been brought into contact here, and that they were engaged in sound serviceable work to mankind to a larger extent than the men in any other town with which he was acquainted. He expressed the confident belief — a conclusion reached from personal observation — that the men of Sheffield were extremely likely to be benefited by having such a museum in their midst as Mr Ruskin contemplated establishing, and that they would enter very heartily and cordially into any organisation for the raising of their position as a class.[255]

That last ambition expressly was not Ruskin's purpose. Rather, he hoped that more knowledgeable, skilled and fulfilled workers would create more useful and beautiful things. He did not seek to make 'a carpenter an artist', but to make 'him happier as a carpenter', as he put it to the National Gallery Site Commission in April 1857.[256]

Ruskin visited Sheffield from 26 to 27 September 1875. He stayed at the Royal Hotel, and Swan showed him the detached cottage and its surrounding land at Bell Hagg Road. Ruskin clearly approved and quickly bought it for £630 from the trustees of the estate of George Wright (c.1797-1874), a local builder. It would serve both as St George's Museum and the Swan family's home for nearly 15 years.

In August 1876, an anonymous Oxford man who visited Ruskin's museum, asked Swan directly why Sheffield had been chosen for its location, and specifically why Walkley had been selected. Swan gave 'what seemed a very satisfactory reply, and as complimentary to the people of Sheffield satisfactory to us'. It is worth quoting in full because it expands on the explanation given in the introduction to this biography.

> It is a fact that, as a rule, Sheffield workmen are more honest and careful in their wish to turn out good work than the workmen of other towns — *e.g.*, of Birmingham or London. The Sheffield

workman, 'like Antonio Stradivari, has an eye/ That winces at false work and loves the true.' [*i.e. quoting from the poem by George Eliot.*]

Again, Walkley is noted for this — that its cottages are chiefly freehold, and their occupants seem to take a pride in the little plots of ground which, for the most part, surround their houses; and they are to be seen after the daily task is ended employed in making the land useful and ornamental by growing vegetables and flowers. No doubt also the general absence of smoke in this locality has been a weighty consideration in causing Mr Ruskin to choose Walkley.[257]

It is highly likely that soon after moving to the town, Henry Swan became involved with the Sheffield Literary and Philosophical Society and the Hall of Science on Rockingham Street, two fertile recruiting grounds for potential local Ruskinians, and lively forums for cultural and intellectual exchange. The latter, in particular, attracted many autodidact artisans. This was precisely the class of person which made up the bulk of the membership of the freehold land societies that built so many of Walkley's houses. These societies afforded their members the opportunity to invest in their own homes. It protected residents from insecure tenure resulting from rising rents and landlords selling out to rich and unsympathetic developers.

Swan was paid for his work as curator of Ruskin's museum from 1 October 1875,[258] though the appointment was officially dated to 1 November.[259] Nevertheless, the Swans did not move into the cottage until some time after 11 November.[260] Ruskin had aptly remarked to Henry on 22 October, 'You and your wife seem to have been sent to Sheffield to be ready for me, to take care of this place'.[261] In February 1876 Ruskin told readers of *Fors Clavigera*:

I have appointed a Curator to the Sheffield Museum, namely, Mr Henry Swan, an old pupil of mine in the Working Men's College in London; and known to me since as an estimable and trustworthy person, with a salary of forty pounds a year, and residence. He is obliged at present to live in the lower rooms of the little house which is to be the nucleus of the museum: — as soon as we can afford it, a curator's house must be built outside of it.[262]

Such a house never came to be built, though there was an extension made to the curator's living quarters in 1882-83. In August 1877, Swan's salary was raised substantially to £100 *per annum*.[263]

The museum may have opened to some visitors as early as November 1875, but it was certainly in operation by April 1876, though in nascent form, and it was still getting on its feet come August.[264] As the months rolled by, Ruskin sent ever more treasures, far more than the single upstairs room of between 12 and 13 square feet — the total extent of the museum — could possibly accommodate. The room was to be painted as white as non-poisonous paint could make it, with removable, washable curtains fastened down.

Generally, Ruskin gave detailed and exacting instructions on how items should be displayed, though sometimes his mind was on other matters, and he did not wish to be bothered with questions. It was always difficult for the Swans to know quite where they stood. But Ruskin specified the dimensions of cabinets and insisted they should be on castors so they could be easily manoeuvred. He stipulated the exact sizes of different drawers and their compartments, precisely how they should lock and slide, and he directed that they should be made of mahogany by a local craftsman. He dictated how items should be arranged and often instructed Henry and Emily on how they could be presented to their best advantage, giving attention to issues such as the colour and material on which items were laid, and concerning himself with the extent to which exhibits were exposed to light. He even wanted the letters and numbers on display labels to be stitched by hand. At other times he bluntly disavowed any interest in what he regarded as trivial minutiae.

Of greatest importance of all to Ruskin were the relationships between items, and how these were shown, as this would demonstrate to the enthusiastic artisan and amateur artist how, for example, the colour and origins of a mineral related to the subject or technical merit of a drawing, painting, or illuminated manuscript, and how far they each taught a valuable moral lesson that revealed the otherwise obscure connections between seemingly unrelated items in the collection. If the workers could be helped to understand the significance and beauty of natural forms, they might produce improved designs that were more deftly executed, an achievement both satisfying to themselves and of advantage for all. It was not an exercise in control, but it was an attempt to influence taste. Still, the museum provided an opportunity to study unfamiliar and rare objects. There was no fee to pay, and nobody was under any obligation to visit.

The lack of space for the museum's growing bounty presented intractable difficulties. In September 1883, just after a temporary gallery was opened in the museum grounds, Emily Swan outlined the potential but exposed the scale of the challenge in a letter to the local press.

> [Ruskin] has himself superintended and had scaffolds erected around the Ducal Palace, Venice, to take casts of the sculpture, also from the cathedrals of Rouen and Amiens, the casts of which are in the storehouse of St George, at Walkley. He keeps

two artists constantly employed in making drawings from the best Continental examples of old masters' works. These drawings are dispersed up and down the country that were done especially for the Museum for the Sheffield people. Many are at the Whitelands College, Chelsea, waiting house room at Sheffield. A valuable shell collection is now in the Nottingham Museum, also awaiting a suitable home.[265] The finest collection of ambers, 60 odd pieces in all, at Mr Dallinger's [Wesley] College; also hidden out of sight.[266] Why? Because there is not room at Walkley to display them. Coins wrapped in silver paper, better examples than there are in the British Museum. Lovely specimens of stuffed birds, presented by Dr Hewitson [sic], of Leeds, still in Leeds, waiting a home.[267] Piles of exquisite examples of all the birds of the world heaped in a corner. Most charming patterns for designers and china painters, bought from the famous Eyton collection, for which Mr Ruskin gave £500; never used. Why? There is no room to display them [...][268]

Yet more material remained with Ruskin at Brantwood. William White (1855-1932), the first curator of the Ruskin Museum at Meersbrook, and effectively the Swans' successor, later wrote that in the Walkley years 'the majority' of the drawings sent from copyists abroad

were kept simply in their mounts, or unmounted, in brown paper parcels packed in cases, to await further treatment. So inconvenient, indeed, did the accumulated store become, that the Master found it necessary to send off several cases both of drawings and minerals to Mr [George] Baker at Bewdley — to be, as he wrote, 'out of my way and in yours'[.][269]

Henry Swan's own *Collected Notes on some of the Pictures in St George's Museum, Sheffield* (1879), a 16-page hand-list, ended with a cautionary footnote that spelt out the reality of the situation at Walkley.

As want of space at present renders it impossible to make rightly visible to visitors more than a few of the drawings in colour relating to St Mark[']s [...] all notice of these has been omitted from this provisional list, which pretends only to meet the immediate requirements of a provisional building.[270]

Although Henry Swan's *Collected Notes* were thus severely limited, a catalogue worthy of the name did eventually appear courtesy of the Swans' remarkable eldest son, Howard.

Howard Swan's compilation of a 64-page *Preliminary Catalogue of the St George's Museum, Walkley, Sheffield* was published by W. D. Spalding & Co. in 1888. It constituted the most significant attempt to date to curate the collection at Walkley in print, but even this pamphlet was severely limited in scope.[271] Howard was then living in London where he worked as an electrical engineer who specialised in lighting and telephony. He was an assistant editor on the journal of the Institute of Electrical Engineers, and contributed to important works on the subject such as *Practical Electrical Engineering* (1890). Politically, he had been involved in the Fellowship of the New Life and was an early member of the gradualist socialist Fabian Society that grew out of it.[272] The *Preliminary Catalogue* was essentially a list of objects, which excluded books, coins, seals, minerals, precious stones and paintings and engravings of birds, fish, and insects — 'of which there are a vast number awaiting mounting and arrangement', Howard explained: only the contents of 13 cases of objects labelled A-M were included, together with volume and page references to Ruskin's published writings where full descriptions could be found, but the passages themselves were not reproduced.[273] However, Ruskin's books could, of course, be consulted in the museum, alongside the objects themselves. But this publication appeared only in the last two years of the museum's life.

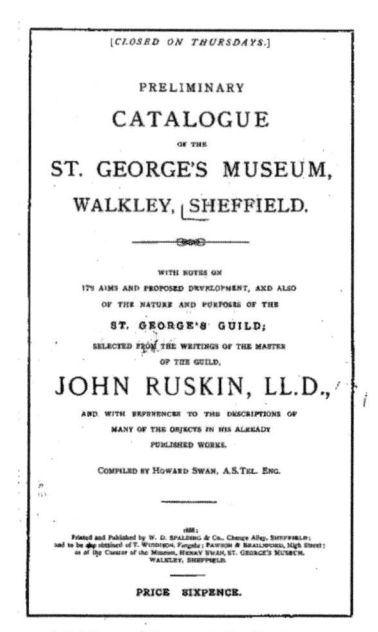

16. Howard Swan, A Preliminary Catalogue of St George's Museum, Walkley, Sheffield *(1888)*.

The Swans seem to have coped with Ruskin's great expectations and the severe practical limitations imposed by the museum's small size and geographical remoteness with general equanimity, but the volume of instructions, the frequency with which Ruskin corrected and even rebuked them, and the endless arrival of ever more acquisitions must have caused frustration and even moral injury. Having apparently caused some offence to Emily, Ruskin once rather feebly explained to her that when he called her 'gushing and romantic' it was meant as a compliment.[274] On 22 August 1877 the Swans made the mistake of turning up unannounced at Brantwood. Given that Ruskin thundered in his diary about a 'quite frightful fit of depression brought on by my curator and his wife coming when they shouldn't', we might assume that they were given a frosty reception.[275] Yet this was the occasion on which Swan is understood to have persuaded Ruskin to sit for a portrait-bust to be sculpted by Benjamin Creswick.[276] The following month Ruskin declared Creswick 'a youth of true genius, greatly surprising and delightful to me, and I have no doubt he will do much. But to do so, he must *leave* Sheffield.'[277] Ruskin considered all large towns and cities essentially irredeemable, Sheffield included.

The life of St George's Museum itself falls largely outside the scope of the present volume, though a sketch of it is given in the introduction. An account of the Swans' contribution to its work is necessarily vital to their biography, however. A short report, published in the *Sheffield Independent* in May 1877, outlines the character of Henry's achievement as curator, and confirms that he lost no time in establishing himself in the role.

> During the afternoon a large number of persons found their way to Mr Ruskin's museum in Bell Hagg road, and although the room in which the art treasures are stored was crowded the visitors were amply repaid for this personal inconvenience by the courtesy of Mr Swan, the curator. They were shown the mineralogical and other curiosities, and the M.SS. and specimens of ancient etching and engraving, together with the modern works of art which have come under the favourable notice of so rigorous a critic as the Master of the Company of St George. Mr Swan furnished them with a great deal of interesting information on subjects commonly imagined too dry and technical ever to become popular, but which, when conveyed in language not that of the schoolroom, is sufficiently intelligible to lead the un-initiated to follow up the enquiry for themselves.[278]

It may sound like faint praise. But Swan's courtesy and the accessible way in which he imparted his considerable store of knowledge and understanding of the museum's treasures and Ruskin's educational purpose in sharing them, were the inseparably paired hallmarks of his curatorship. This point is underscored by a comment published a few months later when the *Sheffield Daily Telegraph* remarked of the collection that 'the interest of the whole is considerably enhanced by the pleasant readiness shown by Mr Swan, the curator, in giving information as to the articles in his charge'.[279]

Visitors from further afield recognised the same quality. 'E. S. P.', writing in the *National Review*, described how Swan was 'talking of "his master", whose sayings he brought forward just like texts of Scripture',[280] while the architect Edwin Seward (1853-1924), reporting on a visit to the museum by the Cardiff Naturalists' Society of which he was a member, referred simply but approvingly to 'the able and earnest Curator'.[281] The Leeds Naturalists' Club and Scientific Association specifically remarked on 'the kindly manner in which the members were received by the Curator (Mr Henry Swann [*sic*]) and his family'.[282] They visited the museum in October 1885 and were met by

Henry and Emily Swan 'who had made unusual arrangements to enable the Club to view the treasures with the greatest possible facility' and 'the Club were greatly indebted' to them for their 'kind attention': their excursion concluded with a heartfelt vote of thanks to Henry, Emily and their family.[283] In a gracious response, Swan reportedly pointed out that 'underlying all Mr Ruskin's teaching was the principle that science and art are only useful as they tend to raise and ennoble society'.[284] Among the club's eminent scientist guests on that occasion was the microscopist and geologist, Dr Henry Clifton Sorby FRS (1826-1908), a former president of the Sheffield Literary and Philosophical Society, a supporter of the museum at Walkley, and a man Ruskin personally respected greatly.

In February 1880, shortly after Swan addressed a meeting of the Ruskin Society of Manchester, the young Ruskinian solicitor, John Ernest Phythian (1858-1935), later a Companion of the Guild of St George, visited the museum and, years later, recalled Swan as 'a devoted yeoman in "St George's" service' who 'would show the treasures and make plain even the darkest and most difficult of "the Master's" sayings'.[285] For the *British Architect and Northern Engineer*, Swan was 'an enthusiastic disciple [of Ruskin], and imbued with the missionary spirit. It is clear', they added, 'that real students will find words of welcome and help when they are at the Walkley Museum.'[286] Unsurprisingly, no word of criticism of Swan and his curatorship is to be found.

Despite the limited availability of public transport and the poor though improving quality of local roads, and the steep walk a visit to the museum therefore necessitated, it is evident from an examination of the museum's visitor books that a large and varied cohort of visitors travelled from far and wide.[287] Local workmen were most likely to find their way to Ruskin's treasures, though how seriously most of them studied the collection is difficult to gauge, but many took their families along with them. Women also visited, often in pairs or groups, or with their children, and there were parties of schoolboys and schoolgirls, as well as trainee and professional teachers. Students went from Oxford and Cambridge, as well as from institutions nearby. Academics, too, and not a few established craftsmen, architects, businessmen and journalists, and men of religion (Anglican and many non-conformist). There were groups of artists and scientists, mostly amateur, but some professional, and many Ruskinians, including Companions of the Guild and members of local Ruskin societies. They went from all over the UK, the USA, many countries across Europe, and as far away as Russia, India, Sri Lanka (Ceylon), China, Egypt, South Africa, Canada, Brazil, Australia and New Zealand.

Some of the locals would go on to become well-known figures in their fields: Benjamin Creswick as a sculptor and master of modelling in Birmingham; Frank Saltfleet as a painter, especially of seascapes; and Omar Ramsden (1873-1939) and Alwyn Carr (1872-1940), who visited separately as schoolboys, went on to form a design partnership in London which produced some of the country's finest silverware. Howard Swan recalled in 1900 that students would

> come out better in inspiration and in technique. Several have been the artists who obtained a start there. Ben Creswick the sculptor, now of the Birmingham School of Art, was a grinder-lad of genius, the spark blown into flame here. Frank Saltfleet, whose exhibition in Bond-street at this moment attests Ruskin's insight when he said, in answer to a question, 'Will he be a master?' 'Why, Swan, Saltfleet is a master.' These from Sheffield — one a grinder, the other a cabinet maker, have risen to high places in art. And others too have received their impulse from that little house on the hill.[288]

Others were already well-established when they visited, such as the artist-craftsman Charles Green (1835-1916), who was a passionate supporter of the museum, and the distinguished woodcarver, cabinet-maker and amateur photographer, Arthur Hayball (1822-1887), a dedicated Ruskinian who crafted much of the museum's furniture (many tables, chairs and picture-frames survive today) and he even designed a proposed museum extension. Henry Bradley (1845-1923) became involved in Ruskin circles when he was working as the correspondence secretary of a cutlery firm in Sheffield, but visited the museum from London in 1888 when he had already begun what would be his lifetime's achievement — his colossal scholarly contribution to what became the *Oxford English Dictionary*.

Inevitably, our interest is piqued by those who were already famous when they visited the museum, and it presumably caused excitement locally and in the Swan household, too, to receive such guests. Oscar Wilde was only 29 when he visited in January 1884 while in Sheffield on a lecture tour, but he was already a celebrity aesthete, though not yet famous for the society comedies that stormed the theatres in the 1890s, let alone notorious for the scandal that led to his imprisonment. The Swans would meet Oscar again in 1888 when they all attended the May Day Festival at Whitelands College, Chelsea, as Ruskin's representatives.[289] William Morris was famous as a poet, a leader of the Arts and Crafts Movement, and a socialist campaigner when he visited in 1886. George Jacob Holyoake — a pioneer of the co-operative movement (also a vegetarian and secularist who had been an early leader of Sheffield's Hall of Science) — was so impressed by the museum when he visited in 1880 that he started a subscription in support of it among his local working-class followers. Even a young teacher named Rolfe visited who would later find fame (or notoriety) as 'Baron' Corvo. The distinguished artist, (Sir) Edward Poynter visited with the local Conservative MP, Charls Stuart Wortley and Wortley's relatives, Lord and Lady Wharncliffe.[290] The Royal Academician, John Callcott Horsley, was among the oldest visitors at 70. Archdeacon Frederick William Farrar, the Canon of Westminster, Chaplain-in-Ordinary to the Queen, and a vegetarian, visited in June 1885 shortly after the opening of the Lyceum Gallery that extended the museum. Ten years later he was appointed Dean of Canterbury Cathedral.

17. Inside the Lyceum Gallery of St George's Museum, dominated by J. W. Bunney's painting of St Mark's, Venice.

At the time Edward Carpenter viewed the treasures, he was building his reputation as a socialist sage and man of letters whose smallholding at nearby Millthorpe, in Derbyshire, served as a secular Mecca for political, religious and sexual radicals. Carpenter's network of youthful disciples, many of whom shared his enthusiasm for Ruskin, were also enticed to the museum at Walkley, among them Charles Ashbee, Goldsworthy Lowes Dickinson, Roger Fry and Cecil Reddie, all of them destined for renown in their different fields.

When Queen Victoria's youngest son, Prince Leopold, visited on 22 October 1879, during a visit to Sheffield to speak in favour of university extension at the opening of Firth College, Ruskin presented him to Swan personally. The Swans' eldest son Howard later recalled how His Royal Highness was shown 'the treasures of this gem of museums by the Professor; the Prince calm and interested, gently beaming; the Professor [...] gazing with affection from lovely opals to the face of his beloved pupil'.[291] A few days earlier, the Prince, who had attended Ruskin's lectures at Oxford, and had become a friend, had accepted as a gift one of Creswick's sculpted busts of the Slade Professor.

Emily Swan seems nearly always to have been present. It is notable that Ruskin called her the museum's 'curatress', and Mark Frost is fully justified in suggesting that the curatorship should be viewed as 'a partnership of talented equals'.[292] There is evidence that she was paid a separate salary: Ruskin wrote to her in April 1880 and asked, 'For how long have I now paid you salary? I must make the Guild refund, through [the Senior Trustee] Mr Baker, and after this, please apply to *him*.'[293] Emily clearly played an important role in displaying the museum's treasures. Her talents were considerable. In 1880, she seems to have made a passable sketch of one of the coins in the collection, Ruskin telling Henry, 'Emily's sketch is clever, and I hope her power may be made really useful': nevertheless, he added, 'I should like her very much to try and make me an outline of the profile' of one of the coins from the reign of William I which he had sent the day before.[294] It is not clear if she ever succeeded, or indeed tried to do so.

That Emily Swan shared her husband's sense of personal loyalty to Ruskin and his dedication to Ruskin's ideals and values should not be doubted. Mark Frost has explained that Ruskin found Emily to be 'a positive, provocative, and interesting person, equally liable to delight and infuriate him, but always capable of making him think'.[295] From time to time she wrote letters to the local press extolling the merits of the collection or giving health bulletins about Ruskin. She also wrote to complain of her frustration about what she considered to be the lacklustre efforts of Sheffield's businessmen to raise funds for the enlargement of the museum. Publicly challenged in October 1883 to do something about it herself, she inaugurated a campaign to inspire a hundred women of Sheffield to collect £10 apiece in fundraising purses with which she supplied them.[296] In doing so, she said that it was the men, not the women, who were guilty of too much talk and not enough action.[297]

It would be a stretch to claim, on this evidence alone, that Emily Swan was some sort of proto-feminist, but she certainly defended her sex and was always prepared to put her head above the parapet to argue her case. It is not difficult to imagine her conversing happily with such campaigners for women's rights, including female suffrage, as Florence Balgarnie (1856-1928), F[rances] Henrietta Müller (1846-1906), and Alice Cliff Scatcherd (1842-1906), all of whom visited the museum at Walkley.

For almost a year following Henry Swan's death, the museum at Walkley remained open, under Emily's dutiful care as sole curator (or 'curatress'). St George's Museum finally closed on Saturday, 8 March 1890.[298] The Ruskin Museum Committee had been set up by Sheffield Town Council in September 1889 to prepare the municipally owned Meersbrook Hall as the new home of the rebranded Ruskin Museum. When the committee purchased an undisclosed number of desk easels from Emily for 10 guineas in October 1889, the official minutes of the meeting carelessly recorded her name as 'Mrs Elizabeth Swan', leaving out or otherwise mistaking her first name.[299] It was symptomatic of her treatment by the council and the Guild. The delicate matter of curatorial succession was not handled sensitively.

An angry letter by someone pointedly calling her or himself 'One Who Loved the Walkley Museum', was published in the *Sheffield Daily Telegraph* on 22 April 1890, shortly after the Ruskin Museum opened at Meersbrook. The writer keenly defended the Walkley Museum's legacy in general, and Emily Swan's vital contribution in particular. Given the sense of personal injury it conveys, it is likely that it was written by Emily herself. At any rate, the author was intimately acquainted with the circumstances and particulars of the case, and complained with some bitterness about people sneering that 'Rachel was weeping over the loss of her curatorship'.

> She is glad to lose it (if lost it is). That cannot be a loss which is given up, and be it known that Mrs Swan wished to resign when Mr Swan died, but was persuaded by Mr Baker 'to keep on and show the people round'.
>
> That is all Mr Baker knows of John Ruskin's intention in a museum.
>
> Mr Baker knows nothing of the 'cultivation of souls' which John Ruskin puts first before the study of stones and pictures.
>
> Mr and Mrs Swan attempted, among very hard hearts, to cultivate the soul [*sic*] life, and it has not failed. Good fruit has, and will still be borne for the 16 [*sic*] years of hard labour at the Walkley Museum.[300]

The plea is no less justified whoever made it.

If the hinted allusion to penal servitude was exaggerated, the singling out of George Baker as the bogeyman seems more rational. Mark Frost has shown that Baker could be a controversial figure who neglected, antagonised and possibly mistreated other servants of the

Guild, particularly those from working-class backgrounds who were engaged in the practical work on the estates at Bewdley, Totley, and Cloughton, near Scarborough. Baker seems to have been possessed of an unenviable lack of sensitivity. The letter-writer's poor opinion of his understanding of Ruskin's intentions in setting up the museum, and by extension, his inability to comprehend and appreciate what the Swans had achieved there, is damning, the more so when one considers that Baker, as the Guild's senior trustee and Ruskin's representative, was most prominently associated with the decisions that led to the removal of the treasures from Walkley to Meersbrook. It is a sad and unworthy postscript to the Swans' tremendous service to Ruskin and the Guild of St George.

Henry and Emily Swan's mission had been to embed in Sheffield an appreciation of the value to the community of Ruskin's exemplary educational art collection. Their efforts were indeed directed at achieving that most nebulous, but vital and precious of things, the cultivation of the soul. They were committed to widening cultural access long before such a concept became familiar. It was thanks largely to them that the museum functioned as a crucible of change that transformed some students' lives forever. It was both a cultural granary and beacon. Moreover, it was a site of Ruskinian pilgrimage that attracted neighbouring residents as well as far-flung travellers. The Swans' achievement was to do the crucial spadework that laid the solid foundations on which others continue to build today.

ELEVEN
BEYOND THE MUSEUM

The Swans were more than Ruskin's museum curators. Their role was greater in scope and importance than nineteenth-century notions of curatorship would lead us to suppose. They were, in a sense, his missionaries, but on a more practical level they were his local agents or representatives. They gave bulletins about Ruskin's health in the local press, for example, such as in March 1878, when Henry publicly shared a letter he had received from the head gardener at Brantwood, David Downs (1818-1888).[301] The message conveyed on that occasion was reassuringly upbeat, though Ruskin had in fact suffered a serious mental-health crisis which incommoded him for months and from which he never fully recovered.

When the Guild of St George held its first general meeting in Birmingham on 21 February 1879, Ruskin felt unable to attend, and his official representative was Henry Swan. This is how Swan came to read to his fellow Companions and their guests Ruskin's report about the organisation's progress and prospects.[302] One of the other speakers at the event was Henrietta Carey (1844-1920), a philanthropist from Nottingham, one of the first Companions of the Guild, and one of Octavia Hill's 'fellow-workers' in social housing. She reached out to Emily Swan after the meeting, rather puzzlingly requesting her to send one of Ruskin's letters so that she might give it to an aunt. In one of the few letters written by Emily Swan and known to have survived, she told Henrietta on 14 March, 'I feel it goes much against the grain as I am sure Master would not like his letters going about', adding limply, 'still I do not like refusing, so I enclose one'.[303] She proceeded to tell Miss Carey that in a recent letter Ruskin had told her that 'the vital power of St <George> must not depend <on personal feelings> over fraternity'. Further, he had insisted, 'the vital thoughts consist in our common sense + the quantity of resulotion [*sic*] to do what we clearly perceive when right'. She quoted directly from several letters Ruskin had written to her, and although she did not always quote them accurately, she caught the gist of Ruskin's message.[304]

For her part, Emily Swan made a rambling request for Henrietta to send the museum in Sheffield a copy of the report Miss Carey had read in Birmingham: 'I did not quite take it in <and I will return it>' she promised, signing the letter 'With love + fraternal <or sisterly> affection (which I know to be needed in spite of what the dear master says altho' it <(St George's work)> must not hang on that) I am sincerely yours'.[305] Emily's warmth, affection and enthusiasm are palpable, but the parenthetical jumble of phrases is also symptomatic of nervous disorder. Unfortunately, though Henrietta sent Emily a copy of the report as requested, it was quickly mislaid, and was perhaps lost altogether. Emily explained in a flustered second letter:

> I lent the report you sent me to a lady who was studying in the [St George's] Museum. I think she must have taken it away [with] her as I cannot see it. She was here yesterday + asked to see it. I had mentioned it to her. I will send it back directly I get it. I am vexed as I wanted to ask you some questions on it + I wanted it to refer to.[306]

Having listened carefully to the report read by Henry Swan in Birmingham, Miss Carey made note of the complaints about the want of space at Walkley and spied an opportunity for Nottingham. 'At the present time', Swan had read, 'a valuable picture, by an old Venetian master, was locked up for the want of room to exhibit it.'[307] Though the picture was not identified, it is clear that he meant *The Madonna and Child* by Verrocchio, bought by Ruskin in 1877. Might not this Old Master painting be exhibited in Nottingham, however temporarily, Miss Carey asked Ruskin? Ruskin replied warmly on 17 March that he would be delighted for her to have the picture at Nottingham 'for a while'.[308] He did not like to risk having it sent by train because it was 'so wholly irreplaceable', he explained. Nevertheless, 'St George must look after it', he concluded, promising that if she sent Henry Swan a receipt and proof of insurance to the value of £100 (the price originally paid for it), she should have it on loan.

Things moved quickly. In her second letter to Henrietta, of 20 March, Emily Swan pointed to Ruskin's remarks on Verrocchio in *Ariadne Florentina* (1876), the printed version of six lectures he gave at Oxford on 'wood and metal engraving' in 1872. Emily's letter was brief because, she explained, 'I have had many [letters] to write + am giddy'.[309] She undertook to write again but no further letters have survived. Ruskin actually said little of Verrocchio in the lectures Emily pointed to, but he did set the painter apart as an old master who 'taught Leonardo da Vinci, Lorenzo di Credi, and Perugino', a remark Emily reproduced at the head of her letter, adding only that Verrocchio was 'a Florentine'.[310] After giving the dimensions of the painting, she added, apparently rather put out by this unexpected turn of events, 'I much wonder at Mr Ruskin sending [the painting] about as it is [*word deleted*] covered with plate glass which is of course very heavy.'

As it turned out, the painting was never sent to Nottingham. From the evidence that can be pieced together, this was owing to honest error and miscommunication, but as Emily Swan's postscript hinted, the

Walkley curators were probably reluctant to risk sending it out on loan even though they did not have adequate space to display it themselves. By the time Prince Leopold visited Walkley in October, Ruskin had reorganised the entire museum around it.

The museum at Walkley quickly developed into a place for discussion as well as study. In the 'Notes and Correspondence' section of *Fors* in November 1876, Ruskin printed portions of a letter from Swan, dated 18 October, in which the curator had given him a long account of a debate on usury among a group of working men, including some of the self-styled 'communists' Ruskin had met at the museum that April. The account was reproduced in the *Sheffield Independent*. It reveals that the museum provided a forum for social, political and religious debate.[311] A report by 'E.S.P.', writing in the *National Review* in 1885, indicated that, at least in an informal way and if only as a result of happenstance, such discussions could involve middle-class women as well as working-class men. The account deserves to be quoted at length, not least because it shows that a crowded room had its merits. The sense of intimacy and growing openness the report conveys is intriguingly suggestive of Victorian ideas of generational, gender, and class boundaries temporarily breaking down or at any rate flexing, even if nineteenth-century prejudices proved harder to shake.

> First some ladies came in, with bright-faced, schoolboy companions, who wanted to look at the collection of stones; and then, in the centre of the small apartment, a little group of men collected, and sat talking, with some numbers of *Fors Clavigera* on the table before them. Altogether there were ten or a dozen persons in the room, and what the atmosphere was like may easily be imagined; but the men and the boys regarded it not at all, and every one knows the equanimity with which mothers and sisters and aunts accept the various holiday experiences in which they may be invited to share.
>
> A little hum of low-voiced talk went forward, neither set of people interfering with the other in any way, except that, in the very limited space at their disposal, they were so crowded that they almost touched. But presently, by some accident, there happened one of those occasional breaks, when every one chances to stop talking at once; and, in the momentary lull, a clear, shrill, eager man's voice suddenly exclaimed: —
>
> 'Christians! In the whole course of my life I have never met with *one!*'
>
> As a rule, it is not well to break into other people's conversation; but sometimes it is impossible to refrain. As much, perhaps, to her own amazement as to that of the speaker, who

was a man of something more than middle age, with an intellectual countenance, the words, 'You have been unfortunate in your experience, sir,' dropped, very softly indeed, from the lips of one of the ladies who were present.

For a single instant he simply looked at her, whilst she, it may be, felt half alarmed at her own audacity; then, whilst his hands rapidly struck open a certain page in *Fors Clavigera*, came the searching question, —

'Are *you* a Christian?'

'Yes.'

'Have you read *this*?'

It was that particular bit in *Fors* which treats of bringing a tramp home to dinner.[312] The lady had read it, and once more briefly answered yes.

Then with finger still on *the* page and increased intensity, —

'Would you do it?'

'No!'

'Ah!'

All the force of 'I told you so' a thousand times repeated was concentrated into that one interjection.

'No, certainly not,' repeated the lady. 'For an honest working-man in trouble I would do anything that lay in my power, but I should *not* ask a tramp to dinner: I have no respect for tramps.'

Two or three of the men round the table were unmistakably working-men. They, too, seemed to have no respect for tramps, for they nodded cordial assent to this remark, and even laughed aloud, and the lady could not help feeling that they considered that she had rather the best of it; but she will not soon forget the effect of missiles firing through the air which these sudden personal questions produced — a curious, novel sensation which one is not often called upon to experience.[313]

It seems improbable that such scenes were commonplace, but the dynamism and daring of such a frank exchange of views between a man and a woman of different classes, speaking in the presence of children and other working men, strikes a progressive note in the context of the 1880s, even if the disdain for 'tramps' that was expressed and tacitly endorsed is apt to offend many people in our changed world today.

Ruskin and the Swans were more tolerant of radical views than a lot of their contemporaries, but the crucial difference was that Ruskin distinctly disavowed the tenets of socialism whereas the Swans certainly appear not to have done so, though they were clear about Ruskin's stance and sentiment and respected it. The most remarkable instance of Ruskin's willingness to engage with working-class radicals through the agency of the Swans, started at the museum and moved beyond it into an actual collaborative land experiment.

Henry Swan was the pivotal and mediating figure. He was personally acquainted with members of a mutual improvement class, mainly consisting of autodidact working men and women. It grew out of the Sheffield Secular Society associated with the Hall of Science on Rockingham Street. The class had become particularly interested in 'communism' and was inspired by socialist ideas about 'co-operative villages', specifically those of the Old Owenite, Dr Henry Travis (1807-1884).[314] This spurred an ambition among some members of the class to secure land near Sheffield on which co-operative principles of food production and husbandry might be practiced.

A senior member of the class, who served its active 'communist' members as their president, was the local Quaker optician, Edwin Priest (1814-1890), a Friend whom Swan appears to have known well. A partner in the spectacles-making firm, Priest & Ashmore, Edwin provided meeting space for the group at his business premises in the town centre. Priest's involvement in a variety of freehold land societies, co-operative schemes and philanthropic enterprises seems to have influenced the group to adopt a joint-stock model of collective ownership, the resulting 'company' eventually calling itself the United Friends Association. Its members made a financial investment by means of a compulsory fee or subscription and additionally contributed what else they could spare. In return, they owned a proportionate number of shares in the company. This was not communism, 'reddest also of the red' in a phrase Ruskin once used about himself, but rather a co-operative investment in a common cause.[315]

Ruskin was keen to meet the workmen of Sheffield, and did so, by Swan's arrangement, first in September 1875, and more consequentially, at the museum in Walkley, on 27 April 1876. Many of the self-styled 'communist' autodidacts attended the meeting and discussed their ideas. Although there was a substantial ideological gulf between Ruskin's more or less feudal ideals and the democratic, co-operative vision of the self-styled communists, both parties overcame their differences and misgivings, at least temporarily, and broadly agreed that Ruskin would provide the land on which the group's plans could be tested. One of the few accounts of the scheme by a participant credited Swan — or perhaps blamed him — as the 'persevering man' who helped broker the agreement.[316]

With Swan's assistance, a plot of between 13 and 14 acres of grassland, with a stone farmhouse, outbuildings and garden, known locally as Badger's Farm after its former owner, was acquired by Ruskin. It was situated on Mickley Lane, Totley, in the Derbyshire countryside a few miles from Sheffield. Characteristically, Ruskin's love of romantic resonance trumped factual accuracy, so that he called it Abbeydale, while the United Friends called it Communist House. The communists had high hopes of realising their dream of founding a rural community where it was possible to live collectively, in sympathy with the natural world, and a comfortable distance from the smoke, squalor, and drudgery of the industrial town.

Swan cannot be said to have acted as co-ordinator, but he was an intermediary and — increasingly — a diplomatist. He undertook some administrative support, too. In the museum's archive is a list, written by Swan, partly in shorthand, headed 'Candidates for Abbeydale' and sub-headed, 'Applicants for Shoe-tuition'. Whilst at least one member of the group was an experienced shoemaker, most were metalworkers with little or no experience of cobbling or farming. Moreover, the group made the decision that most of them would continue to live and work in town as hitherto, not commuting to Totley as part-time colonists as some scholars have suggested, so much as travelling as day-trippers or weekenders pursuing a serious hobby, apparently viewing the project, initially at least, as the cultivation of a large, collective allotment. As such, a manager was hired to live on-site, but disagreements seem to have led to successive changes of staff.

For most of 1877 the quirky arrangements seemed to work well enough, with some unremarkable attempts at shoemaking undertaken. More successfully, the group cultivated fruit and vegetables which were consumed by members, ardent supporters, intrigued visitors to Totley, and market-place consumers back in Sheffield. But the communists' version of Utopia and Ruskin's, though they agreed on some important points, disagreed fundamentally on others. Under the strain of an unworkable alliance, relations soured both between the United Friends and Ruskin, and among the communists themselves.

Swan made hopeful suggestions in an effort to find a way forward, but they all failed in the violent tug-of-war between differing visions. Tensions reached boiling-point early in 1878 just as Ruskin's mental health collapsed, an event to which the difficulties surrounding the Totley experiment probably contributed, and which in turn complicated relations and hastened the end of the collaboration. We observed in chapter eight that one of the potential personal legacies of Totley's communist phase, from Swan's point-of-view, was that the experiment drew him to one of its progenitors and leaders, the shoemaker George Shaw (1834-1914), who had spent time living in America and, crucially, in Australia, and may have introduced Swan to boomerang-throwing. Shaw had also sold musical instruments in his Sheffield shop in the early 1860s, another subject over which he and

Swan might have bonded. Shaw had been one of the men who met Ruskin at the museum in April 1876.

Another man who was present when Ruskin met the workers at Walkley, who was also among the dozen United Friends whose names we know, was the chaotic William Skelton Hunter (1838-1904). Hunter was a metalworker who specialised in surgical instruments. He also keenly shared Swan's interest in spiritualism. Unlike Swan, however, Hunter pursued his enthusiasm with fanatical zeal. He went from offering to give instruction in how to help 'everyone to investigate spiritualism for themselves in their own homes' in 1877 to issuing, 12 years later, a macho challenge to a prominent local anti-spiritualist to debate the subject with him at any time and on any public platform in the town.[317] Beaten up in a street-fight on one occasion, he also had a tempestuous marriage which ended in his wife's suicide, a tragedy to which, the investigating coroner darkly hinted, Hunter's unreasonable behaviour had contributed. Hunter quickly consoled himself by marrying a woman 25-years his junior.

A new phase in the life of the Guild's estate at Totley began as the communists parted ways. Re-named St George's Farm, it was managed by a friend of George Shaw's, a radical of a different stamp named William Harrison Riley (1835-1907) who was an idiosyncratic type of Christian socialist. He had met and worked with Karl Marx, and had even edited the Marxist journal, the *International Herald*. He had also lived in America and was a disciple of Walt Whitman. Influenced by Ruskin, but not uncritical of him, he was the republican sometimes anonymously quoted and often challenged by Ruskin in *Fors Clavigera*. Swan seems to have had less to do with the Totley estate after Riley's arrival, but there is evidence that the two men, both formerly engravers, were on friendly terms. Riley shared the Swans' belief in spiritualism, their vegetarianism and their aversion to alcohol (he had run a teetotal, vegetarian café in Bristol in the early 1870s), though, in contrast, Riley was a heavy smoker. By the turn of the century the Swans' son, Godfrey, was staying with William's son, George Harrison Riley (1861-1954), in Lunenburg, Massachusetts — Godfrey was then working as a gardener, and George as a shoemaker (in the short-term only, in both cases, but appropriately enough for our purposes).

There were other ways in which Ruskin's ideas and values were transmitted and promoted in Sheffield, and the Swans were once again at the heart of these efforts. Most significant was the admittedly short-lived Ruskin Society. A parent body had been formally established in Manchester in 1879 in response to a proposal by a former school-master, Robert Bailey Walker (1839-1885), who led the society's first meeting as chairman. He was a social reformer, a teetotaller averse to tobacco, the first editor of *The Co-operative News*, secretary of the Vegetarian Society and an editor of its journal, the *Dietetic Reformer and Vegetarian Messenger*, to which Swan subscribed and occasionally contributed.[318] Swan addressed the society at Manchester Town Hall on 9 February 1880 and there had been 'a good attendance'.[319] Local branches quickly formed, notably in Glasgow and London. The Ruskin Society of Sheffield was set up early in 1881 and its main object was to study Ruskin's writings. Inevitably, it was intimately bound up with the museum at Walkley, though Swan was clear from the outset that the society was separate and distinct from the Guild of St George of which the museum was a part.[320] The only Guild Companion, beside the Swans, to join the Ruskin Society of Sheffield was Benjamin Creswick.

Nevertheless, at an early stage Swan also expressed the hope that the Sheffield society 'would attract working men within its sphere of operations'.[321] Its meetings took place in the Cavendish Street studio of Arthur Hayball, who served the society as honorary treasurer. Henry and Emily Swan were both involved in the society's work. Henry was one of three members of the society's preliminary committee, and initially served as the society's secretary, in part because his role as resident curator at St George's Museum made him an obvious first point-of-contact for general enquirers, and in fact he continued to answer correspondence on behalf of the society, even after he officially relinquished the secretarial role.[322]

The Swans frequently spoke at society meetings: Henry chaired the first official meeting on 31 March and again in May 1882, and he joined a society excursion to Castleton in July.[323] In March 1882 Emily led a reading-group study session focussing on Ruskin's lecture 'Work', published in *The Crown of Wild Olive* (1866), and Henry took a prominent part in the discussion at a meeting in July, and chaired the discussion on Ruskin's lecture, 'The Future of England', on 6 October 1882.[324]

The study of Ruskin's books eventually provoked complaints from the small but engaged membership about their cost and the inconvenience of applying to George Allen in Kent in order to purchase them. Responding to a resolution of the society, Swan wrote to Ruskin about the matter. In turn, Ruskin told Allen who evidently took it as a personal criticism. Ruskin told Allen:

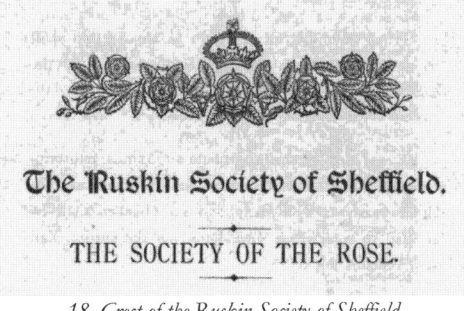

18. Crest of the Ruskin Society of Sheffield.

> Swan ought not to be called a busybody. He does his Museum work entirely well and would do much more, if I gave him the help he deserves. And he is liable to perpetual enquiries about the books, which he cannot but come to *me* [about], not to you.[325]

Allen would have noted the emphasis on 'Museum work', but must surely have felt that he did his own work for Ruskin entirely well and indeed better than well, and would have done even more if *he* had been given the help *he* deserved?

The Ruskin Society of Sheffield had folded by October 1883, partly because the museum was already doing so much of what we would now think of as the 'outreach' and 'engagement' work that the society might otherwise have undertaken. The Swans' energies were invested in the museum, and the seemingly endless and ultimately fruitless campaigns to enlarge it, or otherwise to find or build larger and more accessible premises for the better accommodation of its treasures and the greater convenience of visitors. But they had their own lives to lead, too — lives with which Ruskin and the museum also nevertheless intersected.

TWELVE
QUAKER NETWORKS

In this chapter and the next, our focus will be on the Swans' family life in their adopted county of Yorkshire, and here, we will concentrate on the Quaker networks that helped shape it. It is worth noting that Ruskin often showed an interest in the welfare of the Swan children as well as Henry and Emily themselves. A slightly belated Christmas gift of a pound to each of the children was given in 1875, for example, and Ruskin often sent his greetings to Mabel in particular.[326]

All but the eldest of the Swan children were sent to the Quaker Ackworth School, near Pontefract. Mabel, aged 10, though she was her brother Godfrey's junior, was the first to be enrolled, and was admitted on 2 February 1874.[327] At that time, though the family was listed as living in Sheffield, their meeting house was given as Westminster, a fact which suggests that the move to Sheffield had been relatively recent. Mabel's 'agent' (a respected Quaker sponsor, often but not always an Elder of the community) was George Lynes Neighbour (1818-1879). Neighbour entered his father's business as an oil merchant and Italian warehouseman (a purveyor of fine groceries such as olive oil, pasta, pickles, perfumes, dried fruits, paints and pigments). The firm had premises at 127 High Holborn, about mid-way between the two properties consecutively occupied by Swan's engraving master, W. R. Royle. As Friends, the Neighbours were associated with the Westminster Meeting House. George Neighbour Snr (1784-1865), and GLN's brother, Alfred Neighbour (1826-1890), were innovative and celebrated beekeepers, who sold hives and other beekeeping equipment and supplies from a shop on Regent Street. Alfred also published an important book on the subject — *The Apiary, or Bees, Bee-Hives, and Bee Culture* (1866). Ruskin may well have been aware of the Neighbours, if not through Swan, then independently, as beekeeping was a subject that interested him, and he maintained hives at Brantwood.

Mabel Swan remained at Ackworth School for four-and-a-half years and left on 3 July 1878. Godfrey Swan entered Ackworth on 11 August 1875. By then the Meeting House the Swans attended was given as Balby, on West Laith Gate, Doncaster (demolished in the 1970s).[328] Godfrey left Ackworth less than a year-and-a-half later on 21 December 1876. Leonard was admitted on 1 May 1877 and left just over four years later in July 1881, ending a seven-and-a-half-year association between the school and the Swan children.[329] Whilst all of

Godfrey's and some of Leonard's period of attendance overlapped with Mabel's, the brothers were not there at the same time. Godfrey's and Leonard's agent was Daniel Doncaster of the Balby Meeting House. This was almost certainly Daniel Doncaster Snr (1807-1884) whose business became a significant player in Sheffield's steel trade. Alternatively, the reference might have been to his son, Daniel Doncaster Jnr (1834-1912). Henry and Emily certainly knew some of Daniel Jnr's siblings, as we shall see.

Leonard Swan was a pupil at Ackworth in 1879 when the school celebrated the centenary of its foundation. An account of the jubilee events on 26 and 27 June was written by J. H. Barber who, like George Baker, was an alumnus of Ackworth himself, and someone whom we have already met as the conductor of Henry Swan's funeral service at Walkley in 1889. We shall meet him again presently. Barber's account of the school appeared in a volume which also included a biographical sketch of the school's principal founder, the Quaker and physician John Fothergill (1712-1780). It was written by the Quaker philanthropist James Hack Tuke (1819-1896).[330] Ruskin's editors pointed out that a copy of the book, published by Ackworth School's Centenary Council, was sent to Ruskin by Henry Swan. Ruskin certainly read it, and Cook and Wedderburn reproduced in volume 34 of the Library Edition of Ruskin's *Works* what turns out to be an incomplete summary of an account detailing Ruskin's marginalia.[331] They also omitted the assertion made in the original article on which they based their own account that Swan sent the book in response to a letter from Ruskin 'expressing his sympathy with the work of George Fox and the early Friends', presumably because they could find no evidence to support the claim.[332]

From the 1760s onwards, Fothergill developed an extensive botanical garden at Upton House, in what today is West Ham Park, in which he cultivated many rare plants. Ruskin marked a passage in the book referring to Fothergill's love of botany, an enthusiasm which led Fothergill to correspond with Linnaeus.[333] Next to a woodcut of Fothergill's native Carr End, near Bainbridge, Ruskin wrote: 'quite uniquely beautiful so far as my knowledge reaches in expressing the general character of *old* Yorkshire'.[334] This resonates with one of Ruskin's stated reasons for choosing Sheffield as the location for the museum, in which he credited Yorkshire especially with sharing in an 'old English' tradition of 'Honesty and Piety'.[335] Ruskin also responded positively to an account of two schemes Fothergill inaugurated, one concerning the employment of criminals, the other the feeding of the poor — earning from Ruskin 12 exclamation marks and the adverb, 'Lovely' — and also to Fothergill's interest in mental wellbeing, and his protests against war with France, all matters that concerned and animated Ruskin at various times in his life.[336] It is probably this volume to which Ruskin was referring in a letter to Swan in 1882, in which he wrote, 'I sent you your nice Quaker book with much lineation of passages, and should like it to be kept in the Museum Library'.[337]

The Swans' Quakerism inevitably had a significant impact on the museum itself, because the Quaker circles in which the Swans associated were thereby exposed to its work. On 8 October 1877, for example, a bazaar and exhibition were held at the Friends' Schools at Hartshead to raise funds for a piano to be purchased for the dual purposes of entertainment and instruction. The *Sheffield Daily Telegraph* reported that 'there were a number of most interesting paintings and curiosities of various descriptions on exhibition'. Among them were '[s]ome fine specimens from Mr Ruskin's Walkley Museum' which 'were shown by the Curator, Mr Henry Swan', including 'a cornelian stone, said to be the largest in the world'.[338] Swan's sympathy with the campaign is not to be wondered at bearing in mind his involvement in the Friends' First-Day School Association in the 1850s, his brother John's work as a piano maker in the 1840s and his own engagement with the teaching of singing and reported love of traditional musical instruments. A considerable number of people attended the event, including the steel merchant, David Kenway Doncaster (1837-1881), one of the sons of Daniel Doncaster Snr. The event may well have provided a direct introduction to the museum's collection for many members of the local Quaker community.

Most interestingly of all, the occasion was organised by the Swans' friend, J. H. Barber, who was the main force behind the establishment of the school and chief among its fundraisers. Barber was a tireless supporter of adult education. He was the managing director of the Sheffield Banking Company (with which Swan kept campaign funds for the museum's enlargement), a town trustee, a life-long member of the Liberal Party who sided with Unionism following the split over Irish Home Rule, and he was the father-in-law, through his eldest daughter, Hannah Mary Barber (1845-1913) to Charles Doncaster (1841-1884), the brother of Daniel Jnr and D. K. Doncaster. Among the numerous organisations and institutions that benefitted from Barber's loyal and capable services was the Sheffield School Board, of which he was treasurer from 1870 to 1899.[339]

Other members of the Doncaster family signed the visitor books at Walkley. In June 1883, Helen Doncaster (1833-1920) and her younger sister Phoebe (b. 1847) visited the museum.[340] Both were daughters of Daniel Doncaster Snr, and in 1878, Helen had become the second wife of John Stephenson Rowntree (1834-1907) of the Quaker family of chocolate manufacturers in York. A champion of education in that city, Rowntree was a councillor who had served as Lord Mayor in 1880. He was a prominent author on Quakerism who edited the journal, *The Friend*, from 1875 to 1878. Two children from his first marriage visited the museum in July 1883, Joseph John Rowntree (1864-1883), who would sadly die that September, and James Edward Rowntree (1869-1904), who later owned a café on Lord Street in Southport. The brothers were accompanied on their visit by their maternal step-aunt, Jane Eliza Doncaster (1845-1897).

The Doncasters, Barbers and Rowntrees, all related by marriage, and connected to the Swans by their shared Quaker faith, demonstrate how visitors to the museum were not uncommonly connected in overlapping networks of association. Another Rowntree connection is John Bowes Morrell (1873-1963), for example, who visited the museum as a boy in May 1884 with his brother, Cuthbert (1872-1959), and mother, Lydia (1832-1931). John Morrell joined Rowntrees a few years later at the age of 17, and became a director at 25. Achieving huge success in business — he later owned newspapers including the *Birmingham Gazette*, *Lincolnshire Chronicle* and *Westminster Press* — he was one of York's leading citizens. His achievements are too numerous to list here but include leading roles in the foundation of the University of York, the York Conservation Trust, and the Borthwick Institute for Archives. He was a keen author with a particular passion for York's history. In common with John Stephenson Rowntree, he served as Lord Mayor, first in 1914, and again in 1950.

Among other local Quakers to visit the museum at Walkley were Robert Beacock (1826-1887), a picture framer, Oswald Bradley Baynes (1859-1941) from York, Marion Whitwell (1866-1856) who was a member of the Fry family of chocolate manufacturers in Bristol (and a cousin of Roger Fry's), and, from further afield — visiting from St John's College, Cambridge — John Bull Ridges (1855-1937), later the headmaster of Leighton Park School, Reading. And there were yet others, as we shall see.

Finally, another Quaker connection should be noted. From 1880 the Birmingham-based architect, William Doubleday (1846-1938), a member of a long-established family of Quakers and Liberals in Essex, was involved in efforts to enlarge the museum at Walkley and signed the visitor books at least five times. Doubleday, who like George Baker and the Swan children was a graduate of Ackworth School, was responsible in the 1870s for designing Baker's neo-Gothic fairy-tale mansion, Beaucastle, on the outskirts of Bewdley — with carvings executed later by Benjamin Creswick. According to the *Sheffield Independent*, by March 1880 Doubleday had 'surveyed the ground adjoining the Museum, with the view of ascertaining the best site for the additional accommodation'.[341] The extent of his involvement is unclear, but what is certain is that the complex network of Quaker connections contributed significantly to the work of St George's Museum.

THIRTEEN
LIFE & DEATH IN SHEFFIELD

The most intimate picture of the domestic life of the Swans in Sheffield, and Ruskin's interaction with it, comes courtesy of the eldest of the Swan children, Howard. He described a typical scene confronting Ruskin on his occasional visits to Bell Hagg Road. Howard recalled cups of tea,
> brewed by the mother [*i.e. Emily*], the kettle poured by himself [*i.e. Howard*], in the little homely Yorkshire room, half kitchen, half parlour, in which the geraniums, the harmonium, the iridescent vases, and the pet dog [served] as background to many glinting words and phrases [...]. Outside the Museum were strawberry beds and an orchard tended by the curator's enthusiastic wife and the faithful gardener, whose admiration of the Master was hardly less keen than theirs. So with others, workmen of Sheffield; sometimes irreverently so.[342]

Lest the line about the gardener's admiration for Ruskin be dismissed as careless hyperbole, it is worth noting that the man referred to, George Habershon (1832-1890), was a member of the Sheffield Ruskin Society.[343]

Arthur Hayball's daughter, Mrs Clara Keeling (1852-1954), recalled in old age how she had observed Ruskin's experience of being at home with the Swans.
> Turning towards Mrs Swan [Ruskin] said: 'Emily, I should like my lunch now.'
> 'Yes Master. Where will you have it?'
> 'Here.'
> Soon Mrs Swan came out of the kitchen with a plate of bread and butter, a jug of milk, and a glass on a tray.
> 'I should like a little celery, Emily.'
> Emily brought some. Then, placing the tray before him, she said, 'Isn't this an ugly jug, Master?'
> 'The chief thing about a jug is that it should pour well,' was his reply.[344]

Howard Swan remembered seeing Ruskin 'anxious, engaged, gentle, worried, calm and stormy, deep in stories of Deucalion or laughing over a cup of tea'.[345] Ruskin seems to have felt quite comfortable in the Swans' company,
> drawing the perspective of the cottage outside, and the trees on the window glass of the bedroom in illustration of laws of

perspective. His tall stooping figure was well known there in those years. 'T' Master' or 'Maister Rooskin' he was called — and a mark in the walk like a footstep got to be known as 'T' Maister's Footprint'. May his footprints live long in our hearts! — he was a blessed man, albeit very human. He liked toasted cake and other delicacies. 'Sometimes', he once said to his curator, 'a baked potato and a diet of French prunes have stood between me and the Almighty!'[346] His talk was illuminating, illusive, genial; he was not an irascible man, as some of his writings seem to denote, but very tenderly gentle, sympathetic, thoughtful, full of the best love. He could not bear details as of woodwork and cloth — 'That's what I want. I don't care a rap about tenpenny nails and padding. Make the opal show in the light its lovely colours, and those bands on the chalcedony — never mind the wool'. [...] He was accurate in words and very tenacious of their proper use; and he occasionally — very occasionally — used strong words in the usual way. Once he used a big D— , 'I want the Bible to be *open*!' he said. 'But the nails will scratch the Cloth!' 'Oh, d—n the cloth!' was his ejaculation, which brought forth a laughing 'What, never?' from his astonished listener.[347]

Besides Ruskin's visits, the house on Bell Hagg Road bore witness to the ups and downs of the Swan family's fortunes. Henry and Emily's youngest son, Leonard, moved out in the mid-1880s and found work as a designer and draughtsman in Altrincham, near Manchester. The identity of his employer remains obscure and invites further research, but the leading designer in the town was the Arts and Crafts architect George Faulkner Armitage (1849-1937), an enthusiastic disciple of Ruskin and Morris. Armitage was commissioned in 1890 to oversee the interior decoration of the new Ruskin Museum at Meersbrook Hall.[348] By this time Armitage had taken on Barry Parker (1867-1947) as a pupil, and it is possible that Parker was involved in the museum work, too. Given that Parker's cousin and future professional partner, Raymond Unwin, knew Leonard's brother, Godfrey, the Swan brothers potentially shared an intriguing association with the architects of the Garden City movement, two of England's most influential urban planners.

On Friday, 17 December 1886, Leonard Swan left his lodgings at Springfield Road, Altrincham, to return to his parents and sister Mabel in Walkley. He had been overworking, having in addition to his employment become a volunteer tutor at a school of woodcarving. Overburdened, he felt forced to resign his position. He had been ill with chronic anxiety for some time and saw no improvement in his condition after leaving-off work. He was in very low spirits.[349] Around a quarter-past nine on the morning of 22 December, he was found hanging from a rope attached to a beam in the centre of one of the rooms of the house on Bell Hagg Road. He was discovered by the man described by Howard Swan as the museum's 'faithful gardener', George Habershon, of 254 Burgoyne Road. The alarm was immediately raised. A local man was passing by — a file-cutter in his early 30s named Frank Shelley, who had grown up on Bell Hagg Road and had lived at no. 103 since his wedding two years earlier. He responded to Habershon's call and cut down Leonard's body. It was too late. Leonard had died by his own hand at just 20 years of age.

An inquest held the following day returned a verdict of suicide during temporary insanity. The *Sheffield Weekly Telegraph* reported that '[m]uch sympathy is expressed with the parents of the deceased, who are well known and highly respected'.[350] Leonard was buried on Boxing Day at Walkley Cemetery in a grave in which his father, too, would later be laid to rest. Frank Shelley, who had tried to save Leonard's life, would serve as a pallbearer at Henry's funeral, as we have seen.

Ruskin told Swan at the start of the following March:

I am very thankful for your letter, and for its beautiful expressions of trust in the Future. My own griefs have no such help and always lower rather than better me. There are few more now possible to me — but the closer threat of Death itself.[351]

For Ruskin, the news of Leonard's death no doubt brought back to him haunting memories of the painful losses he had suffered by the deaths of his father, mother and, most recently and painfully of all, the death of the love of his life, young Rose La Touche. Inevitably, for all Swan's courage and positivity, and regardless of whatever comfort spiritualism may have offered, the tragic suicide cast a long shadow. There can be little doubt that this is what Henry was referring to when, in a letter to Ruskin written more than ten months later, in November 1887, he mentioned in a postscript that 'Emily and Mabel are away. None of us can lose sight of what has gone from our life here.'[352]

Leonard's suicide raises the issue of mental health. Emily, in particular, struggled in this respect. Mark Frost, in his analysis of the 30 extant letters from Ruskin to Emily Swan, demonstrates that Ruskin had deep and genuine affection and respect for her energy, sensitivity and diligence.[353] But their personal relationship deepened in 1878 when, as Frost explains,

she suffered some form of mental breakdown only a few months after Ruskin's first episodes of delirium. In August, he wrote simply to say that 'we must stick up for each other now, after we have both been crazy, together'. A day later, in a letter to Henry, he passed on his 'kindest regards to Emily', and his hope that 'we shall both in future, look well after our wits'.[354] Henry and Emily Swan never fully recovered from the loss of their youngest son. On 8 March 1888, Emily's mother, Mary, died at her home at Townshend Villas, Richmond, in Surrey, at the age of 79, leaving a personal estate valued at just over £1,400.[355] Four days later Mary was buried next to her husband in Norwood Cemetery.

Henry's final years were characterized by declining physical health and a general slowdown. Nevertheless, there is no reason to believe that he was seriously ill before the start of March 1889 when he began suffering from a pronounced weakness of the heart. About four weeks later, during a return rail journey from Leeds, he suffered acute stomach trouble. Initially he was not well enough to undertake the journey to Walkley and was forced to stay in the centre of Sheffield. The next day he did manage to get home. But he was dying. He lingered for another few days, remaining conscious until his eldest son, Howard, arrived from London. Given their combined contributions to the museum's success, it was fitting that parents and child should be reunited there before the end came. Finally slipping out of consciousness on the morning of Friday, 29 March, Henry Swan died at five o'clock that afternoon. Howard registered the death on the day of the funeral, 2 April.[356]

During their time in Walkley, the Swans had become a part of an informal network of vegetarians in and around Sheffield. Henry Swan attended a meeting at Brunswick Wesleyan Schools on 31 October 1883.[357] The chairman was Rev. Charles Henry Collyns (1820-1884), a graduate of Christ Church, Oxford (Ruskin's *alma mater*), an Anglican clergyman and former schoolmaster who had translated the works of St Pacian. He was the secretary of the British Temperance League, a member of the Anti-Narcotic League, and he opposed compulsory vaccination. The Collyns family maintained a vegetarian household and reputedly lived on sixpence a day. Collyns visited the museum at Walkley in April 1882 with his wife, Mary, and their teenage children, Spencer, Edith and Arthur.

Collyns spoke passionately at the Sheffield vegetarian meeting. He said that 'man was neither carnivorous nor herbivorous, but frugivorous' and contended that the teeth, jaw, and stomach proved his point. He advanced the case for the benefits of the vegetarian diet to the intellect and personal finances. At the end of the meeting, an auxiliary committee was appointed with Collyns as president, but his death the following year appears to have hindered the attempt to establish a formal Vegetarian Society in Sheffield for several years to come. In the same year in which the *Dietetic Reformer* reported this meeting, the journal carried a classified advertisement promoting a school run by Mrs Rennie, who described herself as a professionally trained teacher, offering to educate 'a few little boys with her own' at her 'beautiful' home, Woodbank Cottage, on Rivelin Street, Walkley, 'one of the most beautifully mountainous' districts, just 'a few minutes' walk from Mr Ruskin's museum' and boasting two acres of field in which each boy might make his own garden.[358]

The vegetables and fruit that were grown in the museum's garden were of particular significance for Swan, as he made clear when he notified readers of the *Dietetic Reformer and Vegetarian Messenger* in July 1877 of recent developments at the museum.

We have just had a small supply of good fruit trees planted here to fill the place which, in front of other museums, would be occupied by evergreens and ornamental shrubs. I hope in course of time that we shall be able to afford practical instructions in the mysteries of grafting, pruning, &c. There are a large number of workmen living on their own little plots of ground, and I have no doubt that a great hindrance to fruit culture arises from the uncertain tenure of the ground now held by many who would otherwise plant for the benefit of their children. Of course, this hindrance will not exist for the tenants of St. George, over whose ground we may reasonably expect to arise many a fine orchard.[359]

Indeed, Emily Swan and the museum gardener cultivated 'a miniature apple-orchard, and bushes of evergreens and old-fashioned flowers' as well as strawberry beds,[360] and a small vegetable allotment where cabbages, cauliflower and celery were grown, and geraniums bloomed in the garden through spring and summer.[361]

The most celebrated local vegetarian was Edward Carpenter, with whom the Swans were certainly acquainted, but among their closest Ruskinian vegetarian friends was the remarkable William Edward Armytage Axon (1846-1913), the librarian, author, antiquary, folklorist, and a journalist on the *Manchester Guardian* for more than 30 years.[362] A member of the Ruskin Society of Manchester, in 1879 Axon published a useful 27-page pamphlet entitled *John Ruskin, a Bibliographical Biography*, originally given, as the subtitle declared, as a paper 'read before Manchester Literary Club' and the Ruskin Society. He was an active vegetarian who had taken official roles in the Vegetarian Society including honorary secretary and vice-president. His anti-narcotics stance and interest in shorthand were presumably other interests over which he and the Swans bonded. Axon signed the visitor books at Walkley in October 1880, September 1881 (when he was accompanied by a group of other Mancunians), and April 1882, when he visited with his daughter, Grace (1867-1952). In December 1881 he visited with his 12-year-old son, Ernest (1868-1947), later Manchester's chief assistant librarian. Father and son would both edit the *Vegetarian Messenger* at different times and in 1889 the older man would write Swan's obituary in the journal.

By the vicissitudes of fate, an organised branch of the Vegetarian Society was officially founded in Sheffield only a matter of days before Henry Swan's death, though its formation owed much to his encouragement and advice.[363] Among the signatures in the visitor books at Walkley is that of Robert Barclay Murdoch (1852-1932). Murdoch had been the foreman in a Glasgow biscuit factory but moved in the 1880s to Heeley in Sheffield and set himself up there as a bookseller and warehouseman. A Quaker who became secretary of the Sheffield Vegetarian Society, he almost certainly went to the museum in order to consult Swan, visiting first on 28 May 1888, and again in July the same year.[364] By the turn of the century he had returned to Scotland where he managed a wholesale furniture warehouse.

The Vegetarian Society of Sheffield held its first public meeting and dinner on 25 April 1889, less than a month after Swan's death. About 90 people gathered at the Silver Grid Café on Bank Street, where a meal of lentil soup, macaroni cheese, potatoes and carrots was served, followed by date pudding — total cost, sixpence. The after-dinner business meeting was chaired by the society's president, William Addy Hall (1824-1908), Inspector of Postmen. Arnold Hills (1857-1927), president of the London Vegetarian Society, and the wealthy managing director of the Thames Iron Works, a large shipbuilding company, spoke on the cause of vegetarianism, which he had done so much in his lifetime to advance. Commending the consumption of fresh fruit, pulses, grains, and nuts, he warned against the use of salt, pepper and mustard, spoke of the dangers of smoking, and the undesirability of drinking tea, coffee and alcohol. Among those present who also spoke in favour of vegetarianism were Emily Swan and the Swans' old family friend, the Rev. T. W. Holmes.[365] The society appears to have flourished for the next decade or so.

On the matter of smoking, it is worth adding a concluding if discordant note. Two of Emily's sisters married men involved in the tobacco trade to which she and Henry objected. Mary Connell (1849-1891) married Frederick Thomas Gush, a cigar merchant in Hastings. More significantly, Kathleen Connell (1845-1922) married Julius Ludwig Sienssen (1838-1923), a German-born tobacco merchant whose firm had such long tentacles that it gave its name to a street in Limbe, Malawi. Julius eventually became a director of his in-laws' firm, G. L. Connell Ltd. of Cheapside. In 1920, he gave the Ruskin Museum at Meersbrook Hall some important gifts, including a volume of proof engravings of animals by the artist John Frederick Lewis (1804-1876), five negatives with views from St George's Museum, Walkley and four manuscript catalogues of the museum's collections from the Walkley days.[366] Emily seems, however, to have been closest of all to her youngest sister, Nora Connell (1851-1926), who evidently took a look at Ruskin's collection herself. She visited Walkley from her home in Richmond, Surrey, and signed the visitor book in October 1880.[367] As close as Emily and Nora seem to have been, the sisters lived very different lives: Nora divorced her husband in 1888 after two years of marriage; the couple's only daughter, Brenda Daines, later became an actress.

As we shall see, for the widowed Emily Swan, a new but final chapter began which took her away from Sheffield. before returning her to Yorkshire.

FOURTEEN
Emily's Retreat

When St George's Museum closed in March 1890, Emily and Mabel, by then the only remaining residents at 75 Bell Hagg Road, went one way, while the treasures went another. Mother and daughter initially moved south to Shrubs Hill, in Sunningdale, near Ascot in Berkshire. It would prove to be the first of many homes in a rather unsettled widowhood. At Sunningdale, towards the end of April 1890, Emily made her last will and testament, touchingly describing herself as the 'widow of the late Henry Swan Curator of the Ruskin Museum Walkley Sheffield'.[368] She bequeathed her entire estate — ultimately valued at only £472 6s. 11d. — to Mabel, whom she appointed sole executrix. The will was witnessed by her solicitor, Arthur Wightman, of Sheffield, and his clerk, Charles Slack, part of the firm used by Ruskin's solicitor as their agent in the town. By 1891, Emily lodged with a gardener, William Stone, and his family, at Rose Cottage, next to the Yew Tree Pub on Reigate Hill, in Surrey. At the turn of the century, she had moved to Hadley Highstone, in Barnet, Hertfordshire. A few years later she moved to 3 Holmdale Mansions, Holmdale Road, West Hampstead, probably shortly after it was built in 1904.

Emily was increasingly infirm as a consequence of heart disease which was understood to disrupt the supply of oxygen to her brain and further undermined her already fragile mental health. In late September 1908, her condition having deteriorated, she was compelled to take up residence at The Retreat on Heslington Road, York, a charitable mental-health hospital for Quakers. There she was placed under the care of medical officer Dr Norah Kemp (1873-1954), a graduate of the University of Glasgow in the city of her birth, and the first woman to work as an asylum doctor in Yorkshire. Between 1898 and 1912 Dr Kemp was responsible for superintending all the female patients at The Retreat. On 4 October, Howard Swan wrote from his home in Vaud, Switzerland, asking staff at the hospital to have 'a message conveyed' to his mother from himself, his 'wife, Mary Swan, and our daughter, Radia, of love + wishes. If', he added, 'it is right to *write* to her I shall do so at once [...]'.[369] The file of family correspondence that survives among Emily Swan's patient records is invaluable not only for the details it reveals of her final illness, but for the sense it gives of the Swans as a close, affectionate and loving family coming to terms with their collective grief.

But coincident with the heart-breaking admission of Emily Swan into The Retreat was another Swan family tragedy. Mary, Howard Swan's wife, had died at Lausanne Hospital after descending into a coma.[370] She had proved 'too weak to recover, and sank in happy peacefulness, conscious [sic] + never knowing she was dying'.[371] 'I could hardly believe it myself', Howard added, writing with affecting poignancy. 'I have often wished this week that I had been more of a doctor so that I could have saved the life of my dear wife Mary in time'. He did not want to tell his mother the upsetting news, he insisted, because she was too ill herself to bear it.

19. Howard Swan, 1892.

By December, Howard seems to have reached England to stay with his sister Mabel in York. He was described as 'overdone with his great trouble', and had been advised to remain quiet and do little or nothing.[372] He nevertheless produced two fascinating and lengthy articles around this time, published in the *Sheffield Independent* in December 1908 and January 1909, describing his residency from August 1900 in Japan, and his work there as an innovative English-language teacher at the Higher Commercial College, in Tokyo.[373] His professional engagements had also included professorships at the Imperial College of Languages, in what was then called Peking, in China, and the University of Southern California, in Los Angeles, USA, where he might have got to know the work of the Ruskin Art Club, founded in 1888 and still thriving today.[374] In 1892 he had co-founded the Central School for Foreign Tongues in London, and had served it as a director and as Principal, teaching the Gouin method of foreign-language acquisition.

Godfrey Swan was living in Massachusetts. He had been a fireman in Lunenburg (1903), where he lived near the former manager of Ruskin's Totley estate, William Harrison Riley. He had also worked for some years as an engineer at the Cushing Academy, Ashburnham, and at hospitals in Gardner and, since October 1906, at Burbank Hospital, in Fitchburg. On hearing that his mother was gravely ill, he set sail across the Atlantic to be with her. He found her 'very ill' and 'in a critical condition', refusing food and medicine, 'extremely irritable' and 'most difficult to nurse'.[375] Staff at The Retreat judged that 'she w[ould] not have much longer to live, as she breathes badly and has other signs of cardiac failure'.[376]

Howard wrote to the hospital at the end of October 1908 to say how glad he was that his 'dear mother ha[d] not gone' and he hoped that it would yet 'prove that she can live some years, at any rate that she w[ould] improve [...]'.[377] He added that Emily had endured two previous operations, and that after the first (major) procedure, he had 'nursed her so completely (+ thoroughly) back to life': 'She has so often recovered when we thought she was going that I hoped it might be so this time [...]'. Returning to America on 21 October, Godfrey wrote to the hospital from Cunard's RMS Ivernia to say, 'I feel perfect confidence in you + if it has not been too much strain for my mother I shall never regret' having visited her.[378]

On the same day Mabel wrote:

I was very glad to hear from the nurse that mother had had a comfortable journey and settled in contentedly at the Retreat. [...] I was glad to hear from my brother that you thought the trouble was more physical than mental, I had thought so myself + felt that what she needed most was kind nursing + quietness.[379]

She tenderly added a request for blankets in place of sheets for her mother to sleep on, explaining that Emily was used to blankets and would otherwise feel the cold; the family would pay, she said, if it meant greater expense in washing.[380]

By December, Mabel had lost her position as a teacher 'owing to the care and attention her mother ha[d] required'.[381] As such, she formally relinquished her role at West Heath School, Hampstead, a progressive co-educational establishment for day-scholars and boarders aged six to 18. She had previously been a governess: at the time of the 1881 census she was a nursery governess to the children of Christopher Barker, a stock broker and chartered accountant, and his wife, Mary, on Wood Lane, Sheffield; by 1891, she served the three young children of a farming family in Brighton in the same capacity; by 1901, she worked as a kindergarten teacher in St John's Wood Terrace, in London's Portland Town.

Mabel moved temporarily to 56 Heslington Road, York, in December 1908, to be close to her mother. Emily was described on Christmas Eve as 'very poorly' but 'certainly a little stronger' than she had been.

The distressing mental symptoms have largely cleared up, and though she says she still has strange delusional thoughts they do not influence her conduct as they did. Consequently, she is much calmer to nurse than she was and she is now very grateful for everything that is done for her.[382]

Yet she remained 'so weak and restless that life is a burden to her, and I rarely see her without her saying that she hopes the end is not far off'.[383]

Movingly, at the end of October 1908, the Swans' old family friend, Rev. T. W. Holmes, wrote from his residence at 3 Oxford Road, Sheffield, on his own behalf and that of his family, to thank the hospital for letting him know that Emily had been admitted there. 'She is a very old + dear friend of ours', he added.[384]

The cost of looking after a patient with a serious chronic condition that caused significant mental distress was considerable. Although Godfrey had promised 25 shillings per week, nothing had been forthcoming, so the hospital applied to the Westminster & Longford Monthly Meeting based then at 52 St Martin's Lane, which Emily had presumably re-joined on moving back to London.[385] Westminster agreed to pay the bills. Eventually, in early November 1909, Godfrey retrospectively sent a cheque for £15 together with a note '[t]hanking thee for all thy kindness + leniency in waiting for the account' to be settled.[386]

Emily Swan died at The Retreat on 15 January 1909, and was buried in the hospital cemetery.[387] After the funeral, Mabel, who had returned to her home in West Hampstead by the end of January, wrote warmly to the hospital authorities on behalf of herself and her brothers.

> We feel we should like a simple little stone at the grave. Mother was 73, not 72 as put on the coffin; it did not matter at all on the coffin, but it would be nice to have it right on the stone. […] Thanking you deeply for all your kindness to our dear mother + to Howard.[388]

Their wish was respected. Godfrey wrote from Massachusetts a month after his sister to

> thank you all for your kindness to my mother, for your letters + everything you have done + hope some day to visit and thank you with a hand-clasp. It was a Retreat[,] but in our case + I know my mother's case[,] one with honour.[389]

On 22 March 1909, the hospital responded.

> I am sure the nurses did all that was possible to make her as comfortable as the painful nature of her malady would allow. It was a very sad and distressing case, but happily towards the end Mrs Swan was able to appreciate the care received and that made things much easier. […] It was to me a source of great satisfaction that we were able to render help to your mother in this way. One feels that in such a case the Retreat is fulfilling its proper function.[390]

The *Sheffield Evening Telegraph* described Emily on her death as an accomplished lady, who exercised a great deal of influence in matters of art during the active period of her life, in collaboration with her husband, who was a very enthusiastic and distinguished disciple of the master. She was also an enthusiastic supporter of Ruskin's ideas and schemes, and used to receive other Ruskin enthusiasts at her pleasant home at Walkley, including such men as the late Prince Leopold and Professor Seeley and Max Müller.[391]

Mrs Swan was also a poet, and was the author of many pieces of sweet and touching verse. She contributed occasionally to the *Pall Mall Gazette* and other publications. In later years her faculties had failed very much, but up to the last she was always full of interesting reminiscences of Professor Ruskin from whom she and her husband had received over 100 letters that have not been published.[392]

Emily's poetry has proved elusive and was presumably published anonymously. William Harrison Riley recalled an occasion when 'Mrs Swan read' him one of her poems: 'Mrs Swan once wrote a poem, addressed to a little lamb, and telling it not to be afraid of the man who was approaching as he was the kind gentle master etc'.[393] A hint of what she was capable of as a writer was given in a letter she wrote during the time that she was the widowed museum curator at Walkley. She was responding to a powerful attack on industrial pollution in Sheffield launched by Edward Carpenter in May 1889.[394] Endorsing Carpenter's argument, she wrote that he had invoked 'the spirit of truth' and, 'like the snowdrop and crocus' which 'breaks through the hard and frosted ground', he had splendidly exposed a reality they were powerless to ignore.[395] People met together and commented on what a lovely day it was, she observed, but only for their friend to reply, 'If we could but see the sun'.

> We know it is shining some four or five miles away, and one's heart aches to see everything starved, and blighted, and blackened, through ignorance, greed, folly, and lassitude. The cuckoo and the skylark are singing, buds bursting. buttercups making the fields one golden splendour.[396]

She followed these Wordsworthian images with lines quoted from the folk song, 'Jockey to the Fair' (though she did not name her source), and proceeded with her lament that in Sheffield 'one's eyes smart, and one's lungs labour to breathe' so that even 'our beloved children' are 'struggling'. Sheffield, she concluded, could be 'as lovely as Bath' if only it were 'as free from pollution of all sorts'. She 'might live', she hoped, 'to see Sheffield pure', and to see all that was now merely 'putty coloured' turned 'to roses'. Alas, it was not to be. But her eloquent paean to the natural world, with its haunted warning about the destructive impact of industrial pollution, makes powerful use of the Ruskinian voice which continues to resonate with us in the twenty-first century.

SWANSONG
THE CULTIVATION OF SOULS

It was aptly observed in the *Pall Mall Gazette* that,
> [w]hatever arrangement Mr Ruskin may make for the future guardianship of St George's Museum, it can safely be said that in ardour and culture he will find it extremely difficult to engage anyone who will be able adequately to take the position so honourably and so zealously filled by poor Henry Swan.[397]

And Emily Swan, too. The press in Sheffield had once expressed the hope that Emily might 'infuse some of her own devotion and zeal for "the Master" into the British public'.[398] The comment came at a moment of great frustration, when the prospect of raising the money needed to fund new museum premises seemed particularly remote. Emily Swan, bitterly disappointed, wrote to the newspapers that while Ruskin 'proffers all this' treasure, the Sheffield public, and especially its leaders, merely
> snap their fingers in his face and say, who are you, we don't want you? Or as good as say it. They think when he says he will be glad of sympathy and help in this work that his society [*i.e. the Guild*] is going down, and he wants money and can't get on without it; and so he can go where he likes, they don't want his stuff and his help, and so the matter stands or sleeps. It is not dead, I know, for I am sure there are many faithful souls longing to see a suitable building erected and Mr Ruskin superintending in person the arrangement of the works on his own plan for the instruction of the rising generation.[399]

Henry and Emily Swan were the finest and most loyal of those 'faithful souls', even if Emily sometimes let her irritation get the better of her. The Swans' concern for 'the rising generation' was sincere and unwavering. It animated their every effort.

Howard Swan wrote eloquently of how Ruskin had gathered
> all the cream, in his conception, the best of the world's art. Sculpture, mosaic, wood-carving, illuminating, oil painting, water-colour [drawing], black and white, prose and poetry; a few specimens of the very finest of the topmost age of each were placed for the world's workmen to see and admire and, if need be, follow.[400]

To make such a priceless educational resource available and intelligible to the widest possible constituency of students was the Swans' motivating purpose.

Ruskin had written to Joan Severn in 1882, when the omens for a new museum in Sheffield were good: 'The old place [at Walkley] will not be sold, but become a centre of quaker St Georgism — which has its qualities — of a sort. The Swans will stay there — the curators of the new museum must be of another sort'.[401] He did not explain exactly what he meant. For 18 months or so before his death, Swan had in fact been working with the Museum and Parks Committee of Sheffield Town Council in a concerted effort 'to increase the usefulness of the museum'.[402] It involved helping Ruskin to provide donations to Meersbrook Hall, which had been purchased by Sheffield Corporation in the hope that it might provide the town with more museum and gallery space. Ultimately, it would become the new home of the re-branded Ruskin Museum, when the connection with Walkley was effectively severed by Swan's death. Swan had always been clear about Ruskin's intentions and he was more consistently confident than Emily in Sheffield's favorable reception of the Ruskin treasures. Inviting Sheffielders to subscribe to a museum building-fund in 1880, he expressed trust in 'their appreciation of Mr Ruskin's design in providing a type of museum to meet the special requirements of the practical student in the little collection' at Upper Walkley.[403]

Henry Swan, though unorthodox in his beliefs, radical in at least some of his opinions, alternative in his way of life, and eccentric in some of his interests and obsessions, was no 'crank', though scholars have tended to think so, and it is the word Ruskin's publisher, George Allen, used to describe him in a private letter written just after the opening of the Ruskin Museum at Meersbrook in April 1890.[404] It is altogether too dismissive a judgement, but it is not to be wondered at that a boomerang-throwing, bicycle-riding, anti-smoking, and teetotal vegetarian, spiritualist and Quaker should be regarded with some suspicion. But the qualities that fed these aspects of his character and personality also funded his endless supply of ideas and fuelled his confident pursuit of them. His appetite for innovation was extraordinary and he demonstrated the courage of his convictions.

Swan was so enthusiastic about shorthand that he literally engraved it on stone so that its inventor, Isaac Pitman, could promote it to a wider public. He not only devised his own 'Regent Method' of musical notation, but used it to teach others how to sing. He patented the 'Clairvoyant', a new hand-held stereoscope with which to create the illusion of three-dimensional imagery. Dissatisfied, he incorporated hand-coloured miniature portraits and viewing device in a single, self-contained 'crystal cube', small enough to wear on a chain — a significant contribution to nineteenth-century photography. He copied illuminated manuscripts well enough to impress John Ruskin. As a thoughtful reader of *Fors Clavigera*, and as someone who also contributed to its pages, he apparently reaffirmed Ruskin's faith in him. It led Ruskin to appoint him to curate his experimental educational art museum, and to locate it in the suburb of the town that the Swans had adopted as their own, namely Walkley, in Sheffield. Having formed a successful printing partnership with his brother, Frank, when the siblings were young men, Henry's marriage was also one of talented equals. Henry and Emily Swan proved their loyalty, ability, and suitability by dedicating the best part of their lives to serving Ruskin as the faithful stewards of his exemplary collection of treasures.

The fact that Henry and Emily Swan were able to pursue Ruskin's aims at Walkley with such constancy and persistence, despite all the challenges, owed more to their faith in the project and the strength of their partnership than to anything else. It was not inevitable. Emily's repeated bouts of acute anxiety sometimes overwhelmed her, but such periodic mental distress was also something over which she bonded with the often-troubled Ruskin. The impressive variety of Henry's activities up to the point that he took on the curatorship was a symptom of chronic restlessness and insatiability which resulted in him moving on from things rather than sticking at them. At last, as Ruskin's missionaries, they were content. No doubt the more settled nature of their minds was also a manifestation of the stage of life the Swans had reached. There seems to have been an element of fate or what Ruskin called '*fors*' in the timing of the venture, at least from the Swans' point-of-view, though good judgement was certainly part of the mix.

Henry was 50 and Emily 40 when the museum was founded. Three of their children would be educated at Ackworth School and, during the life of the museum, all four 'cygnets' matured into adulthood. Howard was the cleverest and shared his father's appetite for multiple professional interests. Mabel seems to have been the steadiest and most emotionally intelligent. Godfrey was the radical who travelled for adventure. Leonard, the youngest, who showed great promise and might have become a leading craftsman, suffered the most serious breakdown in his mental health, and committed suicide at the age of 20. It was a tragedy that cast a shadow over the lives of all of them.

Henry Swan was complex but clear-eyed, energetic but gentle. He had definite opinions but mostly kept them to himself. He was sympathetic, diplomatic, and helpful. And he was multi-talented. His childhood, unlike Ruskin's, was filled with toys.[405] Surrounded by a loving family, he demonstrated selfless courage by saving his friend from drowning, a fact of which none of his obituarists seem to have been aware. It was an act of heroism that was a harbinger of the life he led at Sheffield. After attending Ruskin's drawing class at the London

Working Men's College, and working for him to copy illuminated manuscripts, Swan developed a purposeful, Ruskinian appreciation of art and service. His adoption of Quakerism and vegetarianism in early adulthood was expressive of an unshakeable faith in the merits of a simple, unselfish life. It meant that he was perfectly suited to the role of Ruskin's curator at Walkley. His heart was always in and of the community. For him, the common interest functioned as both motivation and reward.

Fortunately for Ruskin, Swan's sensitivity and skill, his intellectual capacity and practical ability, his artistic talent and his lightness of touch in appropriately and effectively communicating knowledge, were put to use in serving his ideals and values. Fortunately for Swan, Ruskin made him the agent of his extraordinary generosity in sharing an exemplary collection of rare, precious and, above all, beautiful art-treasures, with the workmen and labourers of Great Britain. It provided Swan with a unique opportunity to demonstrate his devotion, aided always by his caring and committed family. Fortunately for Sheffield and far beyond it, the considerable benefits of Ruskin's collaboration with the Swans has bequeathed an enduring cultural legacy.

In 1919, the year in which the centenary of Ruskin's birth was celebrated, the *Sheffield Daily Telegraph* recalled Swan as

a remarkable man in his way. Under his care the museum remained at Walkley, accommodating material in the tiny and hardly accessible cottage — being so to speak in embryo, until the way should be clear for its removal or enlargement [...] [406]

Towards the end of 1883, when hopes were again high that a new, enlarged and more accessible museum for Ruskin's treasures might shortly materialise, Ruskin made it clear that he regarded the cultural granary he had founded as safe in Swan's hands: 'Mr Swan will remain at Walkley, as the head of a branch school and museum *store*, so that we shall let nothing into the Museum itself but what is to stay there.'[407] Ruskin trusted Swan to be the gatekeeper of his collection, the upholder of his values, the teacher of his principles, and the keeper of the flame. A stronger vote of confidence in Swan's comprehensive understanding of the aims and objectives of the Guild and its museum is difficult to imagine.

Ever outwardly graceful, the Swans' hard paddling under the surface went largely unnoticed. Sheffield was seduced. The affection in which the museum at Walkley was held by many of its visitors was matched only by a sense of indebtedness to its curators and founder. Such feelings endured for decades afterwards. It was not only Emily Swan who viewed the museum's function as nothing less than the cultivation of souls. Henry Swan told Ruskin in November 1887 that

[i]t does not matter much that none of the pioneers will see much of this. I have lived not to expect it. We shall see as much as is good for us. There is a power and wisdom beyond ours.[408]

What the Swans realised in Walkley, in a practical sense, was what Ruskin called the 'power to bequeath', and the legacy they helped forge is still felt today, not only in Sheffield, but around the world. The collection first brought together at Walkley has at different times been cherished, neglected, taken for granted, celebrated and ignored; it has delighted and frustrated, puzzled and enlightened. It is appreciated and enjoyed today more fully than it has ever been, vindicating Swan's view that there is a 'power and wisdom beyond' his own that he nonetheless had the perspicacity and strength of faith to recognise and acknowledge. As model custodians and exemplary stewards, the Swans had, as Ruskin saw it, faithfully discharged the most sacred of earthly duties.

'God has lent us the earth for our life'. Ruskin wrote in *The Seven Lamps of Architecture* (1849):

> it is a great entail. It belongs as much to those who are to come after us, and whose names are already written in the book of creation, as to us; and we have no right, by anything that we do or neglect, to involve them in unnecessary penalties, or deprive them of benefits which it was in our power to bequeath. And this the more, because it is one of the appointed conditions of the labour of men that, in proportion to the time between the seed-sowing and the harvest, is the fulness of the fruit; and that generally, therefore, the farther off we place our aim, and the less we desire to be ourselves the witnesses of what we have laboured for, the more wide and rich will be the measure of our success. Men cannot benefit those that are with them as they can benefit those who come after them; and of all the pulpits from which human voice is ever sent forth, there is none from which it reaches so far as from the grave.[409]

ABBREVIATIONS

ATR   Archive of The Retreat (York), RET/6/20/1/18/78 (papers relating to Emily E. Swan)
BF   *The British Friend*
BIA   Borthwick Institute for Archives, University of York
BJP   *British Journal of Photography*
DR   *The Dietetic Reformer and Vegetarian Messenger*
ES   Emily Swan
GRO   General Register Office
GSG   Guild of St George
HS   Henry Swan
INA   Inspire Nottinghamshire Archives
JR   John Ruskin
LE   Library Edition of *The Works of John Ruskin* (39 vols) (London: George Allen, 1903-1912) ed. E. T. Cook and Alexander Wedderburn
LMA   London Metropolitan Archives
PMG   *Pall Mall Gazette*
RRB   *Ruskin Research Blog*
RML   Rosenbach Museum & Library, Philadelphia
RSC   Ruskin-Swan Correspondence, Rosenbach Museum & Library, Philadelphia (RML): EL3. R956, ALsS, John Ruskin to Henry and Emily Swan, 1855-1887 (10 vols), ed. William Allen
SA   Sheffield City Archives
SDT   *Sheffield Daily Telegraph*
SET   *Sheffield Evening Telegraph*
SI   *Sheffield (and Rotherham) Independent*
SMT   Sheffield Museums Trust
SWT   *Sheffield Weekly Telegraph*
WMC   Working Men's College (London)

NOTES

PRELIMINARY NOTE
1. LE, 17.105.
2. LE, 24.371.

INTRODUCTION
3. LE, 34.251.
4. LE, 29.450.
5. LE, 29.397: this is *Fors Clavigera*, letter 88 (March 1880).
6. See <www.ruskinatwalkley.org> (accessed 15 May 2024).
7. See <www.guildofstgeorge.org.uk> (accessed 15 May 2024).
8. LE, 27.13.
9. Public letter by Henry Swan in *SI* (13 March 1880).
10. INA, M/12560: letter from JR to Henrietta Carey (30) (6 August 1883): original emphasis.
11. LE, 30.51-52.
12. LE, 17.171, 27.14, 377.
13. LE, 30.52.
14. LE, 30.52.
15. The Anti-Corn Law Rhymer, Ebenezer Elliott (1781-1849).
16. The Great Sheffield Flood of 1864 devastated parts of the town when the Dale Dyke Dam burst as the reservoir was being filled for the first time.
17. Howard Swan, 'John Ruskin: Reminiscences by a Worker in His Museum', in *Westminster Gazette* (24 January 1900). The bulk of the article was reprinted under the title, 'Mr Howard Swan on Ruskin: Sheffield Reminiscences' in *SI* (26 January 1900). Excerpts were reproduced in LE, notably in 34.718.
18. Edward Bradbury, 'A Visit to Ruskin's Museum', in *Magazine of Art* (December 1879), vol. III, pp. 57-60, specifically p. 57.
19. Bradbury in *Magazine of Art*, p. 57.
20. Bradbury in *Magazine of Art*, p. 58.
21. Qtd in Catherine W. Morley, *John Ruskin, Late Work, 1870-1890: The Museum and Guild of St George, An Educational Experiment* (London & New York: Garland, 1984), p. 59.
22. *SDT* (1 October 1883).
23. *SDT* (23 June 1885).
24. Bradbury in *Magazine of Art*, p. 57.
25. Howard Swan in *Westminster Gazette* (24 January 1900).
26. LE, 30.333: this is from a letter by JR to George Thomson (5 November 1886). On Thomson, see Stuart Eagles, *The Ruskinian Industrialist: George Thomson of Huddersfield* (York: Guild of St George, 2021).

ONE
27. *SDT* (3 April 1889). All details of Swan's funeral are taken from this source.
28. The designer, town-planner and Garden City pioneer Raymond Unwin named Godfrey Swan alongside Edward Carpenter and John Furniss as among the area's socialists in the mid-1880s. See Andrew Lee, *The Red Flag of Anarchy: A History of Socialism & Anarchism in Sheffield 1874-1900* (Sheffield: Pirate Press, 2017), p. 94.
29. *SDT* (3 April 1889).
30. Holmes signed the visitor books between February 1881 and 25 September 1889. He also took his daughter on a visit to the museum in June 1882. For his account of meeting Ruskin, see T.

W. Holmes, 'An Evening with Ruskin at Walkley', reprinted in LE, 30.309-311. The article originally appeared in *The Lamp: a Magazine for Christian Workers and Thinkers,* no. 1 (January 1892), pp. 13-17, and it was extensively quoted in *SI* (5 January 1892).

31. *SET* (2 April 1889).

32. Other mourners included Benjamin Creswick's wife, Fanny (née Goodall) (1855-1931), Mrs Charles Doncaster (née Barber), Messrs Whitehead, H. Whelan, A. Badger (possibly related to the former owners of the farm at Totley), Mrs and Miss Maxfield, plus W. H. Nicol and John Holmes (both of Leeds) and possibly the people Swan was visiting before he fell fatally ill. The last of these was probably John Holmes (1815-1894), a wealthy draper in Methley, Leeds, a radical essayist who was one of the founders of the Leeds Co-operative Society.

33. *SDT* (3 April 1889).

34. *SI* (30 March 1889).

35. *The Companion,* no. 16 (2016), pp. 26, 27. For a full account of the events to mark the creation and unveilings of the plaques, see pp. 24-28.

36. Mark Frost, *Curator and Curatress: the Swans and St George's Museum* (York: Guild of St George, 2013), pp. 34-35. Ruskin called Emily Swan the 'Curatress' in a letter to Henry Swan received 29 January 1878, part of the RSC archive Frost rediscovered at the RML.

TWO

37. *Wiltshire Independent* (18 January 1838).

38. LMA, Royal Humane Society Bronze Medal, case no. 13217 (22 January 1838).

39. *Wiltshire Independent* (13 September 1838).

40. University of London Student Records, 1836-1945.

41. James Waylen, *The Annals of the Royal and Ancient Borough of Devizes, 1102-1900* (Devizes, 1906), p. 36.

42. *Wiltshire Independent* (26 October and 2 November 1837).

43. *Devizes and Wiltshire Gazette* (15 March and 3 May 1838). The toyshop was taken on by Mrs Dodman. Her startling discovery in the winter of 1839 of a burglar who had concealed himself behind the counter was reported in the *Devizes and Wiltshire Gazette* (28 November 1839).

44. George Eliot on *Modern Painter III* in *Westminster Review* (April 1856), pp. 625-633.

45. It has also been speculated that Brabant was among Eliot's earliest lovers. Eliot's visit to Devizes was certainly cut short when Mrs Brabant, who was blind, was warned by her sister that Brabant and Eliot were flirting, leading to Eliot's earlier-than-expected departure.

46. See Victoria Mills, 'The museum as "dream space": psychology and aesthetic response in George Eliot's *Middlemarch*', in *Interdisciplinary Studies in the Long Nineteenth Century,* no. 12 (2011).

47. See *Devizes and Wiltshire Gazette* (12 November 1835).

48. Certificate dated 7 August 1773. See J. H. Chandler, *Meeting House Certificates, 1689-1852* (Wiltshire Record Society, vol. 40) (Devizes: Wiltshire Record Society, 1985), p. 30.

THREE

49. See *Devizes and Wiltshire Gazette*

(2 August 1838) which reported the death of the Swans' eldest daughter, Elizabeth, in London, and described John Swan as 'late of Devizes'. She was buried on 31 July 1838 at the Church of St John the Baptist, Hoxton, which had only opened in 1826.
50. Death certificate of Elizabeth Swan, GRO ref. 2/267, Sep. Q. 1838, Shoreditch.
51. Proceedings of the Old Bailey (19 October 1840) ref. t18401019-2496.
52. UK census (6 June 1841).
53. The 1851 UK census (30 March) gives Henry's occupation only as 'engraver'.
54. See LMA CLC/L/HA/C/ 011/ MS15860/ 010 (City of London, Haberdashers, Apprentices, and Freemen, 1526-1933). The document gives the consideration as £40. However, records in the Royle business archives (held privately) state £63: see Eric V. Royle, *A Printer's Tale* ([No Place]: W. R. Royle Group Ltd, 1991), p. 6.
55. Royle, *Printer's Tale*, p. 5.
56. Royle, *Printer's Tale*, p. 6.
57. *Cambridge Chronicle and Journal* (10 December 1842).
58. *Oxford University and City Herald* (25 April 1846).
59. See *Perry's Bankrupt Gazette* (16 September 1848).
60. See *Bell's New Weekly Messenger* (17 September 1848). The *Gospel Banner* is available online at Google Books (accessed 17 May 2024).
61. See *Morning Post* (8 April 1851).
62. SMT, Ruskin Collection (GSG): St George's Museum Visitor Book, no. 2 (September 1881-December 1882).
63. Death certificate of John Swan Jnr, GRO ref. 3/191, Sep. Q. 1849, Hackney.
64. *SI* (30 March 1889).
65. *The Musical Times and Singing-Class Circular*, vol. 7, no. 152 (1 October 1855), p. 114.
66. *The Musical Times and Singing-Class Circular*, vol. 7, no. 152 (1 October 1855), p. 114.
67. *Directory of 1851 for Hackney, Clapton, Homerton, Dalston, Kingsland, De Beauvoir Town, Shacklewell and Stoke Newington* (Hackney: Caleb Turner, 1851), pp. 62, 246. A Henry Swan listed at 2 Grange Cottages, near Mayfield Road, was in fact an unrelated 50-year-old solicitor.
68. Evidence for 1847 in Supplement to the *Fonotipik Jurnal*, vol. 6 (1847), p. 8; and for 1849 in the *Post Office Directory for 1850*, p. 1033.
69. *BF*, vol. VII, no. 10 (October 1849), p. 264.
70. *BF*, vol. VIII, no. 8 (August 1850), p. 2.
71. *BF*, vol. IX, no. 5 (May 1851), p. 2. *Kelly's Directory of London 1852* also listed the brothers as 'engravers, printers and lithographers' of 13 Liverpool St., Bishopsgate (p. 1013).
72. *The Phonographic Examiner*, vol. 3, no. 36 (December 1855), which was 'ENGRAVED ON STONE, in the Corresponding and Reporting Styles', states on the cover, 'Engraved on Stone, by F. & H. Swan, Kingsland Green, London'.
73. *SI* (30 March 1889).
74. Supplement to the *Fonotipik Jurnal*, vol. 6 (1847), p. 8.
75. Michael Twyman (coincidentally a Companion of the Guild of St George himself during the period that the Ruskin Collection was housed at the University of Reading) provides

useful information in a chapter on Isaac Pitman's publications in his study, *Early Lithographical Books* (London: Farrand Press & Private Libraries Association, 1990), pp. 155, 160, and catalogue entries 5.13, 5.38, 5.43 and 5.48.
76. 'F. & H. Swan imp. Dalston' is written in left-slanting italics on p. 224 of the book.
77. Ruskin asked Swan about Hargrave in August 1880 after receiving a letter from him written at 66 Bower Road: see RML, RSC: letter from JR to HS (17 August 1880).
78. See W[ilfrid] Hargrave, 'The Faithful Steward of the Ruskin Museum (By One Who Knew Him)' in *PMG* (2 April 1889).
79. *SI* (30 March 1889).
80. See *The Phonetic Journal* (20 August 1853), p. 272, and *The Phonetic Journal* (1 October 1859), p. 470, respectively.

FOUR
81. James Adderley, *In Slums and Society: Reminiscences of Old Friends* (London: T. Fisher Unwin Ltd, 1916), p. 199.
82. See 'Origines Collegii' in *The Working Men's College Journal*, vol. 3, no. 55 (July 1895), pp. 240-242, specifically p. 241.
83. Thomas Hancock, 'Henry Swan, The Quaker: Some Personal Reminiscences of Mr Ruskin's "Curator"' in *PMG* (3 April 1889).
84. RML, RSC: letter from JR to ES (14 September 1879).
85. RML, RSC: letter from JR to HS (19 July 1879), and JR to ES (30 April 1879).
86. *SI* (30 March 1889).
87. Hargrave in *PMG* (2 April 1889).
88. Information supplied in a private email to the author from James Gregory, historian of Victorian vegetarianism (15 March 2019).
89. See Hypatia Bradlaugh Bonner, *Charles Bradlaugh: A Record of His Life and Work* (2 vols) (London: T. Fisher Unwin, 1908), vol. 1, p. 19. The suggestion that this was Henry Swan was made in James Gregory, 'The Vegetarian Movement in Britain, c.1840-1900: A Study of its Development, Personnel, and Wider Connections' (University of Southampton Ph.D thesis, 2002), vol. 2, p. 112.
90. On his death in 1873, his estate was officially valued at a handsome £30,000.
91. See James Gregory, *Of Victorians and Vegetarians: The Vegetarian Movement in Nineteenth-Century Britain* (London: I. B. Tauris, 2007), p. 46.
92. On Dornbusch's regimen, see Gregory, *Vegetarian Movement*, p. 78.
93. Benjamin Creswick, a former knife-grinder who frequently visited St George's Museum, where his artistic talents were recognised by the Swans and later nurtured by Ruskin. Creswick was then (March 1879) living in Coniston and was engaged in sculpting portrait busts of Ruskin, one of which was gifted later in the year to Prince Leopold, on the occasion of His Royal Highness's visit to the museum at Walkley.
94. RML, RSC: letter from JR to ES (4 March 1879).
95. Swan's spiritualism is mentioned by Hargrave in *PMG* (2 April 1889), and Dornbusch's in Gregory, *Vegetarian Movement*, pp. 106-107, which also associates

Pierre Baume with socialism.
96. RML, RSC: letter from JR to HS (18 November 1876).
97. Letter from JR to William Ward (26 September 1879) (author's private collection), with thanks to Pavel Chepyzhov.
98. For Dornbusch's fruit-growing colony scheme, see Gregory, *Vegetarian Movement*, p. 45. For the experiment at Totley, see Sally Goldsmith, *Thirteen Acres: John Ruskin and the Totley Communists* (York: Guild of St George, 2016) which draws heavily on Mark Frost, *The Lost Companions and John Ruskin's Guild of St George: A Revisionary History* (London: Anthem Press, 2014).
99. Gregory, *Vegetarian Movement*, p. 55.
100. LE, 30.xliv.
101. LE, 29.434.
102. LE, 29.434-435.
103. LE, 29.435.
104. DR, no. 137 (1 May 1883), p. 114.
105. DR, no. 139 (1 July 1883), p. 181.
106. DR, no. 139 (1 July 1883), p. 181, and LE, 29.435-436.

FIVE
107. HS enrolled on 4 November 1854.
108. F. D. Maurice, *Learning and Working: Six Lectures delivered in Willis's Rooms, London, In June and July, 1854* (Cambridge: Macmillan & Co., 1855), p. xvi.
109. See 'Origines Collegii' in *The Working Men's College Journal*, p. 241.
110. Maurice, *Learning and Working*, p. 66.
111. Frederick Maurice, *The Life of Frederick Denison Maurice, chiefly told in his own letters* (2 vols.) (London: Macmillan & Co., 1884), vol. 2, p. 250.
112. See LE, 10.lx.
113. See Stuart Eagles, 'Morris and John Ruskin' in *The Cambridge Companion to William Morris,* ed. Marcus Waithe (Cambridge: Cambridge University Press, 2024), pp. 259-270.
114. Maurice, *Life*, vol. 2, p. 251.
115. William Ward, *Letters from John Ruskin to William Ward* (2 vols.) (London: printed privately, 1893), vol. 1, pp. xv-xvi.
116. UK census (6 June 1841). Although Ward's attendance at the school is not noted in any published sources, his son says of his paternal grandfather (quoting one of the latter's colleagues): 'He has successively professed — and, I believe, with perfect sincerity — Methodism, Quakerism, Owenism, and every other ism, often changing his religion, yet, I apprehend, without religion ever having changed him.' See William C[lack] Ward, *John Ruskin's Letters to William Ward with a short portrait of William Ward by William C. Ward* (Boston: Marshall, Jones Co., 1922), p. 26.
117. See Ward, *Letters* (1922), p. 31.
118. SA: Ruskin Museum Committee, Minute Book no. 2, p. 23 (minutes of meeting held on 7 June 1894). The price paid was £21.
119. Ward, *Letters* (1893), vol. 1, p. xx.
120. SI (30 March 1889); see also RML, RSC: letter from JR to HS (10 December 1855).
121. Ruskin wrote about the 'Protestant Convent Plan' in letters to William Ward from 1855, see Ward, *Letters* (1922), p. 50.
122. RML, RSC: letter from JR to HS (October 1855). Ruskin wrote

at the end of the letter, 'Thanks for the suggestions about convent.'
123. LE, 30.lv.
124. RML, RSC: letter from JR to HS (1 February 1855).
125. RML, RSC: letter from JR to HS (27 May [1856]): Ruskin's emphasis.
126. Ruskin also entrusted into Hill's care an experimental tea-shop which he had established under the care of former family servants at 29 Paddington Street, see Stuart Eagles, 'Mr Ruskin's Tea-Shop' (*RRB* #34, 30 November 2022) <https://stuarteagles.co.uk/34-mr-ruskins-tea-shop/> (accessed 1 May 2024).
127. See LE, 5.267. Swan would also later engrave a plate for *The Laws of Fesole* (1877-78): 'Construction for Placing the Honour-Points' (see LE, 15.367) for which he was paid £5 (see LE, 28.27).
128. Maurice, *Learning and Working*, pp. 167-169.
129. Maurice, *Life*, vol. 2, p. 233.
130. See William E. Fredeman (ed.), *The Correspondence of Dante Gabriel Rossetti* (10 vols) (Cambridge: D. S. Brewer, 2002-15), vol. 2, p. 258*n*; Alison Chapman and Joanne Meacock, *A Rossetti Family Chronology* (London: Palgrave, 2007), p. 110; and John Holmes, *The Pre-Raphaelites and Science* (New Haven: Yale University Press, 2018), p. 121.
131. See Holmes, *Pre-Raphaelites and Science*, p. 275 *n*33, and John Holmes, *The Temple of Science: The Pre-Raphaelites and the Oxford University Museum of Natural History* (Oxford: Bodleian Library, 2020), p. 119.

132. See 'Museum of Natural History's HOPE for the Future wins National Heritage support' (news release, 27 March 2018) <www.oum.ox.ac.uk/about/HOPE%20for%20the%20Future.pdf> (accessed 22 May 202).
133. Georgiana Burne-Jones, *Memorials of Edward Burne-Jones* (London: Macmillan & Co. Ltd, 1906), p. 189.
134 See Edward A. Tunstall and Antony Kerr, 'The Painted Room at The Queen's College, Oxford' in *The Burlington Magazine for Connoisseurs*, vol. 82, no. 479 (February 1943), pp. 42, 44-47 (with thanks to Matthew Winterbottom for help in making this final connection).
135. For a full analysis of the evidence, see Stuart Eagles, 'A Swan without a Leda' (*RRB* #2, 22 October 2020) <https://stuarteagles.co.uk/2-a-swan-without-a-leda/> (accessed 22 May 2024).

SIX

136. See 'Origines Collegii' in *The Working Men's College Journal*, p. 241.
137. I am grateful to the late Andrew Russell for sharing this information from his research at the Library of the Society of Friends, London.
138. *Eighth Annual Report of Friends' First-Day School Association (presented to the annual meeting held at Ackworth, the 4th of 7th Month 1855* (Bristol: James Ackland, 1855) (not paginated) [p. 10].
139. Ackworth School Admission Register: Mabel Swan (2 February 1874). All information relating to Ackworth School is courtesy of its untiringly helpful archivist, Celia Wolfe, to whom I record

thanks.
140. See 'Origines Collegii' in *The Working Men's College Journal*, p. 241.
141. LE, 17.470: this is in an appendix to Letter 12 (20 March 1867) of *Time and Tide* (1867).
142. SA: Ruskin Museum Committee, Minute Book no. 3 (4 August 1910).
143. John W. Graham, *The Harvest of Ruskin* (London: George Allen & Unwin Ltd., 1920), p. 74.
144. 'I believe [Baker's] whole connexion from first to last with Mr Ruskin has been for self-glorification.' Letter from Egbert Rydings to Mrs F[anny] Talbot (10 December 1910), qtd in Morley, *Late Work*, p. 226.
145. Graham, *Harvest*, pp. 75-76.
146. Graham, *Harvest*, p. 77.
147. Qtd in Morley, *Late Work*, p. 218.
148. Morley, *Late Work*, p. 218.
149. Morley, *Late Work*, p. 219; the quote is from a private letter to Morley from one of Juliet's grandsons, David Morse.
150. Morley, *Late Work*, p. 219.
151. RML, RSC: letter from JR to HS (received 3 April 1876).
152. *The Publishers' Circular* (1 December 1860), p. 718.
153. Swan's patent applications were made between 1858 and 1862 from 5 Bishopsgate Street Without, and he declared himself a 'bookseller's clerk' in the UK census (7 April 1861).

SEVEN
154. Marriage certificate of Henry Swan and Emily Elizabeth Connell, GRO ref. 1b/522, June Q. 1859, Hackney.
155. *Kingsland Times and General Advertiser* (21 December 1861).
156. *The Illustrated London News* (21 July 1851).
157. LMA, ref. CLC/B/057: Connell business papers.
158. See *Sun* (9 December 1846).
159. See *The Letters of Richard Cobden 1860-1865* (Oxford: Oxford University Press, 2007) eds. Anthony Howe & Simon Morgan, p. 112.
160. *London City Press* (21 March 1863).
161. Emily's parents were buried at Norwood Cemetery.
162. Birth certificate of Howard Swan, GRO ref. 1b/265, June Q. 1860, Islington.
163. Birth certificate of Godfrey Swan, GRO ref. 1b/349, March Q. 1863, Hackney.
164. Birth certificate of Mabel Swan, GRO ref. 1b/207, March Q. 1864, Islington; birth certificate of Leonard Swan, GRO ref. 1b/275, June Q. 1866, Islington.

EIGHT
165. British Library: patent no. 2644 (1858).
166. *The Bookseller* (30 November 1859), p. 43.
167. British Library: patent no. 2020 (1859) and British Library: patent no. 559 (1860).
168. Hemry Swan is not to be confused with Sir Joseph Wilson Swan (1828-1914), the patentee of Swan's carbon process in February 1864, and the founder of Swan's Electric Engraving Co., and numerous other initiatives. JWS also invented a successful incandescent light bulb used to illuminate the Savoy Theatre and other public buildings. The two men were not related, but in early photographic journals both were often referred to as 'Mr Swan'.
169. British Library: patent no.

3249 (1862). (Stamp duty of £50 paid.) The US patent (no. 51,906) was issued 2 January 1866.
170. *Morning Post* (22 September 1863).
171. See <https://collection.sciencemuseumgroup.org.uk/objects/co8208587/swans-casket-photograph-stereoscope-collodion-transparency> and <https://collections.vam.ac.uk/context/organisation/A29174/casket-portrait-co.-ltd.> (accessed 14 May 2024).
172. *London Evening Standard* (29 September 1863).
173. *London Evening Standard* (29 September 1863).
174. *Morning Post* (2 October 1863).
175. Will of William Connell, probate: Principal Probate Registry (15 April 1863). The executors were his son, William George Connell, of 83 Cheapside, chronometer maker, and his friend and colleague, George Moore, St John's Square, Clerkenwell, watchmaker. Moore had been in partnership with Francis Bryant Adams, and the Adams family boasted several generations of successful Clerkenwell watchmakers, suggesting a possible (as yet unproven) link with Emily's mother, Mary Hamlin Adams.
176. *Morning Post* (2 October 1863).
177. The image can be viewed online, see <https://www.digitalcollections.manchester.ac.uk/view/MS-ENGLISH-00414-00025-A/1> (accessed 14 May 2024).
178. Birth certificate of Mabel Swan, GRO ref. 1b/207, March Q. 1864, Islington.
179. See *The Athenaeum*, no. 1874 (26 September 1863), p. 386.
180. 'The Casket Portrait' in *The Art Journal* (new series), vol. III, p. 50.
181. *London Evening Standard* (29 September 1863).
182. [William Harrison Riley], 'John Ruskin' in *The Illustrated American*, vol. III, no. 28 (30 August 1890), pp. 347-352, specifically p. 348.
183. *i.e.* printed from ordinary negatives as transparencies on small mica plates.
184. *London Evening Standard* (29 September 1863).
185. 'A New Kind of Miniature' in *The Intellectual Observer*, vol. IV, no. 11 (November 1863), pp. 292-293, specifically p. 293.
186. *Saunders's News-Letter* (21 June 1864) & *Morning Post* (20 June 1864).
187. See Henry Swan, 'Casket Miniature in Relief' in *The Photographic News*, vol. X, no. 400 (4 May 1866), p. 212; and *idem*, 'Casket Miniatures in Relief: On Printing, Colouring, and Mounting the Transparencies' in *ibid.*, vol. X, no. 403 (25 May 1866), p. 248. The two articles were also published in the *BJP* (4 & 18 May 1866), pp. 217, 237 (I am grateful to Andrew Melling for facilitating access to the *BJP*).
188. *Morning Post* (6 December 1864); *The Times* (22 December 1864).
189. *Holborn Journal* (16 December 1865).
190. *The Photographic Journal*, no. 183 (16 July 1867), p. 66.
191. *Illustrated London News* (14 September 1867). His participation is also noted in *Reports of the Paris Universal Exhibition, 1867* (London, 1868), p. 178.
192. See *The Photographic Journal*, no. 160 (15 August 1865), p. 123.
193. *SI* (30 March 1889).
194. *The Photographic News* (20 July

1866), p. 348.
195. Exhibit nos. 639 and 638 respectively.
196. *The Photographic News* (20 July 1866), p. 348.
197. *The Photographic News* (9 November 1866), p. 533.
198. *BJP Annual* (1895), p. 586.
199. *BJP* (4 & 18 May 1866), pp. 217, 237, specifically p. 217.
200. Swan, 'Monopoly through Coalition', in *BJP* (22 November 1872), p. 555.
201. Hargrave in *PMG* (2 April 1889).
202. Hargrave in *PMG* (2 April 1889).
203. See *SDT* (12 May 1869).
204. See *SDT & SI* (12 August 1868).
205. Hargrave in *PMG* (2 April 1889).
206. Tantalisingly, an account of (subsequent Ruskin Museum curator) Gill Parker's popular lecture, 'How the Museum was Established' reported that, 'The history of the museum at Walkley was traced and illustrated by pictures of the rooms in which the collections were housed, and of individuals who were notably associated with the institution at the time.' *SDT* (18 November 1907). A similar report repeated the claim five years later: see *SDT* (18 November 1912). It is difficult to believe that, if Swan was not among these 'individuals', the fact of his absence was not considered worth mentioning. On a different matter, it is worth noting that James S. Dearden speculated in his catalogue of images of Ruskin that one portrait, completed c.1856, may have been the work of Henry Swan. It had been in Swan's possession, was given to the Sheffield craftsman, Charles Green, a regular visitor to the museum at Walkley, and it eventually found its way to Sheffield's Graves Art Gallery. See James S. Dearden, *John Ruskin: A Life in Pictures* (Sheffield: Sheffield Academic Press, 1999), p. 48.
207. Hargrave in *PMG* (2 April 1889).

NINE
208. *BJP* (15 November 1872), p. 549.
209. The correction was given in Swan, 'Monopoly through Coalition', in *BJP* (22 November 1872), p. 555.
210. Coincidentally, the address was later connected with businesses in fields in which the Swans had some involvement and interest. It was the premises of the Rowe Paragon Cycle and Sulky Co. (early 1890s), later still, the Photochromoscope Syndicate, a process engraver, established in 1898, and later still, a watchmaking business (1909).
211. The birth was announced in *BF* (2 April 1860), p. 97.
212. *Clerkenwell News* (23 September 1871).
213. HS's parents, John (died 28 October 1871) and Elizabeth (died 14 May 1882), were buried at St Helier's nonconformist Almorah (or General) Cemetery, on Richmond Road (Plot 2/1/C).
214. Frank Swan's membership number was #1927.
215. *DR* (April 1882), non-paginated advertisement wrappers.
216. A further connection with photography came later in the decade when Emily's younger brother, Frederick Henry Connell

(1839-1911), became a photographer — though this seems to have been a short-lived and probably coincidental connection.
217. *BJP* (15 November 1872), p. 549.
218. *BJP* (10 March 1876), p. 120.
219. The enquirer was Lionel Hartman, see *BJP* (10 March 1893), p. 160.
220. LE, 27.556.
221. LE, 27.554: the letter occupies pp. 554-557.
222. LE, 27.554.
223. LE, 27.542.
224. LE, 27.554, 555.
225. LE, 27.542.
226. LE, 27.497-498.
227. LE, 27.542.
228. LE, 27.542-543.
229. LE, 27.423.
230. For Riley's republican comments referred to by Ruskin here, see LE, 27.423-424.
231. LE, 27.423.
232. LE, 27.542.
233. LE, 27.542.
234. LE, 27.543.
235. LE, 27.542.
236. LE, 27.423. For Ruskin's attack on Smith, the division-of-labour, and the example of pin manufacture, see LE, 10.196.
237. Ruskin invited readers at this point to compare Swan's analysis with his own article, 'Home, and its Economics' which had recently appeared in the *Contemporary Review* (May 1873), reproduced in LE, 17.556-565.
238. This is the Jersey Mercantile Bank which suspended payments on 1 February 1873 after the collapse of the new harbour scheme the previous year. The Jersey Joint-Stock Bank subsequently failed in July 1873. The banking crisis was followed by protracted trade and economic depression.
239. This was the so-called 'bankers' bank' which collapsed in 1866 owing £11m.
240. LE, 27.554-557, the italics, Ruskin tells us, are his own.
241. See LE, 27.417.
242. LE, 27.557.
243. LE, 27.557-558.
244. Henry Swan, 'Monopoly through Coalition', in *BJP* (22 November 1872), p. 555.
245. RML, RSC: fragment of a letter from JR to HS (12 July 1875), qtd in William Allen's introduction.
246. RML, RSC: letter from JR to HS (29 December 1876).

TEN
247. Ackworth School Admission Register: Mabel Swan (2 February 1874). Renewed thanks to Ackworth School's archivist, Celia Wolfe, for kindly supplying so much information about the Swans and the school.
248. RML, RSC: letter from JR to HS (received 7 July 1873, but dated 8 August 1873).
249. RML, RSC: letter from JR to HS (received 15 November 1873).
250. See Stuart Eagles, *Ruskin and the Communists* (forthcoming).
251. RML, RSC: letter from JR to HS (15 November 1873). See Mark Frost, *Curator*, p. 12. We do not have Swan's side of the correspondence, and Ruskin may well have been echoing Swan in writing that the work might be 'useless and vulgar'.
252. Robert Hewison, *Ruskin and His Contemporaries* (London: Pallas Athene, 2018), p. 219.
253. RML, RSC: letter from JR to HS (18 May 1875).

254. *White's General and Commercial Directory of Sheffield, Rotherham...* (Sheffield: William White, 1876).
255. *SI* (22 January 1900).
256. LE, 13.553.
257. *SDT* (12 August 1876).
258. LE, 28.576: *Fors*, Letter 64 (April 1876) detailing 'two quarters' salary to 31 March, 1876', £20.
259. RML, RSC: letter from JR to HS (8 November 1875).
260. RML, RSC: letter from JR to HS (12 October 1875).
261. RML, RSC: letter from JR to HS (22 October 1875).
262. LE, 28.529: *Fors*, Letter 62 (February 1876).
263. See Frost, *Curator*, p. 24.
264. See *SDT* (29 April 1876), *SI* (9 August 1876).
265. The shell collection was given into the care of an early Guild Companion, Henrietta Carey (for more on Miss Carey, see chapter eleven). The shells had been given to Ruskin by the family of the original collector, Mrs Caroline Brereton (1792-1881) of Beverley. They were accepted on loan by Miss Carey on behalf of the Nottingham Kyrle Society and the Nottingham Town and Country Social Guild based at the Social Guild Institute, Upper Parliament Street, where a small museum called the Ruskin Room was freely open to students. It possessed other items gifted absolutely by Ruskin, unconnected with the Guild of St George, and included minerals, pictures and copies of books by himself and others.
266. William Henry Dallinger FRS (1839-1909), an evolutionary biologist, was Principal of Sheffield's Wesley College, president of the Ruskin Society of Sheffield, and a keen Ruskin collector.
267. Henry Bendelack Hewetson (1850-1899), one-time president of the Leeds Naturalists' Club, was a surgeon who specialised in ophthalmology and otology. He was a keen ornithologist. He was a regular visitor to the museum at Walkley and Meersbrook, and a generous donor to the collection. Among the stuffed birds he gifted was the peacock which was later given a prominent position near the entrance to Meersbrook Hall.
268. *SDT* and *SI* (25 September 1883).
269. Qtd in Edith Hope Scott, *Ruskin's Guild of St George* (London: Methuen & Co. Ltd, 1931), p. 45.
270. Henry Swan, *Collected Notes on some of the Pictures in St George's Museum, Sheffield* (Sheffield, 1879), p. 15.
271. See Howard Swan, *Preliminary Catalogue of the St George's Museum, Walkley, Sheffield* (Sheffield: W. D. Spalding & Co., 1888).
272. Norman Mackenzie, 'Percival Chubb and the founding of the Fabian Society', in *Victorian Studies*, vol. 23, no. 1 (Autumn 1979), pp. 29-55, specifically pp. 46, 51.
273. Howard Swan, *Preliminary Catalogue*, [p. 3].
274. RML, RSC: letter from JR to ES (20 October 1876).
275. Helen Gill Viljoen (ed.), *The Brantwood Diary of John Ruskin: together with selected related letters and sketches of persons mentioned* (New Haven, CT: Yale University Press, 1971), p. 42.
276. See M[arion] H. Spielmann, *John Ruskin: A Sketch of His Life, His Work, and His Opinions, With Personal Reminiscences* (Philadelphia:

Lippincott Co., 1900), p. 189.
277. RML, RSC: letter from JR to HS (14 September 1877).
278. *SI* (22 May 1877).
279. *SDT* (16 August 1877).
280. E.S.P., 'Mr Ruskin's Museum at Sheffield' reprinted in *Littell's Living Age*, vol. L, no. 2136 (30 May 1885), pp. 537-542, specifically p. 537.
281. E. Seward, 'Mr Ruskin's Museum at Walkley' in *Cardiff Naturalists' Society: Reports and Transactions*, vol. 18 (1887), p. 28. Seward's paper, delivered at the Queen Street Public Hall, was reported in the *Western Mail* (2 April 1886).
282. *Transactions of the Leeds Naturalists' Club and Scientific Association* (Leeds, 1886), p. 10.
283 'Visit to the Ruskin Museum at Sheffield', in *Transactions of the Leeds Naturalists' Club and Scientific Association* (Leeds, 1886), pp. 35-37, specifically p. 35.
284. 'Ruskin Museum' in *Transactions*, p. 37.
285. *Manchester Guardian* (4 April 1904).
286. 'Mr Ruskin's Museum at Sheffield' in *The British Architect and Northern Engineer*, vol. VIII, no. 9 (31 August 1877), pp. 110-111, specifically p. 110.
287. Seven visitor books have survived, covering an uninterrupted period from September 1880 to the museum's closure in March 1890, with around 1,700 pages noting between 26,000 and 27,000 visits (including return visitors). I have traced the biographies of more than 600 of them.
288. Howard Swan in *Westminster Gazette* (24 January 1900).
289. See Stuart Eagles, 'Living up to their blue china: The Wildes and Ruskin's Sheffield Museum' in *The Wildean*, no. 57 (July 2020), pp. 91-116. The relationship is explored further in Stuart Eagles, '"You are to think of me as of a sand eel": Ruskin's final encounter with Constance and Oscar Wilde' in *The Wildean*, no. 63 (July 2023), pp. 20-61.
290. SMT, Ruskin Collection (GSG): St George's Museum Visitor Book no. 3 (December 1882-June 1884).
291. Howard Swan in *Westminster Gazette* (24 January 1900).
292. Frost, *Curator*, p. 4.
293. RML, RSC: letter from JR to ES (6 April 1880). Ruskin may, of course, have meant 'you' in a general sense, meaning the salary he paid to Henry Swan on behalf of the whole family, but that would make his apparent confusion difficult to explain.
294. RML, RSC: letter from JR to HS (4 June 1880).
295. Frost, *Curator*, p. 31.
296. *SI* (2 October 1883). Emily Swan's idea caught the public imagination and was widely reported, *e.g.* in *DR* (1883), p. 330; *The Literary World* (1883), p. 238; and *The Architect* (1883), p. 192.
297. For example, see *SDT* and *SI* (25 September 1883).
298. This is according to the resolution of the Ruskin Museum Committee. SA: Ruskin Museum Committee, Minute Book no. 1 (6 March 1890).
299. SA: Ruskin Museum Committee, Minute Book no. 1 (24 October 1889).
300. *SDT* (22 April 1890).

ELEVEN
301. *SI* (8 March 1878).
302. See *Birmingham Mail* (21 February 1879). Ruskin's editors

wrongly state that the meeting was held in March and that Ruskin's report was read by George Baker, see LE, 30.14. For a full account of the meeting, see Stuart Eagles, '"An excess of modesty and bashfulness": the first meeting of Ruskin's Guild' (*RRB* #14, 4 June 2021) <https://stuarteagles.co.uk/14-the-first-general-meetiing-of-the-guild/> (accessed 21 May 2024).
303. INA, M/12534: letter from ES to Henrietta Carey (1) (14 March 1879).
304. In fact, her letter to Henrietta throws some light on that correspondence. Ruskin wrote on 6 March 1879, 'Suppose we ever come to be a few thousands — (and I *hope* for thousands of thousands—) how then — if everybody wanted to call on the Master before he could be comfortable in his home?', see RML, RSC: letter from JR to ES (6 March 1879). In her letter to Miss Carey Emily added, from an early part of the Ruskin letter, that if Ruskin always had to meet Companions in person whenever they felt like it, 'it would [simply] render the mastership impossible', though she missed out the word 'simply' in her transcription and did not acknowledge that in the original letter the lines did not follow the others she quoted. What Ruskin scholars have not explored is the context for Ruskin's remark. Emily explained to Henrietta that it was 'in answer to a word or two I said with reference to William Graham's and John Guy's wish to see the master'. These two working-class Companions of the Guild, William Buchan Graham and John Guy, were engaged in working the Guild's estates in Bewdley and Cloughton respectively. Both attended and spoke at the first General Meeting of the Guild at Birmingham, so Henrietta Carey probably remembered having met them there. Graham went on to work at Totley. For more, see Mark Frost, *The Lost Companions and John Ruskin's Guild of St George: A Revisionary History* (London: Anthem Press, 2014). With reference to bothersome visitors, Ruskin later told Henrietta directly, in a different context, that 'nothing turns one's stomach so fatally as an unfortunate — fool — which too many unfortunates are, especially those who want to see me', and added, with reference to an illness from which she was then suffering, 'You won't get better quickly unless you get quite away', see INA, M/12551: letter from JR to Henrietta Carey (21) (18 February 1883). As mentioned elsewhere, Ruskin was none too pleased when the Swans turned up unannounced at Brantwood, either.
305. INA, M/12534: letter from ES to Henrietta Carey (1) (14 March 1879).
306. INA, M/12536: letter from ES to Henrietta Carey (2) (20 March 1879).
307. *Birmingham Daily Post* (22 February 1879).
308. INA, M/12535: letter from JR to Henrietta Carey (6) (17 March 1879).
309. INA, M/12536: letter from ES to Henrietta Carey (2) (20 March 1879).
310. LE, 22.334.
311. See LE, 28.747-748 and qtd in *SI* (6 November 1876).

312. *i.e. Fors,* Letter 82 (October 1877), see LE, 29.245.
313. E.S.P. in *Littell's Living Age,* (30 May 1885), p. 540.
314. See, *e.g.,* Henry Travis, *Effectual Reform in Man and Society* (1875).
315. LE, 27.116.
316. M[ary] A[nn] Maloy, 'St George's Farm' in *The Commonweal,* vol. 5, no. 176 (25 May 1889), pp. 164-165.
317. See *SDT* (14 March 1877) and *SI* (16 April 1889).
318. See *Manchester Guardian* (30 May 1885); *Manchester City News* (6 June 1885). *DR* (March 1879) noted that among other vegetarian members were W. E. A. Axon, Rev. W. A. O'Connor and Mrs Fergusson-Horne (p. 63).
319. *Manchester Courier and Lancashire General Advertiser* (14 February 1880).
320. *SET* (2 February 1881).
321. *SDT* (1 March 1881).
322. *SDT* (1 March 1881). See, *e.g.,* Ruskin Library, University of Lancaster: Abercrombie Archive, vol. 2, p. 71: letter written by HS (17 February [1882]).
323. SA: Arthur Hayball Papers, letter from HS to Arthur Hayball (8 August 1881).
324. *SI* (4 March 1882), *SI* (8 July 1882).
325. Morgan Library & Museum, New York, MA2457.3: letter from JR to George Allen (28 June 1882); qtd in part in Frost, *Curator,* p. 6. I am grateful to Paul Dawson for his help in finding the final sentence of the quote.

TWELVE
326. RML, RSC: letter from JR to HS (31 December 1875). Ruskin's letters to the Swans sometimes included sympathetic professions of affection to Mabel in particular: see RML, RSC: letters dated 17 August and 19 September 1880, 5 September 1882, 2 February 1883 (in which he wrote, 'I am most thankful that Mabel's better'), 19 March 1883, 15 June 1884, and 4 May 1885.
327. Ackworth School Admission Register: Mabel Swan (2 February 1874).
328. Ackworth School Admission Register: Godfrey Swan (11 August 1875). Morley also gives Balby as the Meeting House attended by both Henry and Godfrey Swan, but cites no source, see Morley, *Late Work,* p. 219.
329. Ackworth School Admission Register: Leonard Swan (1 May 1877).
330. See *A Narrative of the Proceedings at the Celebration of the Centenary of Ackworth School, 26th and 27th of Sixth Month, 1879, edited by James Henry Barber. Also a Sketch of the Life of Dr Fothergill by James Hack Tuke* (Ackworth: Centenary Committee, Ackworth School, 1879).
331. See LE, 34.707, originally published in J. Spence Hodgson, 'John Ruskin's Annotations of J. H. Tuke's Memoir of Dr. John Fothergill' in *Proceedings of the Ackworth Old Scholars' Association,* Part V (July 1886), pp. 52-54. The article details 18 marginal notes, of which only half a dozen (but certainly the most interesting) were reproduced by Cook and Wedderburn.
332. Hodgson, 'John Ruskin's Annotations', p. 52. Such a letter from Ruskin has not been traced.
333. See Hodgson's reference to Ruskin's marginal note 15 —

Ruskin's double underlining on p. 73 of the memoir: Hodgson, 'John Ruskin's Annotations', p. 53; not included in Cook and Wedderburn's summary.
334. LE, 34.707. This is the plate opposite p. 53.
335. See Ruskin's 'General Statement explaining the nature and purposes of St George's Guild' (1882) in LE, 30.51-52.
336. Marginal notes on pp. 75-77 of the original volume. Hodgson also refers to a marking by Ruskin on p. 62, also referring to the war with France, and Fothergill's comments about peace, made in response to John Wesley's offer to raise 200 of his converts as a volunteer corp.
337. RML, RSC: letter from JR to HS (5 September 1882).
338. *SDT* (13 October 1877).
339. Henry Swan's involvement in the agricultural experiment at Totley also resulted in local Quakers taking a leading part in its work. Among them were William Scorah (1812-*aft* 1881), at the head of Swan's list of candidates for the venture, a boot and shoe dealer on Old Barrack Lane, who was involved with the Friends' School. (See Morley, *Late Work*, p. 219).
340. SMT, Ruskin Collection (GSG): St George's Museum Visitor Book no. 3 (December 1882-June 1884).
341. *SI* (9 March 1880).

THIRTEEN
342. Howard Swan in *Westminster Gazette* (24 January 1900).
343. See *Third Annual Report of the Ruskin Society* (Manchester: The Ruskin Society, 13 February 1882), p. 5.
344. [Clara Keeling, née Hayball], 'My Recollections of Ruskin: A Woodcarver and a Cauliflower Leaf', in *Yorkshire Post and Leeds Intelligencer* (4 January 1937).
345. Howard Swan in *Westminster Gazette* (24 January 1900).
346. This paraphrases a letter from JR to HS (17 April 1876). A similar statement is recalled by Anthony Hope, author of *The Prisoner of Zenda*, in his memoirs: see Stuart Eagles, 'Ruskin & Morris in Oxford (Part I)', (*RRB* #32, 4 November 2021) <https://stuarteagles.co.uk/32-ruskin-morris-at-oxford-part-i/> (accessed 21 May 2024).
347. Howard Swan in *Westminster Gazette* (24 January 1900) (but not included in the edited down version in *SI*).
348. See Stuart Eagles, 'Ruskin and the Garden City Movement: II, Unwin & Parker, Designing Utopia' (*RRB* #38, 14 May 2024) <https://stuarteagles.co.uk/38-unwin-parker/> (accessed 24 May 2024).
349. See *SDT* and *SI* (23 December 1886).
350. *SWT* (24 December 1886).
351. RML, RSC: letter from JR to HS (2 March 1887).
352. John Rylands Library, University of Manchester, Eng MS 1258 (63): letter from HS to JR (3 November 1887). Courtesy of the University of Manchester.
353. See Frost, *Curator*.
354. Frost, *Curator*, p. 32. The letters quoted were written on 28 August 1878 and 29 August 1878 respectively.
355. Will of Mary Hamlin Connell, probate: Principal Probate Registry (25 June 1888). The executors were her son, William George Connell, of Cheapside,

and Charles Edwin Churchill, a silk agent in the City.
356. Death certificate of Henry Swan, GRO ref. 9c/185, June Q. 1889, Ecclesall Bierlow. The details of Swan's final days are given in *SDT* (30 March 1889).
357. *DR*, no. 144 (December 1883), p. 354.
358. *DR*, no. 140 (August 1883) unpaginated advertising wrappers. More surprisingly, the fabrics produced at Ruskin's 'St George's Woollen Mill at Laxey on the Isle of Man, were recommended to readers on the pretext that it had been 'warmly commended to us by members of our own Society', see *DR*, no. 144 (December 1883), p. 342.
359. *DR*, no. 67 (July 1877), p. 128.
360. Bradbury in *Magazine of Art*, p. 57.
361. Howard Swan in *Westminster Gazette* (24 January 1900).
362. Among other vegetarians sympathetic to Ruskin, known to the Swans and not otherwise mentioned in the main text of this volume are Dr John Balbirnie (1810-1895). Others, possibly not known to the Swans, are Georgina Cowper-Temple (1822-1901), Frederick Furnivall (1825-1910), A. H. Mackmurdo (1851-1942), Hardwicke Rawnslley (1851-1920), John Coleman Kenworthy (1861-1948), Edward Girdlestone (1829-1892), Edmund J. Baillie (1851-1897) from Chester, the artist and craftsman Henry Lindley Fry (1807-1895), Josiah Oldfield (1863-1953), and Henry Salt (1851-1939). Other well-known vegetarians who visited the museum at Walkley include Octavius Shrubsole (1839-1926). Rev. William Sharman (1841-1889), the Radical Unitarian, and early Companion of Ruskin's Guild, seems to have abandoned his early vegetarianism. Born in Sheffield, in 1860 he issued a pamphlet, *Plain Words to the Working Men of Sheffield, now abstaining from dear meat: with an appendix on what to eat and how to cook it*, complete with recipes for cabbage and rice-pudding.
363. See Gregory, *Vegetarian Movement*, p. 54.
364. SMT, Ruskin Collection (GSG): St George's Museum Visitor Book no. 6 (July 1887-August 1889).
365. All details of the meeting were given in *SDT* (26 April 1889).
366. SA: Ruskin Museum Committee, Minute Book no. 3 (26 April 1920).
367. SMT, Ruskin Collection (GSG): St George's Museum, Visitor Book no. 1 (September 1880-September 1881).

FOURTEEN
368. Will of Emily Elizabeth Swan, probate: Principal Probate Registry, London (10 February 1909).
369. BIA, ATR: letter from Howard Swan to The Retreat (4 October 1908): Howard's emphasis.
370. Mary Swan's death occurred on 30 October 1908, but it is incorrectly given as 1909 in the Quaker *Annual Monitor for 1910* (London: Headley Brothers, 1909) p. 173 (covering obituaries for the period from 1 October 1908 to 30 September 1909), an error reproduced in scholarly studies.
371. BIA, ATR: letter from Howard Swan to The Retreat (31 October 1908).

372. BIA, ATR: letter from The Retreat to Godfrey Swan (24 December 1908).
373. See *SI* (3 December 1908 and 6 January 1909).
374. Howard Swan addressed a Friends' Meeting House at Weston-Super-Mare in June 1908 in which he gave a 'witty and humorous' account of his experiences in China and described his attempt to establish a Guild of Literature. See *Weston-super-Mare Gazette* (13 June 1908); see also Howard Swan, 'China and the Language Question' in *Review of Reviews*, vol. 37 (1908), pp. 213-217. His experiences in Japan were detailed in his book, *Flashes from the Far East* (1902). He wrote several books, including *The Facts of Life* (1904), a translation (with Victor Betis) of Francois Gouin's *The Art of Teaching and Studying Language* (1892), and books on conversational Italian (1892), French (1897), German (1897) and Spanish (1903) in the *Travellers' Colloquial...* series published by David Nut.
375. BIA, ATR: letter from The Retreat to Howard Swan (20 October 1908). For an account of Howard's language-teaching method, see W. T. Stead, 'How to Learn a Language in Six Months', in *Review of Reviews*, vol. 5, no. 30 (July 1892), pp. 201-208.
376. BIA, ATR: letter from The Retreat to Howard Swan (20 October 1908).
377. BIA, ATR: letter from Howard Swan to The Retreat (31 October 1908).
378. BIA, ATR: letter from Godfrey Swan to The Retreat (21 October 1908).
379. BIA, ATR: letter from Mabel Swan to The Retreat (21 October 1908).
380. BIA, ATR: letter from Mabel Swan to The Retreat (21 October 1908).
381. BIA, ATR: letter from The Retreat to Westminster & Longford Monthly Meeting (11 December 1908).
382. BIA, ATR: letter from The Retreat to Godfrey Swan (24 December 1908).
383. BIA, ATR: letter from The Retreat to Godfrey Swan (24 December 1908).
384. BIA, ATR: letter from T. W. Holmes to The Retreat (29 October 1908).
385. BIA, ATR: letter from The Retreat to Westminster & Longford Monthly Meeting (11 December 1908).
386. BIA, ATR: letter from Godfrey Swan to The Retreat (2 November 1909).
387. Death certificate of Emily Elizabeth Swan, GRO ref. 9d/9, March Q. 1909, York.
388. BIA, ATR: letter from Mabel Swan to The Retreat (31 January 1909).
389. BIA, ATR: letter from Godfrey Swan to The Retreat (26 February 1909).
390. BIA, ATR: letter from The Retreat to Godfrey Swan (22 March 1909).
391. This is Sir John Robert Seeley (1834-1895), who was appointed Regius Professor of Modern History at the University of Cambridge. A Liberal in politics, he enacted radical educational reforms, spearheading the admission of women into the ancient universities. F. Max Müller (1823-1900), whom Ruskin knew and respected, visited a few weeks before Swan

died, by which time he had effectively retired as Oxford's first Professor of Comparative Philology.
392. *SET* (18 January 1909). The letters are those now preserved in RML, RSC.
393. [William Harrison Riley], 'John Ruskin' in *The Illustrated American*, vol. III, no. 28 (30 August 1890), pp. 347-352. The poem had perhaps been inspired by Ruskin, who wrote to Emily, 'how like you are to a lamb skipping before a broken winded old horse, to please it' (13 March [1876]).
394. Edward Carpenter, 'Correspondence: Smoky Sheffield' in *SI* (25 May 1889).
395. *SI* (28 May 1889).
396. *SI* (28 May 1889).

SWANSONG
397. Hargrave in *PMG* (2 April 1889).
398. *SI* (29 September 1883).
399. *SDT* and *SI* (25 September 1883).
400. Howard Swan in *Westminster Gazette* (24 January 1900).
401. Ruskin Library, University of Lancaster: letter from JR to Joan Severn (25 July [1882]),
402. *SI* (30 March 1889).
403. *SI* (13 March 1880).
404. Morgan Library & Museum, New York: letter from George Allen to John Hobbs (26 April 1890). I am grateful to Paul Dawson for helping me with this source.
405. It must be admitted that Ruskin's claim in *Praeterita* that he had no toys as a child was exaggerated, but his nursery was no toyshop.
406. *SDT* (4 February 1919).
407. Letter from JR to John Francis Moss (7 December 1883) qtd in LE, 30.322.
408. John Rylands Library, University of Manchester, Eng MS 1258 (63): letter from HS to JR (3 November 1887). Courtesy of the University of Manchester.
409. LE, 8.233.

INDEX

Abbeydale (*see also Totley*), 89
Aboriginals, 58
Adams, Francis Bryant, *n*175
Adams, Mary Hamlin (*see also under Connell*), 46, *n*175
Adderley, (Hon. Rev.) James, 27, *n*81
Aesculapius, 32
Alcott, Amos Bronson, 35
Alcott, Louisa May, 35
Alcott House School, Richmond, 35
Allen, George, 34, 91-92, 112, *n*143, *n*325, *n*404
Allen, William, 116, *n*245
Altrincham, 99
   Springfield Road, 99
America (United States of), 10, 12, 52, 61, 90, 106, 107, 108
   California, 106
   Florida, 10
   Massachusetts, 90, 106, 108
      Ashburnham, 106
      Fitchburg, 106
      Gardner, 106
      Lunenburg, 90, 106
   North Dakota, 61
   Southern California, University of (LA), 106
Amiens Cathedral, 74
Anti-Narcotic League, 101
anti-narcotics, 24, 29, 66, 91, 103
anti-vaccination, 24, 30, 101
anti-vivisection, 24, 30
Apiary, or Bees, Bee-Hives, and Bee Culture, The, 93
Architect, The (journal), *n*296
Ariadne Florentina, 85
Armitage, George Faulkner, 99
art, 1, 2, 4, 5, 7, 8, 10, 11, 12, 15, 20, 31, 33-39, 41-42, 43, 47, 48, 50, 51, 52, 53, 55, 57, 77, 78, 79, 83, 109, 111, 113, 114
Art Journal, 50, 53, n180

Art Treasures Exhibition, Manchester (1857), 57
artisans (*see also workers*), 5, 7, 8, 9, 29, 33, 38, 60, 65, 72, 73, 74, 78
Arts & Crafts movement, 47, 79, 99
Ascot, 105
Athenaeum (journal), 50, 53, *n*179
Attlee, Clement, 3
Australia, 58-59, 78, 89
autostereoscope, 51
Axon, Ernest, 103
Axon, Grace, 103
Axon, William Edward Armytage, 102-103, *n*318

Badger's Farm (Totley), 88
Baillie, Edmund J., *n*362
Baker, George, 41, 42, 75, 81, 82-83, 94, 96, *n*144, *n*302
Balby Meeting House (Doncaster), 93-94, *n*328
Bagster, Robert, 21
Bagster, Samuel, 21
Bainbridge, 94
   Carr End, 94
Balbirnie, (Dr) John, *n*362
Balgarnie, Florence, 82
banks, 67-38, 93, *n*238, *n*239
Barber, Hannah Mary, 95
Barber, James Henry, 10, 94, 95, 96, *n*330
Barker, Christopher, 107
Barker, (Mrs) Mary, 107
Barmouth, Wales, 43
Barnet, 105
   Hadley Highstone, 105
Baster, Eliza (HS's grandmother), 18
Baster, Elizabeth (*see also Swan, Elizabeth*) (HS's mother), 18
Baster, Joseph (HS's grandfather), 18
Bath, 24, 109

Bath Stone Firms Ltd, 15
Baume, Pierre, 28, *n*95
Bayley, Robert, 38
Baynes, Oswald Bradley, 96
Beacock, Robert, 96
beauty, 1, 2, 5, 11, 17, 23, 31, 37, 52, 74
beekeeping, 93
Belfast (Queen's College), 25
Bell's New Weekly Messenger, *n*60
Bennett, Alfred William, 44-45, 48-49, 51, 52
 (picture) 44
Bennett, Edward Trusted, 44
Bennett, Mary, 44
Bennett, William, 44
Betis, Victor, *n*374
Beveridge, William, 3
Beverley, *n*265
Bewdley, 75, 83, 96, *n*305
 Beaucastle, 96
bicycles, 25, 58, 112
birds, 75, 76, *n*267
bird prints, 76
Birmingham, 41, 72, 79, 84-85, 96, *n*304
Birmingham Daily Post, *n*302, *n*307
Birmingham Gazette, 96
Birmingham Mail, *n*302
Birmingham School of Art, 79
Blake, William, 43
Bolton Abbey, 7
Bonner, Hypatia Bradlaugh, *n*89
Book of Common Prayer (in shorthand), 24
botany, 37, 94
Brabant, Elizabeth (née Hughes), 17, *n*45
Brabant, Elizabeth Rebecca (Rufa), 17, *n*45
Brabant, (Dr) Robert Herbert, 17, *n*45
Bradbury, Edward, 8, *ns*18-20, *n*22, *n*360
Bradfield, 8
Bradlaugh, Charles, 28, *n*89
Bradley, Henry, 79
Brantwood (*JR's home*), 41, 75, 76, 84, 93, *n*304

Brantwood Diary of John Ruskin, *n*275
Brazil, 78
Brereton, (Mrs) Caroline, *n*265
Bright, John, 57
Brighton, 107
Brighton Aquarium, 5
Bristol, 14, 65, 90, 96
British Architect and Northern Engineer, 78, *n*286
British Association for the Advancement of Science, 54
British Friend (Quaker journal), 23, 40, 116, *ns*69-71
British Journal of Photography, 55, 60, 61-62, 69, 116, *n*187, *ns*198-200, *ns*208-209, *ns*217-219, *n*244
British Journal of Photography Annual, 57
British Museum, 35, 75
British Temperance League, 101
Brooke, Dorothea (*fictional*), 17
Brougham, (Lord) Henry, 56-57
Bunney, John Wharlton, 8, 9, 34
 (picture), 80
Burgess, Arthur, 34
Burne-Jones, Georgiana, 38, *n*133
Burne-Jones, (Sir) Edward, 38, 39
Burns, Robert, 32
Butterworth, George, 34
Byron, Lord, 1

Camberwell, 46
Cambridge, 12, 20, 78, 96, *n*391
 St John's College, 96
Cambridge Chronicle & Journal, *n*57
capitalism (*see industrial capitalism*)
Canada, 78
Canterbury Cathedral, 80
Cardiff Naturalists' Society, 77, *n*281
Carey, Henrietta, 84-85, *n*10, *n*265, *ns*303-306, *ns*308-309
Carlyle, Thomas, 1, 32
Carpenter, Edward, 17, 25, 30, 80, 102, 109, *n*28, *n*394
Carr, Alwyn, 79
Carshalton, 43
 Margaret's Well, 43
cartes de visite, 52

(picture), 56
Casaubon, Edward (*fictional*), 17
Cash, Frederick G., 44
Cash, William, 44
Casket Portrait Company, 51-58, 60-61, *n*180
(picture), 56
Castleton, 91
Catholics, 42
Central School for Foreign Tongues (London), 106
Ceylon (*see Sri Lanka*)
Chandler, J. H., *n*48
Chapman, Alison, 38, *n*130
Charleton, Robert, 65-66
Chartists, 30
chemistry, 15
Chepyzhov, Pavel, *n*97
China, 78, 106, *n*374
  Imperial College of Languages, Peking, 106
Christian Socialism, 27, 33, 90
Christmas, 10, 50, 93, 107
chronometer-making, 46-47, 52, *n*175
Chubb, Percival, *n*272
Church Reformer (*journal*), 27
Churchill, Charles Edwin, *n*356
cinema, 50
Clairvoyant stereoscope, 50
(picture), 50
Claphan, 60
  Clapham Common, 60
  Old Town, 60
  Pavement, The, 60
Clerkenwell, 46-47, *n*175
  Myddelton Street, 47
  St Mark the Evangelist Church, Myddelton Square, 46
  Goswell Road, 46
Clerkenwell News, *n*212
Clockmakers' Pension Society, 48
clockmaking, 47-48
Cloughton, N. Yorks, 83, *n*304
Cobden, Richard, 28, 48, *n*159
Codrington, (Admiral Sir) Edward (MP for Devonport), 15
coffee, 29, 103
coins, 5, 75, 76, 81

cold water-cure, 27, 58
Collected Notes on some of the Pictures in St George's Museum, Sheffield, 75, *n*270
Collingwood, William Gershom, 15
Collyns, Arthur, 101
Collyns, (Rev.) Charles Henry, 101
Collyns, Edith, 101
Collyns, (Mrs) Mary, 101
Collyns, Spencer, 101
colour (in art), 7, 23, 31, 36, 42, 51, 53, 59, 74, 112, *n*187
Commonweal, The (*journal*), *n*316
Communist House (Totley) (*see also St George's Farm*), 89
congregationalism, 10
Coniston Water, 12, *n*93
Connell, (Mary) Christine (ES's niece), 47
Connell, Elizabeth (*see also under Hinds*) (ES's grandmother), 46
Connell, Emily Elizabeth (*see under Swan*)
Connell, Frederick Henry (ES's brother), *n*216
Connell, George (ES's grandfather), 46
Connell, George Lawrence (ES's nephew), 47
Connell, Kathleen (ES's sister), 103
Connell, Mary (ES's sister), 103
Connell, Mary Hamlin (*see also under Adams*) (ES's mother), 46, 101, *n*175, *n*355
Connell, Nora (ES's sister), 104
Connell, William (ES's father), 46-48, 52, *n*175
Connell, William George (ES's brother), 47, *n*175, *n*355
Contemporary Review, 38, *n*237
commercial travellers, 20, 34
Cook & Wedderburn (*JR's editors*), 32, 36, 62, 94, *n*302, *n*331, *n*333
Cooke, Ebenezer, 34
Co-operative News, 91
co-operative movement, 70, 79, 88, *n*32
co-operative villages, 88
copyists (artists), 8, 35, 75

Corn Laws, 8, 24, 48, 57, *n*15
Corsham, 15
Corvo, 'Baron' (*see Rolfe, Frederick William*)
cost-of-living, 66
Court of Common Council (City of London), 45, 47, 48
   Cheap Ward, 47
Cowper-Temple, Georgina, *n*362
craftsmanship, 1, 5, 6, 7, 9, 74, 78, 79, 113, *n*206
craftsmen (*see artisans*)
Creswick, Benjamin, 11, 29, 76-77, 79, 81, 91, 96, *n*32, *n*93
Creswick, Fanny, *n*32
cricket, 59
crime, 19, 94
Crown of Wild Olive, The, 91
   'The Future of England', 91
   'Work', 91
Croydon, 35
Crump, Thomas, 19
crystal cube miniature (*see also Casket Portrait Company*), 51-57, 61, 62, 112
   (picture), 53

Daines, Brenda, 104
Daines, Nora (*see under Connell*)
Dallinger, (Rev. Dr) William Henry, 75, *n*266
Dalston, 19, 20, 21, 22, 28, 46, *n*67, *n*76
   Malvern Road, 28
   Mayfield Road, 20, *n*67
dance, 42
Darwin, Charles, 44
Dawson, Annie Creswick (picture), 11
Dawson, Paul, *n*325, *n*404
Dawson, W. J., 21
Deane & Woodward, 39
Dearden, James S., *n*206
De Beauvoir Town, 48
Dell, Fanny, 48
Dell, John Henry, 48
Dell, John Sutton, 48
democracy, 1, 3, 64, 88

Devizes, Wiltshire, 14-19, 24, 40, 59, *ns*41, *n*43, n45, *ns*47-49
   (picture), 16
   High Street, 15
   Little Brittox, 15-17
      (picture), 16
   Market Place, 15
   Market Street, 15
   St Mary's Independent Chapel, 15, 17-18
Devizes & Wiltshire Gazette, *n*43, *n*47, *n*49
   Dickens, Charles, 36
Dickinson, Goldsworthy Lowes, 80
diet, 28, 31-32, 58, 60, 99, 101-102
Dietetic Reformer and Vegetarian Messenger (*see also* Vegetarian Messenger), 25, 31, 32, 61, 91, 102, 116, *ns*104-106, *ns*357-359
discipleship, 2-3, 24, 64, 78, 80, 90, 99, 109
Dixon, Thomas, 41
Dodman, Mrs, *n*43
Doncaster, 93
   Balby Meeting House (West Laith Gate), 93
Doncaster, Charles, 95, *n*32
Doncaster, Daniel (Snr), 94, 95
Doncaster, Daniel (Jnr), 94
Doncaster, David Kenway, 95
Doncaster, Helen, 95
Doncaster, Jane Eliza, 96
Doncaster, Phoebe, 95
Dornbusch, George, 28-30, 53, *n*92, *n*95, *n*98
   (picture), 29
Doubleday, William, 42, 96-97
Downs, David, 84
drowning, 14-15, 59, 113
Dublin Exhibition, 56
Duke of York's Theatre (London), 40
Dulwich, 35
   Dulwich Wood, 35
   Greyhound PH, 35
Dundas, (Capt.) James Whitley Deans (MP for Devizes), 14
Durant, Susan, 57
Durham Cathedral, 7

eccentricity, 27, 59, 112
Edinburgh, 31, 56
education, 2, 4, 5, 6, 10, 28, 30, 34, 37-38, 43, 44, 63, 70, 77, 83, 95, 96, 102, 107, 111, 113, *n*391
Edwards, Passmore, 28
Egypt, 78
Eliot, George (*see also Evans, Mary Ann*), 17, 73, *ns*44-46
Elliott, Ebenezer, 8, *n*15
engraving, 5, 7, 17, 20, 23-26, 35, 37, 38, 43, 58, 60, 71, 76, 77, 85, 90, 93, 104, 112, *n*53, *ns*71-72, *n*168, *n*216
  (picture), 25
Essex, 96
etchings, 5, 77
Everett, Joseph, 25
Eyton Collection, 75

F. & H. Swan, 23-25, 43, *n*72, *n*76
Fabian Society, 76, *n*272
Farrar, (Archdeacon) Frederick William, 80
Fellowship of the New Life, 76
Fergusson-Horne, Mrs, *n*318
Firth College (*see under Sheffield*)
fish, 76
Fonotipik Jurnal, *n*68, *n*74
Fothergill, (Dr) John, 94, *ns*330-331, *n*336
franchise (extension of), 3, 24, 30, 64
Fredeman, William, 38, *n*130
freehold land societies, 8, 73, 88
freethinkers, 30
Friend, The (*journal*), 45, 96
Friends' First-Day School Association, 40, 95, *n*138
Friends' schools:
  Ackworth School, 93-94, 96, 108, *ns*138-139, *n*247, *n*327, *ns*329-331
  Croydon School (Park Lane), 35
  Sheffield (Hartshead), 95
Frost, Mark, 12, 71, 81, 82, 100, *n*36, *n*98, *n*251, *n*263, *n*291, *n*304, *n*325, *ns*353-354
Fry, Henry Lindley, *n*362

Fry, Roger, 80, 96
Fors Clavigera, 6, 30, 31, 62-70, 73, 86-87, 90, 113, *n*5, *n*258, *n*262, *n*312
Fountains Abbey, 7
Fox, George, 41, 94
fruitarianism, 58, 63, 67, 101-103, 113
Furness Abbey, 7
Furnivall, Frederick, 33, *n*362
Furniss, John, *n*28

Ganthony, Richard, 47
Gamble, Joseph, 11
Gandhi, Mahatma, 3
Garden City movement, 99, *n*28, *n*348
gardens/gardening, 5, 9, 28, 84, 88, 90, 94, 98, 100, 102, 105
Gilpin, Charles, 24, 45, 47
Girdlestone, Edward, *n*362
Glasgow, 91, 103, 105
Golding, Thomas Edward, 53, 55
Goldsmith, Sally, *n*98
Goodall, Fanny (*see under Creswick*)
Gospel Banner and Biblical Treasury (*journal*), 21, n60
Graham, John William, 41-42, *n*143, *ns*145-146
  (picture), 41
Graham, William Buchan, *n*304
Great Exhibition (1851), 47
Gregory, James, 30, *ns*88-89, *ns*91-92, *n*95, *ns*98-99, *n*363
Green, Charles, 24, 79, *n*206
Grouville (*see under Jersey*)
Gouin, Francois, *n*375
Gouin Method (of language acquisition), 106
Guild of Literature, *n*373
Guild of St George, 6-7, 11, 12, 29, 34, 36, 41, 42, 43, 46, 54, 64, 66, 68, 69, 70, 78, 81, 82, 83-84, 90, 91, 111, 114, 116, *n*7, *n*21, *n*75, *n*98, *n*265, *n*302, *n*304, *n*335, *n*355, *n*362,
  Companions(hip), 6-7, 9, 11, 12, 41, 43, 78, 84, 91, *n*75, *n*265, *n*304

Guild of St Matthew, 27
Gull, (Sir) William, 32
Gush, Frederick Thomas, 103
Gush, Mary (*see under Connell*)
Guy, John, *n*304

Habershon, George, 9, 98, 100
Hackney, 46, *n*63
Hall, William Addy, 103
Hall of Science (*see under Sheffield*)
Hampstead (*see also West Hampstead*), 107
   West Heath School, 107
Hancock, Charles, 27
Hancock, (Rev.) Thomas, 27, *n*83
Hardie, (James) Keir, 3
Hare, (Archdeacon) Julius, 33
Hargrave, Wilfrid, 59, *ns*77-78, *n*87, *n*95, *ns*201-202, *n*205, *n*207
Harrow, 27
Hartman, Lionel, *n*219
Harvest of Ruskin, The, 41-42, *n*143, *ns*145-146
Harvey, Thomas Edmund, 42
Hastings, 103
Hawkins, Anthony Hope (*see Hope, Anthony*)
Hayball, Arthur, 79, 91, 98, *n*323
Hayball, Clara, 98, *n*344
Headlam, (Rev.) Stewart, 27
Hemphill, William Despard, 44
Hennell, Charles Christian, 17
Hewetson, Henry Bendelack, 75, *n*267
Hewison, Robert, *n*252
Hill, Ernest, 71
Hill, Miranda, 37
Hill, Octavia, 36-37, 84
Hill & Swann, 71
Hills, Arnold, 103
Hinds, Elizabeth (*see also under Connell*) (ES's grandmother), 46
Historic Society of New York, 57
Hodge, William, 19
Hodgson, J. Spencer, *ns*331-333, *n*336
Holborn, 20, 93
Holborn Journal, *n*189
Holloway, 48

Belgrave Road, 48
Holmes, John, 38, *ns*130-131
Holmes, John (of Leeds), *n*32
Holmes, (Rev.) Thomas William, 10, 103, 108, *n*30, *n*384
Holyoake, George Jacob, 79-80
homoeopathy, 32
Hood, Robin (*fictional*), 56
Hope, Anthony, *n*346
Hope, Frederick William, 38
Horsley, John Callcott, 80
Howarth, Elijah, 11
Howe, Anthony, *n*159
Howitt, Mary, 52
Howitt, William, 48
Huddersfield, 9, *n*26
Hunt, William Holman, 35
Hunter, William Skelton, 90

Ibbotson, Thomas, 58
ice-skating, 14
illuminated manuscripts, 5, 7, 35, 36, 58, 74, 112, 114
Illustrated American (journal), *n*182, *n*393
Illustrated London News, 56, *n*156, *n*191
India, 78
industrial capitalism, 1, 6, 34, 65, 109-110
insects, 38, 76
Institute of Electrical Engineers, 76
Intellectual Observer, 55, n185
International Herald, 90
Ivernia, RMS, 107
Irish Home Rule, 24, 95
Ironside, Isaac, 30
Isle of Man, *n*358
   Laxey, *n*358
Islington, 27, 48, 60,
   Mildmay Park, 48
   Milner Square, 27
Islam, 42
Ives, Samuel, 20-21
Ives & Swan, 20-21
   (picture), 21

Japan, 106, *n*374

Higher Commercial College
  (Tokyo), 106
Jersey (Channel Islands), 60-63, 66-
  70, 71, *n*214, *n*238
  economy of (HS's letter on), 66-
    68
  Grouville, 61
    Nora House, 61
  St Helier, 60-61, *n*213
    Almorah Cemetery, 61, *n*213
    David Place, 60, 61
    Mont à l'Abbé, 60, 61, 63
    Portrait Establishment, 61
    Royal Hotel, 60
    St Mark's Church, 60
    Undercliff, 61
  St Saviour, 61
    Langley House, 61
Jersey Joint-Stock Bank, *n*238
Jersey Mercantile Bank, *n*238
Jersey Times, 61
jewellery, 52
'Jockey to the Fair' (*folk song*), 109
*John Ruskin, a Bibliographical
  Biography*, 102
John Ruskin: A Sketch of His Life ...,
  *n*276
Judaism, 42

Keeling, (Mrs) Clara (*see under
  Hayball*)
Kelmscott Press, 34
Kemp, (Dr) Norah, 105
Kemmet & Avon Canal, 14
  Drew(e)'s Wharf, 14
Kent, 91
Kenworthy, John Coleman, *n*362
Kerr, Antony, *n*134
King William I, 81
Kingsland, 19, 22, 23, 27, 40, 48,
  60, *n*67, *n*72
  Kingsland Green, 22, 23, 27,
    *n*72
  Kingsland Ragged School, 48
  Mayfield Road, 20
  Pleasant Place, 19
  Shrubland Grove, 22
*Kingsland Times and General
  Advertiser*, *n*155

Kingsley, (Rev.) Charles, 34
Kirk, (Rev. Prof.) John, 63-64
Kropotkinites, 30
Kyrle Society, 37, *n*265

Labour Party, 3
La Touche, Rose, 29, 100
Laws of Fesole, The, *n*127
Leaman, Samuel (HS's brother-in-
  law), 16, 61
Leeds, 75, 78, 101, *n*32
  Methley, *n*32
Leeds Co-operative Society, *n*32
Leeds Naturalists' Club & Scientific
  Association, 78, *n*267, *ns*282-283
Leonardo da Vinci, 85
Leopold (Prince), 8, 80, 86, 109,
  *n*93
Lee, Andrew, *n*28
Letters of Richard Cobden, *n*159
Lewis, John Frederick, 104
Liberal Party, 24, 37, 45, 48, 95, 96,
  *n*391
Liberal Unionist, 95
libraries, 21, 55, 71, 95, 102, 103
Lincoln Cathedral, 7
Lincolnshire Chronicle, 96
Linnaeus, Carl, 94
Literary World (*journal*), *n*276
lithography, 20, 23, 24, 25, 69, *n*71,
  *n*75
Littell's Living Age, *n*280, *n*331
Little Women, 35
Livesey, Dora, 43
Lomas, John Arthur Mease, 47
London, 19-26, 33-40, 44, 46-49,
  51-53, 56, 93, 104, 107
  Bedford College, 44
  Bishopsgate, 23, 40, 44, 48, *n*71
  Bishopsgate Steet (Without), 44,
    51, *n*153
  Charing Cross, 40, 52, 53, 56
  Cheapside, 47, 52, 104, *n*175,
    *n*355
  Freeman of the City, 47, 48
  Great Coram Street, 56
  High Holborn, 20, 93
  Hoxton, *n*49
  King Street, 20

Liverpool Street, 23-24
Paternoster Row, 20, 21, 25
Portland Town, 107
Red Lion Square, 33
Regent Street, 52, 93
Rolls Buildings (Fetter Lane), 20, 23
St Botolph without Bishopsgate, 44
St Bride's (Fleet Street), 46
St Martin's Lane, 40, 108
St Paul's Cathedral, 20
(The) Strand, 20
London, University of, 15, *n*40
London City Press, *n*160
London Evening Standard, 51, 53, *ns*172-173, *n*181, *n*184
Lorenzo di Credi, 85
Lyceum Gallery (*see under St George's Museum*)

Mackenzie, Norman, *n*272
Mackmurdo, A.H., *n*362
Magazine of Art, *ns*18-20, *n*22, *n*360
Malawi, 103
Maloy, Mary Ann, *n*316
Manchester, 28, 41, 43, 48, 57, 78, 90, 91, 99, 102-103, *n*177
  Dalton Hall, 41
  Moss Side, 43
  Town Hall, 91
Manchester City News, *n*318
Manchester Courier & Lancashire General Advertiser, *n*319
Manchester Guardian, 102, *n*285, *n*318
Manchester Literary Club, 102
Marylebone, 37
Maurice, Frederick, *n*111, *n*114, *n*129
Maurice, Frederick Denison, 33-34, 37-38, 40, *n*108, *ns*110-111, *n*114, *ns*128-129
Marx, Karl, 90
May Day Festival (*see also Whitelands College*), 79
Meacock, Joanne, 38, *n*130
medicine, 15, 36, 106
Meersbrook, 5, 35, 75, 82, 83, 99, 104, 112, *n*267

Meeting Houses (Society of Friends)
  Balby (Doncaster), 93, 94, *n*328
  Devonshire House, 40, 44
  Stoke Newington, 40
  Weston-Super-Mare, *n*374
  Westminster, 40, 93
Melling, Andrew, *n*188
metalworkers, 5, 72, 89-90
Methodism, 24, 34, 75, 101, *n*116, *n*266, *n*336
Middlemarch, 17, *n*46
Mills, Victoria, 17, *n*46
Millthorpe, 30, 80
mines, 67
Modern Painters, 17, 37
Moore, George, *n*175
Morgan, Simon, *n*159
Morley, Catherine W., 43, *n*21, *n*144, *ns*147-150, *n*328, *n*339
Morning Post, 50, 51, 52, 55-56, *n*61, *n*170, *n*174, *n*176, *n*186, *n*188
Morning Star, 57
Morrell, Cuthbert, 96
Morrell, John Bowes, 96
Morrell, (Mrs) Lydia, 96
Morris, William, 3, 34, 38, 39, 46, 65, 79, 99, *n*113, *n*346
Morse, David, *n*149
Morse, Sydney, 42-43
Morse, Juliet, 42-43
Moss, John Francis, *n*407
Müller, F[rances] Henrietta, 82
Müller, F[riedrich] Max, 109, *n*391
Munro, Alexander, 39
Murdoch, Robert Barclay, 103
music, 22, 26, 41, 42, 55, 89, 95, 112
  pianofortes, 22, 95,
  musical instruments, 22, 89, 95
  Regent Method, 22, 26, 55, 112
Musical Times, 22, *ns*65-66
mutton-chop, 30, 31, 32

Napoleon, Prince Louis, 56
Napoleonic Wars, 14
National Education League, 71
National Gallery Site Commission, 72

National Review, 77, 86
National Trust, 37
Nature (journal), 45
Neal, William, 19
Neale, Vansittart, 38
Neighbour, Alfred, 93
Neighbour, George (Snr), 93
Neighbour, George Lynes, 93
New Zealand, 78
Newcastle-upon-Tyne, 54
Nisbet, Andrew, 31
Nisbet, Catherine, 31
Nisbet, Helen (née Currie), 30-32
    letter to Ruskin from, 31-32
Nisbet, (James) Hume, 30-31
    Ruskin's letter to, 31
Nisbet, Iverlyn, 31
Nisbet, Margaret, 31
Nisbet, Noel, 31
nonconformism (religious), 15, 18, 29, 30, 34, 61
Norton, 30
Norwood Cemetery, 101, *n*161
Nottingham, 75, 84, 85, *n*265
    Ruskin Room, *n*265
    Social Guild Institute, *n*265
    Upper Parliament Street, *n*265
Nottingham Kyrle Society, 37, *n*265
Nottingham Town & Country Social Guild, *n*265
Nutter, Ruth, 12

O'Connor, (Rev) W. A., *n*318
Old Bailey (Central Criminal Court), 19, *n*51
Oldfield, Josiah, *n*362
optics, 55, 59
oranges, 10, 31
Orpheus, 32
Overend-Gurney, 68
Owenite socialism, 30, 86-88, *n*116
Oxford, 5, 8, 20, 38-39, 72, 78, 79, 85, 101
    Bodleian Library, 5
    Christ Church College, 101
    Drawda Hall, 39
    Oxford Union Society, 38
    Oxford University Museum of Natural History, 39, *n*131
    Queen's College (The), *n*134
    University College, 39
    University of, 5, 20-21, 38, 72, 78, 81, 85, 101, *n*391
Oxford English Dictionary, 79
Oxford University & City Herald, *n*58
oysters, 32

Pall Mall Gazette, 12, 25, 58, 109, 111, 116, *n*78, *n*83, *n*87, *n*95, *ns*201-202, *n*205, *n*207, *n*397
Paris, 66-67
Paris Universal Exhibition, 56, *n*191
Parker, Barry, 99, *n*348
Parker, Gill, *n*206
patents (of HS), 50-51, 52, 53, 55, 56, 58, 62, 71, 112, *n*153, *n*165, *ns*167-169
    (pictures), 50, 53
Perugino, 85
Pestalozzian education, 24, 35, 44
peace movement, 24, 29, 44
Pentonville (*experimental garden at*), 28
People's College (*see under Sheffield*)
Perry's Bankrupt Gazette, *n*59
Phonetic Institute Building Fund, 26
Phonetic Journal, 25, *n*80
Phonetic Society, 24
phonetics, 24, 25, 26, 55
Phonographic Corresponding Society, 24
Phonographic Examiner (and Aspirants' Journal), 24-25, n72
    (picture), 25
Phonographic Magazine, 24
Phonographic Star, 24, 45
phonography (shorthand), 7, 24-25, 26, 89, 102, 112
Photochromoscope Syndicate, *n*210
Photographic Journal, The, *n*190, *n*192
Photographic News, The, 55, 56, *n*187, *n*194, *ns*196-197
Photographic Society of Scotland, 56

photography (*see also stereoscopy*), 7, 26, 35, 44, 48-61, 62, 69, 79, 112, *n*168, *n*216
  (pictures), 53, 56
phthisis, 21
Phythian, John Ernest, 78
Pitman, Benn, 25
Pitman, Frederick, 25
Pitman, Henry, 25
Pitman, (Sir) Isaac, 7, 24-26, 28, 43, 45, 58, 112, *n*75,
Playfair, (Dr) Lyon, 37, 38
Plato, 1, 64
Political Reform League, 28
Pollen, John Hungerford, 39
pollution, 6, 73, 89-90, 109-110
Pontefract, 93
porridge, 31
Portrait Establishment (*see under Jersey*)
Poynter, (Sir) Edward, 80
Praeterita, *n*405
Practical Electrical Engineering, 76
Preliminary Catalogue of the St George's Museum, Walkley, Sheffield, 75-76, *n*271, *n*273
  (picture), 76
Pre-Raphaelites, 38-39, 43, *ns*130-131
Priest, Edwin, 88
Priest & Ashmore, 88
Prince of Wales (later King Edward VII), 55
printing trade, 20, 23-26, 43-46, 69-70
Prisoner of Zenda, The, *n*346
Proctor, Adelaide Anne, 35
Protestant Convent Plan, 35-36
Proust, Marcel, 3
Publishers' Circular, The, *n*152
Pullen, Louise, 12
Puttock & Simpson (auctioneers), 21

Quakerism, 7, 10, 23, 24, 26, 29, 34, 40-45, 47, 52, 57, 58, 63, 65, 88, 93-97, 103, 105, 112, 114, *n*116, *n*339, *n*370
Queen Victoria, 8, 81

Queen's College, Harley Street, 35

raisins, 32
Ramsay, A. B., 42
Ramsden, Omar, 79
Randell, James, 15
Randell, James Saunders, 15
Randell, Winter, 14-15, 16, 17
Randell & Saunders, 15
Rawnsley, Hardwicke, *n*362
Reading, Berkshire, 15, 96
  Leighton Park School, 96
Reading (University College/University of), 15, *n*75
Reddie, Cecil, 80
Reed, Thomas Allen, 24
Regent Method (*of teaching singing at sight*), 22, 55, 112
Reigate Hill, 105
Rennie, Mrs, 102
Retreat, The (*see under York*)
Review of Reviews, The (*journal*), *ns*374-375
Richmond, Surrey, 35, 61, 101, 104
Ridges, John Bull, 96
Riley, George Harrison, 90
Riley, William Harrison, 54, 64, 90, 106, 109, *n*182, *n*230, *n*393
ritualism, 42
Rivelin Valley, 8
Rolfe, Frederick William, 80
Rome, 17
Rossetti, Dante Gabriel, 38, *n*130
Rouen Cathedral, 74
Rowe Paragon Cycle & Sulky Co., *n*210
Rowntree, James Edward, 96
Rowntree, John Stephenson, 95-96
Rowntree, Joseph John, 96
Royal College of Physicians, 55
Royal Humane Society, 14
  bronze medal (picture), 14
Royal Microscopical Society, 45
Royal Navy, 14-15, 47
Royle, Eric V., *ns*54-56
Royle, William Richard (HS's master), 20, 23, 93, *ns*54-56
rugby football, 43
Ruskin (*origins of the surname*), 68

Ruskin, John, 1-13, 15, 17, 25, 26, 27, 28, 29, 30, 31, 32, 33-39, 41-45, 46, 52, 53, 54, 58, 59, 62-95, 98, 99, 100, 102, 104, 105, 106, 109-115 (picture), 2
　on education, 1-5, 6, 34, 37-38, 43, 63, 70, 77, 83, 111, 113,
　on heroism, 4
　on industrial capitalism, 1, 6, 34, 65, 109-110
　influence of, 1-3, 7, 33, 64, 74, 90
　on La Touche, Rose, 2, 29, 100
　on museums, 5, 74
　pen-portrait by Howard Swan, 98-99
　and philanthropy, 10, 29, 114
　political philosophy of, 1-3, 5-6, 34, 65, 109-110
　as Slade Professor of Fine Art at Oxford, 5, 81
　on spiritualism, 29-30
　on stewardship, 3, 12, 15, 113, 115
　on teetotalism, 29, 63-64
　on vegetarianism, 29-32
　at the Working Men's College, 33-39
　writings (*indexed individually by title*)
Ruskin at Walkley (online reconstruction, 6, *n*6
Ruskin, John James, 2, 29, 100
Ruskin, Margaret, 2, 43, 100
Ruskin Art Club (LA), 106
Ruskin Lecture, 12
Ruskin Museum (Meersbrook), 35, 75, 82, 99, 104, 112
Ruskin Museum Committee, 11, 41, 82, *n*118, *n*142, *n*s298-299, *n*366
Ruskin Room (*see under Nottingham*)
Ruskin Society —
　of Glasgow, 91
　of London, 91
　of Manchester, 90, 102
　of Sheffield, 9, 90-92, 98, *n*266, *n*343
　　(picture), 91

Ruskin's Guild of St George, *n*269
Ruskin-in-Sheffield (*project*), 12
Russell, Andrew, *n*137
Russell Institute, 56
Russia, 78

St Bernard, 32
St Benedict, 32
St George's Copying Fund, 36
St George's Company/Guild (*see Guild of St George*)
St George's Farm (Totley) (*see also Communist House*), 90
St George's Museum Walkley), 4-12, 21, 57, 70-87, 91-92, 94-96, 98, 100, 102-104, 111-112, 114, 115
　(pictures) *cover, frontispiece*, 4, 80
　Appointment of HS as curator, 71, 73
　arrangement of exhibits, 11, 76, 78
　Collection of, 5-8, 10-12, 15, 25, 35, 57, 74-78, 80-81, 83, 86, 91, 92, 95, 104, 111-112, 114, 115
　decoration and furniture, 73-74, 79, 99
　garden of, 5, 9, 98, 100, 102,
　location, 7-8, 72, 76-77, 78, 92, 94, 114
　Lyceum Gallery, 4, 9, 80, (picture), 4, 80
　online reconstruction of, 6, *n*6
　opening of, 73-74
　presentation of exhibits, 73-74
　size, 8-9, 70, 74, 76, 86,
　visitors to, 5, 8, 9, 10, 21, 72, 77-81, 82, 86-87, 95-96, 98, 101, 102-103, 104, *n*18, *n*30, *n*62, *n*93, *n*206, *n*268, *n*283, *n*287, *n*290, *n*340, *n*362, *n*364, *n*367, *n*391
St George's Woollen Mill (Laxey) *n*358
St Helier (*see under Jersey*)
St Mark's Rest, 2
St Pacian, 101
St Saviour (*see under Jersey*)
Salt, Henry, *n*362
Saltfleet, Frank, 11, 79

Samuel Bagster & Son, 21
Saunders's News-Letter, 55, *n*186
Savoy Theatre, *n*168
Scarborough, 83
Scatcherd, Alice Cliff, 82
science, 5, 37, 49, 51, 54-55, 59, 73, 77-78, 79, 114
Scorah, William, *n*339
Scott, Edith Hope, *n*269
Scott, (Sir) Walter, 1, 32, 44
sculpture, 5, 7, 52, 56-57, 74, 111
sectarianism, 79, 80, 88
Selby Abbey, 7
Seeley, (Prof. Sir) John Robert, 109, *n*391
Seven Lamps of Architecture, The, 115
Severn, Joan, 11, 112, *n*401
Seward, Edwin, 77, *n*281
Shacklewell, 46
  Warwick Lodge, Amhurst Road, 46
Sharman, (Rev.) William, *n*362
Shaw, George, 59, 89-90
Shelley, Frank, 10, 100
Shelley family, 100
Sheffield, 4, 5, 6, 7, 8, 10, 11, 12, 15, 17, 21, 30, 36-38, 58, 59, 71-75, 77, 78, 80-82, 85, 86, 88, 90, 91, 94, 96, 98-105, 108-109, 111-112, 114-115
  Bank Street, 103
  Bell Hagg Road, 5, 10, 71, 72, 77, 98, 99, 100, 105
  Bole Hill Road, 5, 12
  Bow Street, 58, 71
  Bramall Lane, 58
  Brunswick Wesleyan Schools, 101
  Burgoyne Road, 100
  Cavendish Street, 91
  Dale Dyke Dam, *n*16
  Firth College, 81
  Graves Art Gallery, *n*206
  Hall of Science, 73, 79, 88
  Heeley, 103
  Hollow Meadows, 30
  Millennium Gallery, 5
  Nether Edge, 71
  Old Barrack Lane, *n*339
  Oxford Road, 108
  People's College, 38
  Rivelin Street, 102
  Rockingham Street, 73, 88
  Silver Grid Café, 103
  Wesley College, 75, *n*266
  West Street, 71
  Weston Park Museum, 11
  Wood Lane, 107
Sheffield Banking Co., 95
Sheffield Bicycle Club, 58
Sheffield Corporation, 112
Sheffield Daily Telegraph, 77, 82, 95, 114, 116
Sheffield Flood, Great, 8, *n*16
Sheffield (& Rotherham) Independent, 11, 24, 72, 77, 86, 96, 106, 116
Sheffield Literary and Philosophical Society, 73, 78
Sheffield Museum & Parks Committee, 112
Sheffield Secular Society, 88
Sheffield School Board, 95
Sheffield Town Council, 30, 82, 112
Sheffield Vegetarian Society, 101, 103
sherry, 29, 64
Shoreditch, 19
shorthand (*see phonography*)
Shrubsole, Octavius, *n*362
Shuttleworth, (Canon) Henry Carey, 27
Sienssen, Julius Ludwig, 103-104
Sienssen, Katheleen (*see under Connell*)
Slack, Charles, 105
Smith, Adam, 65
Smith, George Hinde, 19
Smith, Henry Dixon, 20
Smith, Theophilus, 48
socialism, 1, 28, 30, 34, 64, 65, 76, 79, 80, 87-88, 90, *n*28, *n*95
Society for Psychical Research, 29, 44
Society for the Abolition of Capital Punishment, 45
Social Politics in Great Britain and Ireland, 63-64

Sorby, (Dr) Henry Clifton, 78
South Africa, 78
Southall, J. E., 42
Southgate, 60
    Chase Side, 60
    College House School, 60
Southport, 96
    Lord Street, 96
spelling reform, 24, 26, 55
Spielmann, Marion H., *n276*
spiritualism, 29, 50, 58, 90, 100, 112, *n95*
Sri Lanka, 78
Stead, W.T., *n375*
Steelopolis (*see also Sheffield*), 6
Stereoscopic Treasury, 50
stereoscopy (*see also Casket Portrait Company, crystal cube miniature, Swan's Patent Clairvoyant*), 7, 44-45, 49-59, 62, 112
stewardship, 3, 12, 15, 113, 115
Stoke Newington, 40
    Meeting House, 40
    Park Street, 40
    Yoakley Road, 40
Stirling, Scotland, 31
Stone, William, 105
Stones of Venice, The, 33, 65
    'The Nature of Gothic', 33, 65
Stradivari, Antonio, 73
Sun (periodical), *n*158
Sunday League, 30
Sunderland, 41
Sunningdale, 105
    Shrubs Hill, 105
Swan, Ann (HS's sister), 16
Swan, Elizabeth (Snr) (*see also under Baster*) (HS's mother), 17-18, 22, 23, 40, 46, 48, 51, 60, 61-62, *n*50, *n*213
Swan, Elizabeth (Jnr) (HS's sister), 16, 19
Swan, Emily Elizabeth (*see also under Connell*) (HS's wife), 2, 3, 7, 9, 10, 12, 17, 27, 28, 29, 30, 36, 46-49, 60, 74, 78, 81-83, 84-85, 91, 93, 94, 98, 100-101, 102, 104, 105-110, 111, 112, 114, *n296, n304, n368, n387, n393*

birth, 46
contribution to museum work, 12, 29, 74, 78, 81-83, 84-85, 111
as curator, 82-83
death, 108
and environment, 108-110
family background, 46-49
fundraising efforts, 81
as gardener, 9, 102
as host, 98
illness of, 105-108,
and mental health, 100-101, 105-108
obituary, 108-109
as poet, 109-110
and Quakerism, 94
and the Ruskin Society, 91
and spiritualism, 29, 100
as vegetarian, 103
and women (role of), 81-82
Swan, Emma (HS's sister), 16
Swan, Fanny (HS's sister), 16, 48, 51, 60-61
Swan, Francis Benet (Frank) (HS's brother), 16, 19-20, 22-29, 33, 35, 36, 40, 45, 51, 60-61, 63, 71, 99, 113, n214
Swan, Godfrey (HS&ES's son), 10, 48, 60, 61, 90, 93-94, 99, 106, 107, 108, 113, *n28, n163, n328, n372, n378, ns382-3, n386, ns389-390*
Swan, Henry, 2-3, 4, 6-7, 8-9, 10-12, 13-104, 111-114
(picture of grave), 11
appearance, 59
apprenticeship, 20
baptism, 16
and bicycles, 25, 58, 112
birth, 16
and boomerangs, 58-59, 89, 112
as boy hero, 14-15
at the British Association for the Advancement of Science, 54-55
as curator, 3-4, 6-7, 8-10, 71-88, 111-115
death, 11, 101
diet, 30-31, 58, 63, 67
and Devizes, 14-19

eccentricity, 27, 59, 112
as engraver, 23-26
and F. & H. Swan, 23-25
funeral, 11-12
health, 11, 27-28, 30-31, 101
and illumination, 35-37, *n*127
and Jersey, 62-69
letters to Ruskin, 62-69, 86, 114-115
and London, 19-27, 33-40, 44, 46-49, 51-53, 56, 60, 93, 104, 107, *n*67, *n*72
and music, 22, 55, 89-90, 95, 112
patents, 50-51, 52, 53, 55, 56, 58, 62, 71, 112, *n*153, *n*165, *ns*167-169
personality, 14-15, 18, 65, 77-78, 113-115
and phonography, 24-26, 28, 45
and photography/stereoscopy, 50-59, 61-62
and Pitman, 24-26, 28
as Quaker, 40-41, 93-97
and spiritualism, 29, 90, 100
as teacher, 22, 77
as teetotaller, 29, 58, 63-64, 90
as vegetarian, 28-29, 101-103
and the workers, 86-91
and the Working Men's College, London, 33-39
Swan, Howard (HS&ES's son), 7, 8, 10, 48, 60, 75-76, 79, 81, 98, 100, 101, 105-106, 107, 108, 111, 113, *n*17, *n*23, *n*162, *n*271, *n*273, *n*288, *n*291, *n*342, *n*347, *n*361, *n*369, *n*371, *ns*374-377, *n*400
(picture), 106
catalogue of St George's Museum, 76
(picture), 76
Swan, John (HS's great uncle), 18
Swan, John (Snr) (HS's father), 15-18, 20-22, 23, 25, 40, 46, 48, 51, 59, 60, 61, *n*50, *n*213
Swan, John (Jnr) (HS's brother), 16, 21-22, *n*63
Swan, Joseph, 39
Swan, (Sir) Joseph Wilson, *n*168

Swan, Leonard (HS&ES's son), 10, 48, 60, 85, 93-94, 99-100, 113, *n*164, *n*329
(picture of grave), 11
Swan, Mabel (HS&ES's daughter), 10, 48, 52, 60, 93-94, 99-100, 105, 106, 107, 108, 113, *n*139, *n*164, *n*178, *n*247, *ns*326-327, *ns*379-380, *n*388
Swan, (Mrs) Mary [HS&ES's daughter-in-law], 105, *n*370
Swan, Radia (HS&ES's granddaughter), 105
Swan, William (HS's grandfather), 18
Swan, William (HS's great grandfather), 18
Swan, William (HS's 2xgreat grandfather), 18
Swan, William T., 28
Swan's Electric Engraving Co., *n*168
Swan family, 10, 19, 20, 42, 61, 72, 99, 106
Swan's Patent Clairvoyant, 50, 112
(picture), 50
Swedenborg, Emmanuel, 24
Switzerland, 105-106
Lausanne Hospital, 106
Vaud, 105

Talbot, (Mrs) Fanny, 43, *n*144
tea, 29, 35, 44, 67, 98, 103, *n*126,
teetotalism, 29, 58, 90, 112
Thames Iron Works, 103
theatre, 14, 40, 42, 79, *n*168
theft, 19
theological books, 20-21
Thompson, S., 44
Thomson, George, 9, 41, *n*26
Thomson, James Rodway, 60
Thomson, Matthew, 60
Time & Tide, 41
Times, The, 55-56, *n*188
Togue, John, 19
Tolstoy, Leo, 3
Totley, 25, 30, 54, 59, 83, 88-91, 106, *n*32, *n*98, *n*304, *n*339
trade unionists, 30

Trafalgar (Battle of), 15
Travis, (Dr) Henry, 88, *n*314
Trowbridge, 24
Tuke, James Hack, 94, *ns*330-331
Tunstall, Edward A., *n*134
Turner, J. M. W., 1, 34, 35
  Sheffield from Derbyshire Lane (c.1797), 35
Turks, 42
Twopenny (Aboriginal, football (soccer) player), 58
Twyman, Michael, *n*75
Tylor, Alfred, 43
Tylor, Juliet (*see also under Morse*), 43
typhus fever, 22

Unto this Last, 1
Unwin, Raymond, 99, *n*28, *n*348
Upton House, 94
usury, 42, 86

Vegetarian Association (of London), 28
Vegetarian Cottage (Dalston), 28-29
Vegetarian Messenger (*see also* Dietetic Reformer...), 25, 31, 91, 102, 103, 116
Vegetarian Society, 24, 25, 35, 91, 101, 102, 103
vegetarianism, 7, 24, 25, 26, 28-29, 30-32, 35, 44, 53, 58, 61, 63, 79, 80, 90-91, 101-103, 112, 114, 116, *ns*88-89, *ns*91-92, *n*95, *ns*98-99, *n*214, *n*318, *ns*362-363
Venice, 9, 74, 80
  St Mark's, 74, 80
Verrocchio, Andrea del, 85
  'Madonna and Child', 85
Viljoen, Helen Gill, *n*275
vignettes, 52
Vinci (*see Leonardo da Vinci*)
votes for women, 30, 82

Waithe, Marcus, 6, *n*113
Walkley, Sheffield, 4, 5, 6, 7, 8, 10, 12, 15, 17, 21, 36, 37, 58, 59, 71-75, 77, 78, 80, 82, 85, 86, 88, 90, 91, 94, 96, 98, 99, 100, 101-102, 104, 105, 109, 112, 114-115
  Bell Hagg Road, 5, 10, 71, 72, 77, 98, 99, 100, 105
  Bole Hill Road, 5, 12
  St Mary's Church, 71-72
  Walkley Cemetery, 10, 100
    (picture), 11
Walker, Robert Bailey, 90
Walthamstow, 46
  Clay Street/Forest Road, 46
  William Morris Gallery, 46
Wandle Basin, 43
Ward, Helen, 30
Ward, William (Snr), 34-35, *n*116
Ward, William (Jnr), 29-30, 34-35, *n*97, *ns*115-117, *n*119, *n*121
  (picture), 35
Ward, William Clack, *n*116
watchmaking, 46-47, *n*175, *n*210
Watts, Richard, 12
Waylen, James, *n*41
W. D. Spalding & Co., 76, *n*271
Wealth of Nations, The, 65
welfare state, 3
Wertheim, Benjamin, 20
West Ham Park, 94
West Hampstead, 105, 108
  Holmdale Road, 105
Western Mail, *n*281
Westminster Abbey, 80
Westminster Gazette, *n*17, *n*23, *n*288, *n*291, *n*342, *n*345, *n*347, *n*361
Westminster & Longford Monthly Meeting, 108, *n*381, *n*385, *n*400
Westminster Meeting House, 40, 93
Westminster Press, 96
Westminster Review, *n*44
Weston-super-Mare Gazette, *n*374
Wharncliffe, Lord & Lady, 80
Wheatstone, Charles, 49
Whistler, James McNeill, 43
White, William, 75
Whitelands College (Chelsea), 75, 79
Whitman, Walt, 90
Whitwell, Marion, 96
Wightman, Arthur, 105
Wilde, Oscar, 79, *n*289

Wilkins, Silvanus, 42
Wilmer, Clive, 12
Winterbottom, Matthew, *n*134
Wilson, John, 20
Wilson, William, 20
Wiltshire, 14-18, 19, 24, 40, 59
    Devizes, 14-18, 19, 24, 40, 59, *n*41, *n*45, *n*49
        (picture), 16
    Trowbridge, 24
Wiltshire Independent, *n*37, *n*39, *n*42
Wright, George, 72
Wolfe, Celia, *n*139, *n*247
women's rights, 30, 44, 82
woodcarving, 79, 99, 111, *n*344
W. R. Royle (& Son), 20, *n*54
Wordsworth, William, 1, 109
workers (*see also artisans*), 1, 2, 5-6, 7, 25, 30, 33-39, 63-64, 71, 72, 74, 84, 89
Working Men's College (London), 7, 26, 27, 29, 33-39, 40, 41, 52, 63, 65, 73, 114,
Working Men's College Journal, *n*82, *n*109, *n*136, *n*140

Worshipful Company of Clockmakers, 47
Wortley, Charles Stuart (MP for Sheffield), 80

Xenophon, 1

York, 7, 57, 96, 105-108
    Borthwick Institute for Archives, 96
    Heslington Road, 105, 107
    Retreat, The (*Quaker hospital*), 105-108, *n*369, *ns*371-372, *ns*375-386, *ns*388-390
    University of, 96
York Conservation Trust, 96
York Minster, 7
Yorkshire, 4, 7, 10, 93, 94, 98, 104, 105
Yorkshire Fine Art and Industrial Exhibition, 57
Yorkshire Post & Leeds Intelligencer, *n*344